THE CHARTERED INSTITUTE OF MARKETING

Professional Diploma in Marketing

STUDY TEXT

The Marketing Planning Process

Valid for assessments up to September 2013

The Chartered
Institute of Marketing

First edition July 2012

ISBN 9781 4453 9145 8

e-ISBN 9781 4453 7618 9

British Library Cataloguing-in-Publication Data
A catalogue record for this book
is available from the British Library

Published by

BPP Learning Media Ltd
Aldine House, Aldine Place
142-144 Uxbridge Road
London W12 8AA

www.bpp.com/learningmedia

Printed in the United Kingdom by Polestar Wheatons

Hennock Road
Marsh Barton Industrial Estate
Exeter, Devon
EX2 8RP

Your learning materials, published by BPP Learning
Media Ltd, are printed on paper obtained from
traceable sustainable sources.

We are grateful to The Chartered Institute of Marketing for
permission to reproduce in this text the unit syllabus.

Lead Author: Neil Towers

Contents

Page

Introduction

Studying for The Chartered Institute of Marketing (CIM) qualifications ▪ The Professional Diploma Syllabus ▪ Assessment ▪ The Magic Formula ▪ A guide to the features of the Study Text ▪ Additional resources ▪ Your personal study plan · · · v

Chapters

Section 1: Marketing planning to deliver marketing strategies · · · 1

1   The different roles of marketing and its cross-functional interaction within organisations · · · 3

2   The synergistic planning process · · · 13

3   The role of the marketing plan in relation to the organisation's philosophy · · · 29

4   The relationship between corporate, business and marketing objectives at an operational level and the influences on objectives · · · 39

Section 1: Senior examiner's comments · · · 55

Section 2: The marketing audit and strategic outcomes · · · 57

5   The practicalities of undertaking a marketing audit · · · 59

6   Auditing the market environment · · · 69

7   The external marketing environment · · · 81

8   The internal marketing environment · · · 103

Section 2: Senior examiner's comments · · · 123

Section 3: Creating marketing strategies through segmentation, targeting and positioning · · · 125

9   The role of marketing strategies and market segmentation · · · 127

10   Market targeting · · · 145

11   Marketing positioning · · · 157

Section 3: Senior examiner's comments   169

Section 4: Adapting marketing planning in different contexts   171

12   Key dimensions of implementing marketing planning in practice   173

13   Approaches to implementing the process of marketing planning   197

Section 4: Senior examiner's comments   223

Key terms / Index   227

Review form

1 Studying for The Chartered Institute of Marketing (CIM) qualifications

There are a few key points to remember as you study for your CIM qualification:

(a)   You are studying for a **professional** qualification. This means that you are required to use professional language and adopt a business approach in your work.

(b)   You are expected to show that you have 'read widely'. Make sure that you read the quality press (and don't skip the business pages), *Marketing*, *The Marketer*, *Research* and *Marketing Week* avidly.

(c)   Become aware of the marketing initiatives you come across on a daily basis, for example, when you go shopping look around and think about why the store layout is as it is; consider the messages, channel choice and timings of ads when you are watching TV. It is surprising how much you will learn just by taking an interest in the marketing world around you.

(d)   Get to know the way CIM write their exam papers and assignments. They use a specific approach (the Magic Formula) which is to ensure a consistent approach when designing assessment materials. Make sure you are fully aware of this as it will help you interpret what the examiner is looking for (a full description of the Magic Formula appears later).

(e)   Learn how to use Harvard referencing. This is explained in detail in our CIM Professional Diploma Assessment Workbook.

(f)   Ensure that you read very carefully all assessment details sent to you from CIM. There are strict deadlines to meet, as well as paperwork to complete for any assignment or project you do. You also need to make sure have your CIM membership card with you at the exam. Failing to meet any assessment entry deadlines or completing written work on time will mean that you will have to wait for the next round of assessment dates and will need to pay the relevant assessment fees again.

2 The Professional Diploma Syllabus

The Professional Diploma in Marketing is aimed at anyone who is employed in a marketing management role such as Brand Manager, Account Manager or Marketing Executive. If you are a graduate, you will be expected to have covered a minimum of a third of your credits in marketing subjects. You are therefore expected at this level of the qualification to be aware of the key marketing theories and be able to apply them to different organisational contexts.

The aim of the qualification is to provide the knowledge and skills for you to develop an 'ability to do' in relation to marketing planning. CIM qualifications concentrate on applied marketing within real workplaces.

The complete qualification is made from four units:

- Unit 1 The Marketing Planning Process
- Unit 2 Delivering Customer Value through Marketing
- Unit 3 Managing Marketing
- Unit 4 Project Management in Marketing

CIM stipulates that each module should take 50 guided learning hours to complete. Guided learning hours refer to time in class, using distance learning materials and completing any work set by your tutor. Guided learning hours do not include the time it will take you to complete the necessary reading for your studies.

The syllabus as provided by CIM can be found below with reference to our coverage within this Study Text.

Unit characteristics – The Marketing Planning Process

This unit is designed to provide a detailed understanding of marketing planning, including the synergistic planning process and its links with the delivery of marketing strategy. It also considers a thorough assessment of the dynamic and complex nature of the marketing environment and its impact on developing marketing plans to achieve strategic outcomes and competitive advantage in the market place.

The unit includes significant consideration of segmentation, targeting and positioning, with a view to developing sophisticated approaches to targeting customers and the development of effective positioning strategies, all based upon a sound assessment of market segment opportunities and value.

By the end of this unit, students should be able to apply the concept of the marketing planning process to a variety of organisational contexts and sectors, and to account for their varying goals when developing marketing plans. They should be able to demonstrate their ability to relate the challenges posed by a dynamic marketing environment to the marketing planning needs of different organisations and to devise appropriate, innovative positioning strategies in response to environmental changes.

Overarching learning outcomes

By the end of this unit students should be able to:

- Evaluate the role of the marketing planning process and the marketing plan implementation in a range of marketing contexts including that of the organisation's strategy, culture and broader marketing environment.

- Evaluate the interconnectivity between corporate, business and marketing objectives and consider the impact of the external marketing environment and the organisation's resources on their development and achievement.

- Conduct a marketing audit including a detailed analysis of the internal and external marketing environments.

- Assess the findings of the audit and develop a marketing plan that is responsive to market and organisational changes and underpins the organisation's marketing strategy.

- Determine the importance of segmentation, targeting and positioning and their relative interdependencies and develop effective segmentation, targeting and positioning strategies which are innovative, cost effective, valuable and maximise the potential marketing opportunities successfully.

- Utilise a range of positioning platforms including price, quality, service and brand perception, to establish an organisation's marketing positioning strategy.

- Recognise the significance of retaining existing customers through relationship marketing when developing strategies to achieve marketing objectives.

SECTION 1 – Marketing planning to deliver marketing strategies (weighting 25%)

		Covered in chapter(s)
1.1	Critically evaluate the different roles of marketing and its cross-functional interaction within organisations <ul><li>Marketing as an organisation function and orientation</li><li>Marketing as a co-ordinating force in the organisation</li><li>Marketing's interface with other organisational functions</li><li>Exchange, transactions and relationships</li><li>Markets, customers, competition and value creation</li><li>Marketers as planners, strategists and tacticians</li><li>Marketing in theory and in practice</li></ul>	1
1.2	Critically evaluate the synergistic planning process including the different components of the marketing plan and its links with delivering the organisation's corporate, business and marketing strategies <ul><li>The purpose of marketing planning</li><li>Achieving a sustainable competitive advantage</li><li>The stages of the marketing planning process: analysis, planning, implementation and control</li><li>Sequential, cyclical, and iterative approaches to planning</li><li>The outcomes of planning and plans</li><li>Contents of a marketing plan</li><li>Documentation and reality</li></ul>	2
1.3	Critically evaluate the role of the marketing plan in relation to the organisation's philosophy and an organisation's strategic intent <ul><li>The marketing plan as means of conveying organisational purpose and future vision</li><li>The marketing plan as vehicle for setting direction and focus</li><li>The marketing plan as an operational framework</li><li>The marketing plan as a method of resource and budget allocation</li><li>The marketing plan as a tool for performance measurement</li></ul>	3
1.4	Evaluate the relationship between corporate, business and marketing objectives at an operational level and describe how they impact upon the activities associated with the marketing plan <ul><li>Identifying a hierarchy of objectives</li><li>Objectives at varying levels and time scales</li><li>Different types of objectives: organisational, innovation, financial, market, relationship-focused, societal, non-profit</li><li>Consistency of plans with objectives</li><li>Resource issues and constraints</li></ul>	4

		Covered in chapter(s)
1.5	Assess the external and internal influences on the formulation of objectives and specify the key environmental drivers of organisational change	4
	■ Recognition of environmentally driven marketing planning and the resource-based view of the firm	
	■ Identify internal influences on objectives including objective setting process, corporate mission and strategy, culture, resources, capabilities	
	■ Identify external influences on objectives including economic conditions, markets, competition, industry life cycle, technological development	
	■ Identify drivers of organisational change including innovation, evolving consumer behaviours, globalisation, ethical consumption and corporate social responsibility, sustainability relationship management, stakeholder relations, globalisation	
1.6	Critically evaluate the wider impact of external and internal environmental forces on the setting of objectives at different levels and the process of planning marketing	4
	■ Macro-environment: political, cultural, social, economic, technological, legal, ecological, ethical	
	■ Micro-environment: market, customers, competitors, industry structure and dynamics, suppliers, intermediaries	
	■ Internal environment: capabilities in functional areas, assets and core competences, product and service portfolio, innovation, business relationships and strategic partnerships, current market position and past performance, dynamic capabilities, competitive advantage	

SECTION 2 – The marketing audit and strategic outcomes (weighting 30%)

		Covered in chapter(s)
2.1	Critically evaluate the practicalities of undertaking a marketing audit including resource limitations and implications within the organisational context	5
	■ Conducting a marketing audit in practice	
	■ Scope, timing and frequency	
	■ Responsibilities and objectivity	
	■ Constraints and issues	
2.2	Assess the concept of the organisation as an open system faced with changing environmental conditions and internal capabilities	5
	■ Complex and dynamic external environment	
	■ Variability in organisational resource, asset and competence base	
	■ Controllable and uncontrollable influences	
	■ Responding to external and internal change	
	■ Shaping strategy and plans proactively	
2.3	Appraise the process of auditing the marketing environment and make recommendations for the utilisation of various approaches in a range of different organisational contexts and sectors	6
	■ Past, current, and future-oriented perspectives	
	■ Organising information for planning	
	■ Marketing audit structures eg environment, strategy, organisation, systems, productivity and functions audits	
	■ External and internal sources of information	
	■ Organisational and sectoral constraints	
	■ Using models and frameworks to facilitate understanding	

The Chartered Institute of Marketing

		Covered in chapter(s)
2.4	Evaluate the external marketing environment through detailed analysis using a variety of marketing audit tools and techniques ■ The evolving nature and extent of external environmental change ■ Marketing intelligence and environmental scanning ■ Marco- and micro-environmental analysis frameworks ■ Gauging the impacts of external forces on marketing planning ■ Identifying key external issues and assumptions ■ External audit tools eg PESTEL, Porter's Five Forces, and strategic group mapping	7
2.5	Assess the internal marketing environment of an organisation through an audit process using a range of evaluation processes and approaches ■ The evolving nature and extent of internal organisational change ■ Developing resource-based planning and strategy ■ Internal environmental analysis frameworks ■ Establishing the effects of organisational resources and capabilities on marketing planning ■ Identifying key internal issues and assumptions ■ Internal audit tools eg product life cycle, portfolio models, and the value chain	8
2.6	Utilise the planning gap as a means to identifying and assessing key marketing planning requirements to fulfil the organisation's marketing strategy ■ Establishing objectives and the planning gap ■ Generating alternative strategic options ■ Filling the planning gap with new and existing strategies ■ Evaluation of marketing opportunities and the achievement of competitive advantage	8
2.7	Assess the issues and constraints arising from the marketing audit and consider the consequences for the organisation in order to develop its marketing plan ■ Prioritising issues and executing SWOT analysis ■ Specifying marketing objectives, strategies and plans ■ Consideration of timescales for implementation	8

SECTION 3 – Creating marketing strategies through segmentation, targeting and positioning (weighting 25%)

		Covered in chapter(s)
3.1	Critically evaluate the role of marketing strategies and demonstrate how they can be used to develop competitive advantage, market share and growth ■ Marketing strategies for meeting marketing objectives through satisfying customer requirements ■ Marketing strategies as product 'offers' providing benefits to customer segments ■ Identifying customers and offers for future development	9
3.2	Assess the importance of market segmentation as a basis of selecting markets to achieve the organisation's business and marketing objectives via customer satisfaction ■ Defining local, national, international and global markets and their parameters ■ Principle of market segmentation, targeting, and positioning ■ Benefits and costs of market segmentation ■ Conditions for successful segmentation	9

		Covered in chapter(s)
3.3	Critically evaluate the different segmentation approaches available to organisations in different organisational contexts and sectors and make recommendations for their use ■ Segmentation variables for consumer markets ■ Segmentation variables for business markets ■ Profiling segments and defining customer types ■ Critical evaluation of segmentation techniques ■ Contemporary methods of segmentation such as relationship-based approaches and online behaviours	9
3.4	Assess the value of 'targeting' markets as an approach to achieving customer satisfaction, competitive advantage and retention ■ Focused effort and resource efficiency ■ Potential for achieving short-, medium-, and long-term objectives ■ Potential for achieving competitive advantage ■ Scope for competitive advantage through distinctive positioning	10
3.5	Critically evaluate a range of targeting coverage strategies for different organisational contexts and sectors ■ Undifferentiated marketing ■ Differentiated marketing ■ Concentrated marketing ■ Customised marketing	10
3.6	Assess the attractiveness and value of selected market segments ■ External and internal criteria for evaluation: size, growth, profitability, relationship potential, competition, capabilities ■ Segment evaluation process: factor weighting and ranking of alternatives ■ Fit between potential and internal considerations	10
3.7	Examine the concept of marketing positioning strategy and how it can be used to convey the organisation's value proposition ■ Differential advantage, customer value, and organisational benefits ■ Consideration of alternative positioning strategies ■ Relationship positioning strategies ■ Competitive positioning strategies ■ Selection of target markets and point of differentiation ■ Positioning and perceptual maps	11
3.8	Critically evaluate positioning options and their implementation within the context of the organisation and its markets ■ Criteria for effective positioning and competitive advantages ■ Positioning and the marketing mix ■ Positioning and repositioning in practice	11

The Chartered Institute of Marketing

SECTION 4 – Undertaking marketing planning in different contexts (weighting 20%)

		Covered in chapter(s)
4.1	Assess the significance of the key dimensions of implementing marketing planning in practice ■ Organisational structures, systems, and processes ■ Forecasting and budgeting ■ Time-scales and responsibilities	12
4.2	Critically evaluate the barriers and constraints to implementing marketing planning, and consider how they may be addressed by organisations ■ Managerial, organisational, and cultural shortcomings ■ Planning inadequacies ■ Poor and inadequate organisational resource ■ Lack of innovation ■ Failure to integrate into corporate planning systems ■ Monitoring performance metrics and control mechanisms ■ Contingency planning ■ Internal marketing	12
4.3	Propose and justify approaches to implementing the process of marketing planning in different contextual settings ■ Marketing planning for different stakeholder groups ■ Planning in consumer and business-to-business markets ■ Services marketing planning ■ Issues of marketing planning in large and small organisations ■ Internal marketing segmentation ■ Marketing planning in non-profit organisations ■ The international and global dimension of marketing planning ■ Marketing planning in highly competitive markets ■ Facilitating relationship-based marketing planning and customer retention ■ Planning marketing in the virtual marketplace	13

3 Assessment

The unit covered by this Study Text (Unit 1 The Marketing Planning Process) is assessed using a work-based assignment. In order to help you focus specifically on your assessment we have also written a Professional Diploma in Marketing Assessment Workbook which is available either through your usual book retailer or our website www.bpp.com/learningmedia.

4 The Magic Formula

The Magic Formula is a tool used by CIM to help both examiners write exam and assignment questions, and you, to more easily interpret what you are being asked to write about. It is useful for helping you to check that you are using an appropriate balance between theory and practice for your particular level of qualification.

Contrary to the title, there is nothing mystical about the Magic Formula and simply by knowing it (or even mentioning it in an assessment) will not automatically secure a pass. What it does do, however, is to help you to check that you are presenting your answers in an appropriate format, including enough marketing theory and applying it to a real marketing context or issue.

The Magic Formula for the Professional Diploma in Marketing is shown below:

Figure A   The Magic Formula for the Professional Diploma in Marketing

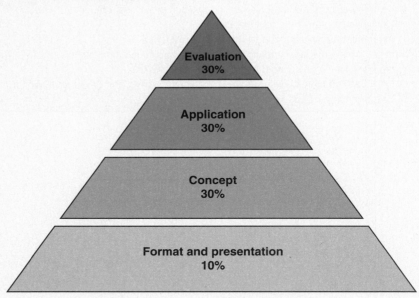

You can see from the pyramid that for the Professional Diploma marks are awarded in the following proportions:

- **Presentation and format – 10%**

  You are expected to present your work professionally which means that assignments and projects should **always** be typed. Even in an exam situation attention should be paid to making your work look as visually appealing as possible. CIM will also stipulate the format that you should present your work in. The assessment formats you will be given will be varied and can include things like reports to write, slides to prepare, emails, memos, formal letters, press releases, discussion documents, briefing papers, agendas and newsletters.

- **Concept – 30%**

  Concept refers to your ability to state, recall and describe marketing theory. The definition of marketing is a core CIM syllabus topic. If we take this as an example, you would be expected to recognise, recall and write this definition to a word perfect standard to gain the full marks for concept.

- **Application – 30%**

  Application based marks are given for your ability to apply marketing theories to real life marketing situations. For example, a question may ask you to discuss the definition of marketing and how it is applied within your own organisation. Here you are not only using the definition but are applying it in order to consider the market orientation of the company.

- **Evaluation – 30%**

  Evaluation is the ability to asses the value or worth of something, sometimes through careful consideration of related advantages and disadvantages, or weighing up of alternatives. Results from your evaluation should enable you to discuss the importance of an issue using evidence to support your opinions.

  For example, if you were asked to evaluate whether or not your organisation adopts a marketing approach you should provide reasons and specific examples of why you think they might take this approach, as well as considering why they may not take this approach, before coming to a final conclusion.

  You should have noticed that for the Professional Diploma, you are expected to consider the equal weightings of concept, application and evaluation in order to gain maximum marks in assessments.

5 A guide to the features of the Study Text

Each of the chapter features (see below) will help you to break down the content into manageable chunks and ensure that you are developing the skills required for a professional qualification.

Chapter feature	Relevance and how you should use it
Introduction	Shows why topics need to be studied and is a route guide through the chapter
Syllabus reference	Outlines the syllabus learning outcomes covered in the chapter
Chapter topic list	Study the list, each numbered topic denotes a numbered section in the chapter
Key Term	Highlights the core vocabulary you need to learn
Activity	An application-based activity for you to complete
The Real World	A short case study to illustrate marketing practice
Exam tip/Assessment tip	Key advice based on the assessment
Chapter roundups	Use this to review what you have learnt
Quick quiz	Use this to check your learning
Further reading	Further reading will give you a wider perspective on the subjects you're covering

6 Additional resources

To help you pass the Professional Diploma in Marketing we have created a complete study package. The **Professional Diploma Assessment Workbook** covers all four units of the Professional Diploma level. Practice questions and answers, tips on tackling assignments and work-based projects are included to help you succeed in your assessments.

Our A6 set of spiral bound **Passcards** are handy revision cards and are ideal to reinforce key topics for The Marketing Planning Process work-based assignment.

7 Your personal study plan

Preparing a Study Plan (and sticking to it) is one of the key elements to learning success.

CIM has stipulated that there should be a minimum of 50 guided learning hours spent on each unit. Guided learning hours will include time spent in lessons, working on distance learning materials, formal workshops and work set by your tutor. We also know that to be successful, students should spend **approximately 100 hours** conducting self study. This means that for the entire qualification with four units you should spend 200 hours working in a tutor-guided manner and approximately 400 hours completing recommended reading, working on assignments, and revising for exams. This Study Text will help you to organise this 100-hour portion of self study time.

Now think about the exact amount of time you have (don't forget you will still need some leisure time!) and complete the following tables to help you keep to a schedule.

	Date	Duration in weeks
Course start		
Course finish		Total weeks of course:

Project received	Submission date	Total weeks to complete:

 The Chartered Institute of Marketing

Content chapter coverage plan

Chapter	To be completed by	Considered in relation to the assignment
1 The different roles of marketing and its cross-functional interaction within organisations		
2 The synergistic planning process		
3 The role of the marketing plan in relation to the organisation's philosophy		
4 The relationship between corporate, business and marketing objectives at an operational level and the influences on objectives		
5 The practicalities of undertaking a marketing audit		
6 Auditing the market environment		
7 The external marketing environment		
8 The internal marketing environment		
9 The role of marketing strategies and market segmentation		
10 Market targeting		
11 Marketing positioning		
12 Key dimensions of implementing marketing planning in practice		
13 Approaches to implementing the process of marketing planning		

BPP
LEARNING MEDIA

Section 1: Marketing planning to deliver marketing strategies

Section 1 covers essential content relating to marketing and marketing planning, their purpose within the organisation and how they relate to marketing strategy development in fulfilling organisational goals. The focus is therefore on the role of marketing within organisations, the purpose and process of marketing planning, the function and structure of marketing plans, and the fit with objectives at different levels of the organisation.

You should be able to examine marketing planning from the point of view of how it enacts marketing within organisations as an integrated process which provides strategic direction towards specific goals.

It is important to recognise that the level of this qualification is a step up from previous studies and requires evidence of an ability to explain, apply and evaluate the marketing planning process and its various dimensions. It is especially important therefore that a critical approach to the application of marketing planning and the development of plans is adopted, which takes account of the environment, resources, and objectives and practical implementation issues in a range of contexts.

CHAPTER 1

The different roles of marketing and its cross-functional interaction within organisations

Introduction

This chapter covers the part of the syllabus which relates to the role of marketing, the relationship with other functional departments and the role of marketers. The reader will be introduced to marketing as a function, an activity and as an orientation.

Topic list

The marketing function	1
Marketing as an orientation	2
Marketing's interface with other organisational functions	3
Marketers as planners, strategists and tacticians	4
Marketing in theory and in practice	5

1.1	Critically evaluate the different roles of marketing and its cross-functional interaction within organisations

- Marketing as an organisational function and orientation
- Marketing as a co-ordinating force in the organisation
- Marketing's interface with other organisational functions
- Exchange, transactions and relationships
- Markets, customers, competition and value creation
- Marketers as planners, strategists and tacticians
- Marketing in theory and in practice

1 The marketing function

> ▶ **Key term**
>
> **Marketing** is the management process responsible for identifying, anticipating and satisfying customer requirements profitably. (The Chartered Institute of Marketing)

The marketing function is concerned with the management of the marketing mix, involving the various tools and techniques available to marketing managers. The marketing mix being, product, price, promotion and place (the four Ps). Increasingly, the mix includes additional elements: people, physical evidence and processes (the extended services mix or seven Ps). Depending on the organisation it can also involve the integrated planning of marketing together with any research that is undertaken into markets, customers, competitors, or on initiatives such as new products.

Marketing as a stand-alone function appears to have been transformed, replaced in an increasing number of organisations with marketing as a philosophy, ie a way of doing business that focuses on the customer. This could include sales, customer service, customer relationship management and customer intelligence, for example. Increasingly, a marketing orientation is seen as critical to the success of organisations, as it drives the organisation towards its goals through delivering value to customers (van Raaij and Stoelhorst, 2008). Marketing orientation contains elements of market intelligence generation, dissemination and use, with the aim to create value for customers (Lafferty and Hult, 2001).

From the mid-twentieth century marketing grew as 'the whole business seen from the point of view of its final results, that is, from the customer's point of view' (Drucker, 1954, p36). According to Dibb *et al*. (2006, p5) 'marketing consists of individual and organisational activities that facilitate and expedite satisfying exchange relationships in a dynamic environment through the creation, distribution, promotion and pricing of goods, services and ideas'.

McDonald (2007) agrees there is considerable confusion about what marketing is.

He suggests that marketing is the process for:

- Defining markets
- Quantifying the needs of the customer groups (segments) within these markets
- Determining the value proposition to meet these needs
- Communicating these value propositions to all those people in the organisation responsible for delivering them, and getting their buy-in to their role
- Playing an appropriate part in delivering these value propositions (usually only communications)
- Monitoring the value actually delivered.

There needs to be a clear distinction between marketing as an activity or business function and marketing as a concept, often referred to as a marketing orientation.

The Chartered
Institute of Marketing

Dyson is a British technology company, founded in 1992 by Sir James Dyson, which designs and manufactures vacuum cleaners, hand dryers, bladeless fans and heaters. It sells machines in over 50 countries and employs 3,100 people worldwide. The company prides itself on engineering products which work in different and better ways than their predecessors. Success has been achieved by understanding the value proposition through a marketing orientation and then marketing innovative products to a broad customer base.

2 Marketing as an orientation

> ▶ Key term
>
> **Marketing orientation** is where the current and future customer's requirements are embedded within all the organisation's activities.

Marketing orientation consists of five key cultural aspects according to Narver and Slater (1990):

- Customer focus
- Competitor focus
- Integrated functional co-ordination
- Organisational culture
- Long-term profits.

All of these aspects enable the business to, in theory, achieve sustainable competitive advantage through fulfilling customer requirements, and the cultural market orientation perspective is seen to be predominant in fulfilling this, particularly with regard to co-ordinating the organisation's resources.

Kotler *et al* (2009, p25) define the marketing concept as follows:

'The marketing concept and philosophy states that the organisation should strive to satisfy its customers' wants and needs while meeting the organisation's profit and other goals'.

Organisations need to be marketing orientated, which means that there must be a clear focus throughout the organisation on customer needs and wants, and how these needs are met constantly.

A marketing orientation involves multiple departments or functions sharing information about customers and pursuing activities to meet customer needs and wants. An organisation that has a marketing orientation see the requirements of customers and potential customers as crucial and this drives all strategic decisions.

Kohli and Jaworski (1990) define market orientation in terms of three behavioural dimensions.

- The generation of market information about the needs of customers and external environmental factors
- The dissemination of such information across organisational functions
- The development and implementation of strategies in response to the information.

Similarly this intelligence-management approach enables the firm to fulfil the desires of customers in a way which leads it towards its aims and objectives.

Select an organisation that you are familiar with and identify the market information required to assess the needs of customers and external environmental factors.

There are three main alternatives to adopting a marketing orientation as shown in Table 1.1.

Table 1.1   Different business orientations

Sales orientation	The emphasis is on selling more of the products and services they have to customers. Little attention is paid to identifying and satisfying customer needs and wants.
Production orientation	Maximising output to obtain economies of scale to maximise profits.
Product orientation	The emphasis is on the product, but ignoring customer tastes may result in product failures or lost market to competitors.

If a marketing orientation is to develop within organisations, attention should be given to each of the following:

- Create a customer focus throughout the business
- Listen to the customer
- Target customers precisely
- Measure and manage customer expectations
- Build customer relationships and loyalty
- Commit to continuous improvement
- Manage profitability
- Manage the marketing culture.

3 Marketing's interface with other organisational functions

▶ **Key term**

Marketing planning is the series of activities that formulate the plans to achieve sustainable competitive advantage for an organisation.

Marketing planning will require a co-ordinated approach with plans such as production, finance and personnel linking with the marketing plan.

The complex nature of marketing means that there are many interfaces with other functional areas. Marketers in their own right cannot meet all the requirements of customers; they need to work with other parts of the organisation, especially where physical production processes are involved, and equally when people deliver intangible services.

Functional areas will each have their own concerns and constraints. Managers frequently find that those obstructing the implementation of marketing plans are not marketers themselves but staff from other functional areas. The marketing planner must take these concerns and constraints into account if plans are to be successfully executed.

Decisions made by the marketing function will have repercussions on many other functional areas.

- A decision on a promotion, changing the credit terms, will have profound effects on credit collection and cash flow, concerns of the finance function

- A promise by marketing to meet a delivery date will have implications on production in terms of production planning

The Chartered
Institute of Marketing

- Improvements in service delivery will depend on the co-operation and communication between the human resources and marketing functions.

Functional areas will have information that is of value to marketing and therefore a good relationship is essential to ensure the flow of information for decision making, monitoring and control.

The co-ordination and communication between marketing and the finance function is considered by many to be the most critical of all the functional relationships. Pricing will require costing information from the finance function. Performance measurement will require data from the finance function on promotional expenditure for future decision making.

An understanding of the areas of potential conflicts is useful, as given in Table 1.2.

Table 1.2   Organisational conflicts between marketing and other functions

Department	Emphasis	Emphasis of marketing
Production	Standard orders Long lead times Long runs	Customised orders Short lead times Frequent model changes
Inventory management	Economic stock levels Fast-moving items Narrow stock range	Targeted stock levels Broad product range
Accounting	Standard transactions	Special terms and discounts
Finance	Firm budgets Price to cover total costs	Flexible budgets for changing needs Price for market growth
Credit	Lower credit risks Tough credit terms Tough collection procedures	Medium credit risks Easy credit terms Easy collection procedures

A marketing orientation is only achieved when:

- Departments engage in activities geared towards understanding customers' current and future needs;
- There is sharing of this knowledge and understanding across departments;
- Departments engage in activities designed to meet or exceed customer needs.

Market orientation requires organisation-wide generation, dissemination and responses to marketing intelligence. Marketing has a critical role in the co-ordination, and communication between, all of the functions.

ACTIVITY 1.2

Within an organisation that you are familiar with, list the necessary co-ordination and communication issues required between marketing and the finance function.

4 Marketers as planners, strategists and tacticians

Marketing planning is a systematic process involving the assessment of resources and the marketing opportunities and threats. The marketing planning process requires marketers to take a critical planning perspective.

The marketing planning process enables information, aims and ideas to be developed into a document that can be easily understood, evaluated and implemented. The marketing planning outcome will be a plan for the future with objectives, strategies, identified resources and timings. Therefore, the plan acts as a 'road map' or blueprint for the organisation into the future.

Planners research, collect information, evaluate alternative courses of action and make decisions, whatever field the planner operates in. Marketers research the macro-and micro-environment. They collect information on customers and competitors. Alternative strategies are evaluated, such as market penetration compared with market development. Decisions are made on strategies, marketing programmes, organisational structures and resourcing.

Marketers play a key role as strategists within organisations, asking and finding solutions to questions such as:

- Which market should we be in?
- How should we compete in this market?
- How can we embrace new technologies to sustain our current markets?
- What is the best way to deal with the threat of a new competitor?
- How should we address changing consumer needs?

The marketing strategist will seek the best way to deploy the resources available. Furthermore, tactical decisions will be made on when to gain the best position against the competition. If the organisational objectives are to be achieved then strategies will need to be formulated. However, changing circumstances will require changes in strategies if the objectives are to be achieved.

ACTIVITY 1.3

Outline the markets that are to be serviced by your organisation and describe the requirements for each of the customers.

The marketer will formulate a strategy to deal with the competitive threat; an offensive or defensive response? Retrenchment to protect the current position or make opportunities for growth? Would a better strategy be to outflank the competitor by attacking selected segments of the market where the competitor is weak? What impact will our actions have on our current market segments?

Marketers will also act as tacticians in day-to-day matters or operational matters. They will make short-term decisions on tactics within the longer-term framework provided by the marketing plan. In so doing, they will address questions relating to operational matters such as:

- How do we respond to a competitor's price cut?
- Should we use price competition or non-price competition?
- Should this product be withdrawn?

These are all examples of tactical decisions.

5 Marketing in theory and in practice

The theory of marketing is relatively straightforward – customer focus, co-ordinating resources, competitive advantage, planning towards goals – all appear to be sound principles for any business or organisation to adopt. However the reality of marketing in the dynamic and ever-changing real world, faced with constant international, national and local competitive pressures, is much more difficult. As we will see as our investigation of the marketing planning process unfolds, putting it into practice involves a great deal of skill and knowledge, especially when encountering implementation issues in particular marketing contexts.

THE REAL WORLD

Virgin (Virgin.com) is one of the world's most recognised and respected brands. Conceived in 1970 by Richard Branson, the Virgin Group has gone on to grow very successful businesses in sectors ranging from mobile telephony to transportation, travel, financial services, media, music and fitness. According to their web site, Virgin stands for value for money, quality, innovation, fun and a sense of competitive challenge. They claim to deliver a quality service through a marketing orientation by empowering their employees and by facilitating and monitoring customer feedback to continually improve the customer's experience through innovation. When exploring new opportunities they ask fundamental questions such as: is this an opportunity for restructuring a market and creating competitive advantage? What are the competitors doing? Is the customer confused or badly served? Is this an opportunity for building the Virgin brand?

▶ Assessment tip

Understand the underpinning theories of marketing orientation and relate examples to reinforce your understanding. Recognise how the whole organisation contributes to this approach and how the internal functional interfaces in an organisation are very important to delivering customer expectations.

Summary

This chapter has introduced marketing as a function, activity and business orientation. The benefits of marketing as a way of doing business based on satisfying customer requirements have been outlined and the relationship of the marketing function with other business functions explored. Marketing success depends critically on the way the marketing concept is applied and how this translates into practical reality within organisation. Investigating how this is achieved in a range of different organisational settings will be explored in the remainder of this text.

CHAPTER ROUNDUP

- The scope and purpose of the marketing function and the marketing orientation
- The marketing's interface with other organisational functions
- The key role of marketers as planners, strategists and tacticians

FURTHER READING

Doyle, P. (2004) *Marketing Management and Strategy*. 3rd Edition. London, Prentice-Hall.

Hollensen, S. (2007) *Global Marketing*. 4th Edition. London, Prentice-Hall.

REFERENCES

Dibb, S. *et al* (2006) *Marketing: Concepts and Strategies*. 5th edition. Boston, Houghton Mifflin.

Drucker, P. (1954) *The Practice of Management.* New York, Harper and Row.

Kohli, A.K. and Jaworski, B.J. (1990) Market orientation: the construct, research propositions, and managerial implications. *Journal of Marketing*, 54 (April), pp1-18.

Kotler, P. *et al* (2009) *Marketing Management*. London, Pearson education.

Kotler, P. and Keller, K.L. (2006) *Marketing Management*. 12th edition. Englewood Cliffs, NJ, Prentice-Hall.

Lafferty, B. and Hult, G. (2001) A synthesis of contemporary market orientation perspectives. *European Journal of Marketing,* 35 (1/2) pp92-109.

McDonald, M. (2007) *Marketing Plans: How to Prepare Them, How to Use Them*. 6th edition. London, Butterworth Heinemann.

Narver, J.C. and Slater, S.F. (1990) The effect of a market orientation on business profitability. *Journal of Marketing*, 54(October), pp20–35.

van Raaij, E. and Stoelhorst, J. (2008) The implementation of a market orientation: a review and integration of the contributions to date. *European Journal of Marketing*, 42 (11/12), pp1265-1293.

QUICK QUIZ

1. What advantages does the marketing orientation have over other organisational philosophies: product, production and sales?

2. Outline the benefits that a marketing orientation can offer the following organisations: a high-street retailer, a charity and a global fast-moving consumer goods brand.

3. List three of the five cultural aspects for a marketing orientation.

4. List the three requirements to achieve a marketing orientation in your organisation.

5. Quantify the needs of the customer groups (segments) within the markets your organisation serves.

ACTIVITY DEBRIEFS

Activity 1.1

Marketing information will enable the chosen organisation to identify and prioritise the needs of the customer and the factors from the external environment that impact upon the customer's choice. Such examples could be based on attitude, preferences, dislikes and desires of the potential customers.

Activity 1.2

The necessary co-ordination and communication issues would relate to how the finance department is geared towards understanding customers' current and future needs. The list should include examples such as ensuring payment dates to suppliers are adhered to, refunds for customers are paid promptly and the internal financial procedures are customer-facing.

Activity 1.3

A list of the markets should be established by some criteria such as geographical location, gender or product type and then an assessment made on their worth by sales, market share etc. For each defined market the range of customer needs should be described. This will be useful when performance of each market is reviewed to gain an understanding of the market trends over time.

QUICK QUIZ ANSWERS

1   A marketing orientation has the customer's point of view at the centre of the organisation's activity.

2   The benefits are realised by only undertaking activities that are beneficial for the customer:

- High street retailer: Understands target customer and tailors relevant products and services
- Charity: Relates support to client requirements in partnership with other support agencies
- Global fast-moving consumer goods brand: Positions brand to match customer's expectation and arranges internal organisation to deliver the experience.

3   The five cultural aspects are: customer focus, competitor focus, integrated functional co-ordination, organisational culture and long-term profits.

4   The three requirements are:

- The generation of market information about the needs of customers and external environmental factors
- The dissemination of such information across organisational functions
- The development and implementation of strategies in response to the information.

5   These could include product range requirements, product functionality, ease of use, accessibility of stores and product price point.

CHAPTER 2

The synergistic planning process

Introduction

In this chapter, we are going to explore the marketing planning process. Why plan? What is the purpose of the marketing plan? What are the barriers? What should be included in a marketing plan? How do we obtain a competitive advantage from our planning?

The marketing plan contains the following stages:

- Mission, corporate goals and objectives
- Assessment of the current internal and external situation
- Internal analysis
- Segmentation, targeting and positioning
- Marketing strategy
- Tactical marketing plan
- Marketing budget
- Implementation and performance evaluation

In order to complete an effective marketing plan, all these sequential stages need to be undertaken.

Topic list

The synergistic planning process   (1)

The purpose of marketing planning   (2)

Achieving a competitive advantage   (3)

The stages of the marketing planning process: analysis, planning, implementation and control   (4)

Sequential, cyclical and iterative approaches to planning   (5)

Outcomes of planning and plans   (6)

Contents of the strategic marketing plan   (7)

Barriers to planning   (8)

1.2	Critically evaluate the synergistic planning process including the different components of the marketing plan and its links with delivering the organisation's corporate, business and marketing strategies
	■ The purpose of marketing planning
	■ Achieving a sustainable competitive advantage
	■ The stages of the marketing planning process: analysis, planning, implementation and control
	■ Sequential, cyclical and iterative approaches to planning
	■ The outcomes of planning and plans
	■ Contents of a marketing plan
	■ Documentation and reality

1 The synergistic planning process

▶ **Key term**

Synergistic planning

Synergistic planning is the rational process of determining future actions based on a realistic consideration of the current situation and the outcome that is desired.

■ Desired outcome
■ Analysing the current situation
■ Designing possible routes
■ Deciding what to do and how to do it.

The process of planning must start with a clear statement of what is to be achieved.

It is only when objectives are clearly defined that alternative courses of action can be evaluated and eventual success or failure measured.

Planning must take into account the current circumstances that will affect the achievement of the objective.

So the first step is to establish the current situation. It is important to establish the current internal strengths and weaknesses and identify the external opportunities and threats for the future.

The next step is to analyse the information gathered and to generate potential strategies.

When a range of possible plans has been outlined, it then becomes necessary to go through a process of selection, normally by considering such factors as those below:

■ Probability of success
■ Resources required
■ Acceptability of the proposed action and its implications
■ Potential obstacles.

The process of planning is not complete when a course of action has been chosen. It is essential to prepare detailed plans for all the groups and individuals involved, which must be integrated in such a way that all action undertaken supports the attainment of the overall objective through implementation of the plan. It is an iterative process that is dynamic, responsive and challenging.

Finally, performance measures and control mechanisms must also be established if the plans are to be successfully executed.

2 The purpose of marketing planning

McDonald states that marketing planning is necessary because of:

- Increasing turbulence, complexity and competitiveness
- The speed of technological change
- The need for the marketing planner to
  - identify sources of competitive advantage
  - force an organised approach
- The need for superiors to inform
- The need for non-marketing functions to get support
- The need for subordinates
  - to get resources
  - gain commitment
  - to set objectives and strategies.

Organisations need a strategic marketing plan in order to adapt to changing business environments. Organisations must continually adapt and develop if they are to remain successful.

The marketing plan should provide a systematic framework with which to analyse the marketplace and supply a well-defined way to pursue strategic goals.

Drummond *et al*. (2008) summarises the reasons for planning as follows.

- **Adapting to change**
  Planning provides an opportunity to examine how changes in the business environment have affected or will affect the organisation. It will enable management to focus on strategic issues as opposed to day-to-day operational problems.

- **Resource allocation**
  No plan can succeed without appropriate resources. When a strategic perspective is taken, organisations are better placed to marshal the resources required to meet the strategic opportunities. Planning allows the organisation to deploy resources to meet threats and take advantage of opportunities.

- **Consistency**
  A marketing plan provides a common base to work from, enhancing the decision-making process. The use of standard methods and formats should improve internal communication.

- **Integration**
  As a strategic process, planning should facilitate the integration and co-ordination of all marketing activities. Where there is a strategic focus, it should be possible to generate synergy from the individual elements of the marketing mix.

- **Communication and motivation**
  The plan should clearly communicate strategic intent to employees and other stakeholders. Clear objectives and an understanding of the individual and group contributions to the process will serve to generate 'ownership' and motivation.

- **Control**

    All monitoring and control activities are based on some predetermined plan. The planning process should set meaningful targets and timescales, thus defining the criteria by which success is measured.

It is important to remember where the marketing plan fits into overall corporate strategy.

The corporate strategic plan and the marketing plan are not the same thing. The difference is largely of scope. The corporate plan has to consider all aspects of the organisation's business while the marketing plan is principally concerned with the marketing activities. The marketing plan is thus derived from the corporate plan. However, the marketing plan should be closely linked to the corporate plan and should support it.

Strategic decisions are concerned with:

- The long-term direction of the organisation
- Defining the scope of the organisation's activities in terms of what it will do and will not do
- Matching the activities of the organisation to the environment in which it operates, so that it optimises the opportunities and minimises the threats
- Matching the organisation's activities to its resource capacity.

The differences between strategic and marketing planning are given in Table 2.1.

There are two types of marketing plan – the strategic and the tactical. The strategic plan takes a longer time frame and will provide a broad framework for the organisation's marketing activities.

Table 2.1 Differences between strategic and marketing planning

Strategic planning	Marketing planning
Concerned with overall, long-term organisational direction	Concerned with the medium-term and the day-to-day performance
Provides a long-term framework for the organisation and the strategic business units	Concerned with one aspect of the organisation's development
Overall orientation needed to match the organisation to its environment	The functional orientation tends to be the main emphasis
Goals and objectives are evaluated from the perspective of the overall organisation	Goals and objectives are converted to specific targets
Emphasis on financial performance measures	

Strategic marketing will focus on defining market segments and the positioning of products to obtain a competitive position. Plans will consider the changing business environment, changing market dynamics and the strategies and products of competitors. Broad strategies will be developed for distribution, product development, communications and pricing.

Tactical marketing takes a shorter time frame and will be concerned with day-to-day activities and budgetary controls. The broad strategic marketing objectives and strategies will be developed into operational objectives and strategies. Problems are often repetitive and will deal with the individual aspects of the marketing mix such as pricing and promotions.

The differences between strategic and tactical marketing are given in Table 2.2.

 The Chartered Institute of Marketing

Table 2.2   Differences between strategic and tactical marketing

	Strategic marketing	Tactical marketing
Time frame	Long term	Short term
Focus	Broad	Narrow
Key tasks	Defining market and competitive position	Day-to-day operational marketing activity
Information and problem solving	Unstructured, external aspects	Structured, internal, repetitive
Examples	Market development, new product development	Promotions, price discounting

(Adapted from Drummond *et al*, 2008)

> **THE REAL WORLD**
>
> The influence of globalisation has had a significant impact on how marketers approach overall long-term organisational direction. The global economic cycle plays an important part in deciding how the organisation will develop its marketing plan. The global economic downturn which started in 2009 has had a major influence in how organisations have had to adapt to increasing competitive pressures and low levels of consumer confidence. Consequently the tactical plan became very important with a focus on cash flow and customer service. A key requirement is to constantly analyse the marketplace, adapt to changes and supply a well-defined way to pursue strategic goals. For the organisation it is very important to constantly learn from the operational experiences and to modify the strategic plan as necessary.

3 Achieving a competitive advantage

▶ **Key term**

Competitive advantage: anything that a firm does especially well compared to rival firms.

Marketing strategy and the concept of competitive advantage are intrinsically linked.

Competitive advantage is the process of identifying a fundamental and sustainable basis from which to compete. Marketing strategy aims to deliver this advantage in the marketplace.

Porter (1985) identified three fundamental sources of competitive advantage. These are:

- Cost leadership
- Differentiation
- Focus.

Let us examine each of these sources of competitive advantage, or generic strategies as they are called.

3.1 Cost leadership

One source of competitive advantage is to pursue an overall cost leadership position. The focus of strategic activity is to achieve and maintain a low cost structure.

The organisation will be pursuing economies of scale, applying new technology, global sourcing of materials, minimising R&D expenditure and keeping a firm control of overheads.

Maintaining a competitive advantage through cost leadership can be difficult. Cost leadership with high volume will require high levels of investment. Better financed and resourced competitors may enter the market. Economies of scale may fall and overheads rise if market share is lost.

3.2 Differentiation

The product offered here is differentiated from the competition. The product offering must be perceived as unique. The source of differentiation should be on the basis of customer value and ideally should offer the opportunity for charging a price premium.

Maintaining a competitive advantage through differentiation can be difficult. The costs of differentiation can exceed the benefit of increased revenues. Differentiation and innovations may be replicated by competitors.

Common sources of differentiation include:

- Product performance
- Product perception
- Product augmentation.

3.3 Focus

The aim is to specialise in specific market segments and develop detailed knowledge of customer requirements. This approach may be based on factors such as:

- Geographic area
- End-user focus
- Specialist products.

Competitive advantage may be achieved by effectively meeting the needs of the chosen segments better than competitors. However, the advantage may be eroded as new competitors, perhaps better resourced and financed, are attracted to profitable niches.

Porter (1985) advises organisations to pursue competitive advantage through the adoption of one generic strategy and thereby avoiding the danger of 'stuck in the middle' positions which are perceived as having low profitability.

In order to be sustainable, the competitive advantage must be:

- Relevant – It must be appropriate to current and future market needs. It must also be relevant to the organisation – it must be achievable given the resources available to the organisation.

- Tenable – The competitive advantage must be difficult to replicate, otherwise competitors will simply copy.

So what are the barriers that prevent competitors from copying a successful formula? There are two major barriers.

- Asset-based barriers – These are tangible assets controlled by the organisation such as location, plant and machinery, finance and brands.

- Skilled-based barriers – These are skills and resources which utilise assets effectively and efficiently. Examples would include product design, quality management and brand development.

Davidson (1997, p153) states that competitive advantage is achieved 'whenever you do something better than competitors. If that something is important to consumers, or if a number of small advantages can be combined, you have an exploitable competitive advantage'.

Davidson identified a number of sources of competitive advantage (Table 2.3).

The Chartered Institute of Marketing

Table 2.3   Sources of competitive advantage

Source of competitive advantage	Examples
Product performance	Strong, easy-to-use, economic
Perception of product	Product positioning, brand image
Low-cost operations	Location, economies of scale, buying power
Legal advantage	Patents, copyright, contracts
Alliances and relationships	Networking
Superior skills	R&D, design
Flexibility	Customised solutions
Attitude	Focus on delivering value, innovation

(Adapted from Davidson, 1997)

ACTIVITY 2.1

List three companies that have pursued competitive advantage based on:

1.   Cost leadership
2.   Differentiation
3.   Focus.

4 The stages of the marketing planning process: analysis, planning, implementation and control

Marketing planning appears to be a simple logical step-by-step process. It is seen as a series of activities leading to the setting of marketing objectives and the formulation of plans for achieving them. However, in reality it is a multi-faceted, complex, cross-functional activity that touches on every aspect of organisations.

In small organisations the process may be informal but in larger organisations the process is likely to a formal system. Once started, marketing planning becomes part of the annual planning cycle.

The standard approaches to the planning process are:

- **Top–down**: Senior management develop objectives and strategy which managers at an operational level then implement.

- **Bottom–up**: Senior management devolves authority and responsibility for the formulation and implementation of strategy. Senior management then monitors the agreed objectives.

However, hybrid systems are also common, where the objectives are 'top–down' and the responsibility for formulation and implementation is devolved.

The stages of the marketing planning process are:

- **Analysis**: This covers the analysis of the marketing environment, both macro and micro, the industry, markets and competitor analysis

- **Planning**: This covers formulation of strategies and marketing programmes with the identification of resources and timing

- **Implementation**: This covers the practical execution of the plan, with any changes required to achieve this

- **Control**: This covers monitoring against planned targets, control mechanisms and performance metrics.

5 Sequential, cyclical and iterative approaches to planning

Marketing planning is a systematic process that involves assessing marketing opportunities and resources, determining marketing objectives and strategies, and developing marketing programmes and plans for implementation and control.

The marketing planning cycle is a circular process that runs in two directions, with planning running one way and feedback the other. There is a need for continuous feedback so that monitoring and control with modifications of the plan can take place (Figure 2.1).

Most organisations produce marketing plans each year. Once the system is up and running, the process will involve the revision of the previous year's plan, updating the marketing analysis and revising the strategies.

The Chartered Institute of Marketing

Figure 2.1   The marketing planning cycle

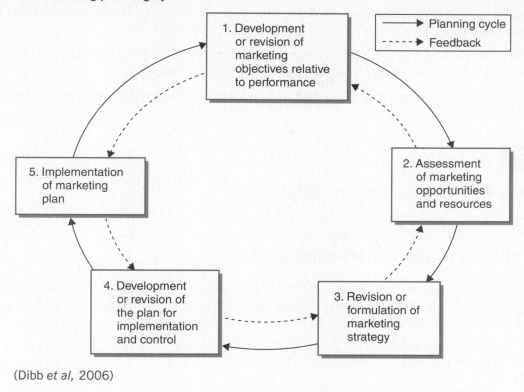

(Dibb *et al*, 2006)

6 Outcomes of planning and plans

Planning is often seen as a restrictive process based on the programming of events and the generation of paperwork. Nothing could be further from the truth.

So what are the outcomes?

The outcomes of planning and the marketing plan are:

- A vision for the future of the organisation
- A mission to communicate
- Organisational objectives covering a range of time periods
- Objectives for each of the functional areas of the organisation.

Strategies to follow to pursue the objectives

- Identification of market segments
- Decision on which segments to target
- A positioning statement
- Plans for each element of the marketing mix with resources and timing:
    - product
    - place
    - price
    - promotion
    - people
    - physical evidence
    - processes
- Identification of performance metrics
- Identification of methods and times of monitoring
- Control measures
- Contingencies.

The marketing plan should be a concise yet complete document providing a summary of the environment, the marketplace and the organisation's position together with the recommended strategy and detailed plans for the marketing mix.

The plan should be informative and must set out clearly the marketing activities that should be pursued to implement the desired strategy to achieve the organisational objectives.

The really successful marketing plan should be a vehicle for communication to managers throughout the organisation.

ACTIVITY 2.2

Using the marketing planning cycle, list an activity for each component.

7 Contents of the strategic marketing plan

So what does the strategic marketing plan look like? The content, structure, detail and complexity will vary from organisation to organisation. However, strategic plans tend to have common elements and the following components would be expected:

- External analysis
- Industry analysis
- Internal analysis
- Opportunity identification
- Objective setting
- Formulation of strategy
- Proposed marketing programmes
- Implementation and control.

A typical structure for a marketing plan is shown below (adapted from McDonald, 2007):

1.0   Executive summary
    1.1   Current position
    1.2   Key issues
2.0   Corporate strategy
    2.1   Corporate mission/objectives
    2.2   Summary of overall position and corporate strategy
3.0   External and internal analysis
    3.1   Overview of market
    3.2   Competitor analysis
    3.3   Future trends
    3.4   SWOT
4.0   Marketing objectives
    4.1   Financial objectives
    4.2   Marketing objectives
5.0   Marketing strategy
    5.1   Market segmentation
    5.2   Competitive advantage
    5.3   Marketing strategy
    5.4   Specific marketing programme 7Ps
       - Product
       - Place
       - Price

The Chartered
Institute of Marketing

- Promotion
- Physical evidence
- People
- Processes

6.0 Implementation
  6.1 Schedule of key tasks
  6.2 Resource allocation
  6.3 Budgets
  6.4 Contingency
7.0 Control and forecasting
  7.1 Assumptions made in the plan
  7.2 Critical success factors
    - Benchmarks
    - Metrics
  7.3 Financial forecasts
    - Costs
    - Revenues

Whilst formats, conventions and content may differ, the key purpose of the strategic marketing plan is to generate action. The marketing planning process should address the critical issues of the organisation in a manner which is relevant to that individual organisation.

THE REAL WORLD

A synergistic planning process for a fictitious Italian restaurant includes the following approach:

- Decide desired outcomes
- Situation analysis
- Decide on possible routes to desired outcome
- Decide what course of action to take and how to get there

Sigmund's Gourmet Pasta will be the leading gourmet pasta restaurant in Eugene with a rapidly developing consumer brand and growing customer base. The signature line of innovative, premium, pasta dishes include pesto with smoked salmon, pancetta and peas linguini in an alfredo sauce, and fresh mussels and clams in a marinara sauce. Sigmund's Gourmet Pasta also serves distinct salads, desserts, and beverages. Sigmund's Gourmet Pasta will reinvent the pasta experience for individuals, families, and take-out customers with disposable income by selling high quality, innovative products at a reasonable price, designing tasteful, convenient locations, and providing industry-benchmark customer service.

Sigmund's Gourmet Pasta is close to entering its second year of operation. The restaurant has been well received, and marketing is now critical to its continued success and future profitability. The restaurant offers an extensive offering of gourmet pastas. The basic market need is to offer individuals, families, and take-out customers fresh, creative, attractive, pasta dishes, salads and desserts. Sigmund's uses homemade pasta, fresh vegetables, and premium meats and cheeses.

Market trends

The market trend for restaurants is headed toward a more sophisticated customer. The restaurant patron today relative to yesterday is more sophisticated in a number of different ways.

Food quality. The preference for high-quality ingredients is increasing as customers are learning to appreciate the qualitative differences.

Presentation/appearance. As presentation of an element of the culinary experience becomes more pervasive, patrons are learning to appreciate this aspect of the industry.

Health consciousness. As Americans in general are more aware of their health, evidenced by the increase in individuals exercising and health club memberships, patrons are requesting more healthy alternatives when they eat out. They recognise that an entree can be quite tasty, and reasonably good for you.

Selection. People are demanding a larger selection of foods; they are no longer accepting a limited menu.

Keys to Success

Location, Location, Location.

Sigmund's site selection criteria are critical to success. Arthur Johnson, former VP Real Estate, Starbucks, helped us identify the following site selection criteria:

- Daytime and evening populations.
- Shopping patterns.
- Car counts.
- Household income levels.

Critical issues

Sigmund's Gourmet Pasta is still in the speculative stage as a retail restaurant. Its critical issues are:

Continue to take a modest fiscal approach; expand at a reasonable rate, not for the sake of expansion in itself, but because it is economically wise to. Continue to build brand awareness which will drive customers to existing outlets as well as ease the marketing efforts of future outlets.

Difficulties and risks:

Problems generating visibility.

Overly aggressive and debilitating actions by competitors.

An entry into the Eugene market of an already existing, franchised gourmet pasta restaurant.

Worst case risks may include:

Determining that the business cannot support itself on an ongoing basis.

Having to dispose of equipment or intellectual property to cover liabilities.

ACTIVITY 2.3

For Sigmund's Gourmet Pasta, write a vision statement that captures the strategic marketing requirements for the Italian restaurant.

---

8 Barriers to planning

We have seen that marketing planning is a logical sequence of steps and activities which lead to the setting of marketing objectives and the formulation of plans for achieving them. There are, however, many practical obstacles to be overcome. Many of the barriers to successful marketing planning are related to the human aspects of management.

While marketing planning has many clear benefits, it can create tension and barriers within the organisation. The newly defined strategies may create considerable change, involving new structures, systems, processes and even changes in staffing.

- **Culture**: The prevailing culture may not be amenable to marketing plans. There is often resistance to change and a gradual return to the 'old practices'.

- **Power and politics**: All organisations are subject to internal politics. The development of a strategic marketing plan may become a battlefield where vested interests fight over proposals, resources and status.

The Chartered Institute of Marketing

- **Analysis not action**: Time and energy can be wasted by the process of analysing data and planning for action without actually taking any action. Many planning systems are more concerned with reviewing progress and controlling activities rather than tackling strategic issues.

- **Resource issues**: A major aspect of the planning process is to match resources to strategic aims. Managers must take a realistic view of the resource position and endeavour to ensure resources are not needlessly withheld or overcommitted.

- **Skills**: Managers may not have the skills to make the best use of the planning process and the opportunities for business development are missed opportunities.

McDonald (2007) identifies the following ten principal barriers:

- Confusion over marketing tactics and strategy
- Isolating the marketing function from operations
- Confusion between the marketing function and the marketing concept
- Organisational barriers – the tribal mentality – failing to define SBUs correctly
- Lack of in-depth analysis
- Confusion between process and output
- Lack of knowledge and skills
- Lack of a systematic approach to marketing planning
- Failure to prioritise objectives
- Hostile corporate cultures.

Whilst marketing planning may be considered a series of simple steps, in practice the process is complex and challenging.

▶ **Assessment tip**

Understand the concept of the synergistic planning process and how it is important to identify what is achievable and possible. Learn the different approaches to competitive advantage and the stages of the marketing planning process: analysis, planning, implementation and control and the potential barriers

---

Summary

This chapter has explored the systematic marketing planning process and the nature of strategic marketing. It has identified the sources of competitive advantage as a basis for developing marketing strategies. The elements of a marketing plan are then considered and an overview of barriers to marketing planning presented.

CHAPTER ROUNDUP

- Understand the synergistic planning process and the purpose of marketing planning
- Recognise how to develop a competitive advantage and the stages of the marketing planning process: analysis, planning, implementation and control
- Determine the outcomes of planning and plans and the contents of the strategic marketing plan
- Understand the barriers to marketing planning

FURTHER READING

Doyle, P. (2002) *Marketing Management and Strategy*. 3rd Edition. London, Prentice Hall.

Lynch, L (2006) *Corporate Strategy*. 4th Edition. London, Prentice Hall.

Mplans.com (2012) Free marketing plans & more. Mplans, http://www.mplans.com/ [Accessed on 19 June 2012]

REFERENCES

Davidson, H. (1997) *Even More Offensive Marketing*. London, Penguin Business.

Dibb, S. *et al* (2006) *Marketing: Concepts and Strategies*. 5th edition. Boston, Houghton Mifflin.

Drummond, G. *et al* (2008) *Strategic Marketing Planning and Control*. 3rd edition. Oxford, Butterworth Heinemann.

McDonald, M. (2007) *Marketing Plans: How to Prepare Them, How to Use Them*. 6th edition. Oxford, Butterworth Heinemann.

Porter, M. (1985) *Competitive Advantage*. London, The Free Press.

QUICK QUIZ

1   What is meant by the synergistic marketing planning process?

2   What is the content of the strategic marketing plan?

3   How can differentiation assist in developing a competitive advantage?

4   Explain how a luxury brand company such as Burberry (www.uk.burberry.com) sustain their competitive advantage?

5   What human aspects of management could act as a barrier to successful marketing planning.

Activity 2.1

1. Cost leadership: Low-cost airline such as Easyjet or Ryanair
2. Differentiation: Meets needs better than others such as McDonald's or Audi cars
3. Focus: Luxury brand such as Bentley cars or Burberry

Activity 2.2

Using the headings of the marketing planning cycle typical examples would be:

1. Marketing objectives: Gain an addition % market share in 3 years
2. Assessment of marketing opportunities: Review staffing level requirements to achieve objectives
3. Formulation of marketing strategy: Decide on long-term plan such as growth or differentiation
4. Development of the plan: Determine implementation and control issues
5. Implementation the plan: Manage the resources and timing considerations for the organisation

Activity 2.3

The vision statement should capture the experience and service delivery of innovative, premium pasta lines at a high quality and reasonable price. An example would be:

Mantinelli's; a fine Italian experience of premium pasta dishes!

Mantinelli's provide innovative, premium pasta dishes created by our talented chefs with the highest quality, fresh ingredients in our finest restaurant. We aim to provide a memorable Italian experience to enjoy our famous dishes in a relaxed atmosphere.

QUICK QUIZ ANSWERS

1. Synergistic planning is the rational process of determining future actions based on a realistic consideration of the current situation and the outcome that is desired.

2. The strategic marketing plan includes:

   - External analysis
   - Industry analysis
   - Internal analysis
   - Opportunity identification
   - Objective setting
   - Formulation of strategy
   - Proposed marketing programmes
   - Implementation and control

3. Underlying differentiation is the concept of market segmentation. By standing out from your competition a higher price will be sought for the additional benefits.

4. Burberry will sustain their competitive advantage through constant innovation of desirable and exclusive new products.

5. A number of potential barriers exist including culture, power and politics, analysis not action, skills and resource issues.

CHAPTER 3

The role of the marketing plan in relation to the organisation's philosophy

Introduction

In this chapter, we will look at ways in which organisations attempt to communicate their purpose, through mission, vision and corporate values statements. A statement of the direction and purpose of the organisation is the key foundation on which objectives (see Chapter 4) and strategy (see Chapter 5) will be based. Many marketers argue that a marketing plan is incomplete without some reference to the organisation's mission or vision.

Topic list

The marketing plan as a means of conveying organisational purpose and future vision	1
The marketing plan as a vehicle for setting direction and focus	2
The marketing plan as operational framework	3
The marketing plan as a method of resource and budget allocation	4
The marketing plan as a tool for performance measurement	5

1.3	Critically evaluate the role of the marketing plan in relation to the organisation's philosophy and an organisation's strategic intent
	▪ The marketing plan as means of conveying organisational purpose and future vision
	▪ The marketing plan as vehicle for setting direction and focus
	▪ The marketing plan as an operational framework
	▪ The marketing plan as a method of resource and budget allocation
	▪ The marketing plan as a tool for performance measurement

1 The marketing plan as a means of conveying organisational purpose and future vision

Mission statement

The mission of the organisation is the unique purpose that distinguishes it from other organisations and defines the boundaries or scope of its activities.

Vision

Greater emphasis is now being given to creating a vision. The vision is a picture of the organisation in the future, perhaps five years ahead.

Organisational values

Organisations are now including statements on organisational values in their annual reports and other literature.

The organisation's aims and aspirations are the results of a series of influences. Johnson *et al*. (2005) identify these as:

- **Corporate governance** – To whom should the organisation be accountable? What is the regulatory framework within which executive decisions are made? These corporate governance issues relate to the accountability of the organisation and they exist to constrain management and protect the rights of stakeholders.

- **Stakeholders** – These include groups such as shareholders, suppliers of finance, employees, suppliers, customers and the wider community. Organisations may try to further the interests of particular groups depending on the power and influence of such stakeholders.

- **Business ethics** – Ethics will affect the mission and the objectives of organisations. This will mainly shape the response to issues of corporate social responsibility.

- **Cultural context** – The cultural environment will influence the mission of the organisation. National cultures, organisational culture and individual employees will all have differing levels of influence on the organisational mission.

Stakeholders are able to influence purpose and strategies. However, power is shared unequally between the different groups of stakeholders. There are many different sources of power, as shown in Table 3.1.

Table 3.1   Sources of stakeholder power

Within organisations	For external stakeholders
Hierarchy (formal power)	Control of strategic resources, eg materials, labour, money
Influence (informal power) eg charismatic leadership, control of strategic resources	Through internal links, eg informal influence
Possession of knowledge and skills eg finance specialists, computer specialists	Possession of knowledge or skills, eg subcontractors, partners
Control of human environment	Involvement in strategy implementation eg distribution outlets, agents
Involvement in strategy implementation	

(Adapted from Johnson *et al,* 2005)

The values, mission and objectives will be the result of a complex mix of negotiations and pressures from stakeholders who have varying degrees of power or influence.

Before writing a mission statement, the marketing planner needs to consider the purpose of the organisation. This involves asking questions such as:

- Why does the organisation exist:
    - To create wealth for the owners?
    - To satisfy the needs of stakeholders?
    - To pursue some higher goal (scientific advancement)?
- What are the organisation's capabilities?
- What are the internal and external constraints?
- What are the current opportunities?
- What are the opportunities that might develop?

Bart and Baetz (1998) argue that a well-crafted mission statement has the following advantages:

- Provides direction
- Provides a basis for objectives and strategies
- Serves as a focal point
- Ensures unanimity of purpose
- Arouses positive feelings about the firm
- Resolves divergent views among managers.

Clear mission statements play an important part in helping to frame marketing strategies. Poorly or wrongly defined mission statements can create strategic limitations which may result in loss of competitiveness and failure.

Pearce and David (1987) suggest that the mission statement should contain the following aspects:

- Customers (the target market)
- Products/services (offerings and value provided to customers)
- Geographic markets
- Technology
- Concern for survival/growth/profits
- Philosophy (organisation's values, ethics and beliefs)
- Public image (contribution to society/communities)
- Employees (importance of management and employees)
- Distinctive competence (how the organisation is better than or different from its competitors).

David and David (2003) undertook a study that found that many organisations failed to include many of the above aspects. Key areas of markets, technology, philosophy, public image and employees were frequently omitted or given little attention.

BPP LEARNING MEDIA   3: The role of the marketing plan in relation to the organisation's philosophy | **31**

Mission statements that are very tightly defined may create problems in the future. As markets are evolving rapidly, a tightly defined mission may prevent the organisation developing a broader target market.

Mission statements provide a focal point and a sense of direction but many have been criticised for being too general ('to be the best') or over-ambitious ('to be a global leader').

Wilson and Gilligan (2005) suggest that 'visioning' has been most successful where there has been clarity of managerial thinking in areas, including:

- The size of the organisation, business unit or brand in three to ten years' time
- The corporate and brand values that will be developed
- The nature of the customer base and the customer segments that will be served
- How these customers should perceive the organisation or brand
- The geographic coverage that will have been achieved
- The overall position within the market and the competitive stance
- The links with other organisations.

Hamel and Prahalad (1989) have discussed vision in terms of a strategic intent. They have defined strategic intent as involving the following:

- A dream that energises the organisation
- A long-term ambition which provides a sense of direction
- Offering a new goal for employees to work towards
- Provides coherence to the strategic plans
- Implying a stretch for the organisation.

These authors argue that strategic intent requires a demanding purpose which will leverage the organisation's resources and capabilities. It is not sufficient to simply match resources with objectives. Strategic intent involves the setting of challenging goals that will stretch the organisation, requiring creativity to make the most of the limited resources.

In developing a vision, there is a need to understand both the organisation's competences and the future likely changes in the environment. There is also a need to understand the organisational values.

Values relate to the organisation's culture and the beliefs that are embedded within the organisation.

Values often include the principles of business:

- Commitment to customers
- Commitment to employees
- Commitment to suppliers
- Commitment to the environment
- Ethical governance.

THE REAL WORLD

Welcome to The World of Airbus

Airbus is the world's leading aircraft manufacturer whose customer focus, commercial know-how, technological leadership and manufacturing efficiency have propelled it to the forefront of the industry.

Airbus' modern and comprehensive product line comprises highly successful families of aircraft ranging from 107 to 525 seats: the single-aisle A320 Family, the wide-body long-range A330/A340 and the all-new next generation A350 XWB Family, and the ultra long-range, double-decker A380 Family. The company also continues to broaden its scope and product range by applying its expertise to the military market. It is also extending its portfolio of freighter aircraft that will set new standards in the general and express freight market sectors.

(Airbus, 2012)

Select an example of each of the organisations below and identify their mission statement.

(a)   A major retailer
(b)   An oil company
(c)   A construction company
(d)   A charity.

THE REAL WORLD

British Airways (BA) is a global flag carrier airline of the United Kingdom that is now part of the International Airlines Group (IAG). BA is a founding member of the oneworld airline alliance, along with American Airlines, Cathay Pacific and Qantas.

Business plan

We have built our business plan to both advance our Global Premium Airline strategy, and to ensure British Airways fulfils its role within IAG.

Central to the business plan is the effort to adapt British Airways in order to realise these synergies through:

Deliver outstanding customer service and continue to invest in our products

Our customer-facing staff have long been passionate about delivering outstanding customer service.

Grow revenue with our airline partners

We will work with both Air Berlin and Kingfisher Airlines to support their introduction to oneworld. Where appropriate we will seek to deepen partnerships through the extension of codeshare relationships and the development of joint businesses.

Secure the right assets and infrastructure

We will prepare the airline for the arrival of our new Boeing 787 and Airbus A380 aircraft, involving development of the airport infrastructure, provision of enhanced IT, and a significant programme of training.

Achieve a cost base that enables us to compete and grow

Despite achieving structural change in our cost base, we face significant cost pressures over the life of the plan, with a projected rise in fuel costs, above-inflation increases in many airport and over-flight charges, as well as inflationary pressures on wages and supplier costs.

Create the culture and capabilities to succeed

All elements of the plan rely on engaged, motivated people. A comprehensive People Strategy has been developed that will transform the way people are led, developed, rewarded and engaged.

Set the standard for responsible aviation

British Airways has led the industry in adopting a responsible approach through our award-winning One Destination Programme. This brings together all of our work on the Environment, Community, Diversity and Inclusion.

(IAG 2010 Financial Report, 2012)

The vision provides a focus and direction for the organisation while the values provide guidance for the behaviour of management and employees.

Using the same organisations you selected in Activity 3.1, compare their vision and value statements.

2 The marketing plan as a vehicle for setting direction and focus

The marketing plan serves as a vehicle for setting the direction of the organisation and as a focus for the management and employees.

The marketing plan, incorporating a mission and vision, maps the direction the organisation should take — both now and in the future. Management, having created the mission and vision, can then focus on specific objectives and strategies within a long-term framework. The statement of strategic intent, or mission, provides a reference point when making strategic decisions and when setting objectives. This should help to focus and prevent decisions which are not appropriate to the long term.

The marketing plan should be communicated widely if it is to provide the focus for both management and employees.

3 The marketing plan as operational framework

The marketing plan provides a framework for the operations of the organisation. Beyond the mission and the statement of strategic intent, the marketing plan sets out plans for each aspect of the strategies to be pursued towards the organisational objectives.

The marketing plan identifies the objectives together with the strategies to be adopted to achieve those objectives at the different levels of the organisation. The marketing plan will outline the strategies and tactics for each area of the marketing mix.

The marketing plan provides a detailed route map for the different aspects of the marketing mix and provides guidance for other functional areas of the organisation, for example, production and human resources.

The marketing plan provides not only an effective route map for what should be done but also outlines how the organisation should monitor and control the implementation of the plan.

Milestones or points where reviews should be carried out are identified and the metrics to be used should be stated within a marketing plan.

Time is an important aspect of marketing planning. The marketing plan should identify the timing of the various activities. Organisations may be successful if the timing of various activities is not right. Critical issues are:

- Time to develop new products
- Timing and speed of entry into new markets
- Timing and speed of response to competitor challenges
- Timing of marketing communications.

The marketing plan not only outlines strategies but also provides a detailed guide for the implementation of the plan, with activities, timing, resources and costs.

The marketing plan is not just some vague vision but a detailed plan for a range of activities that should be put into operation in pursuit of the organisational objectives.

The Chartered
Institute of Marketing

Using the organisations you selected in Activity 3.1, compare their approach to ethical issues using information from recent company reports.

4 The marketing plan as a method of resource and budget allocation

> **Key term**
>
> **Budget allocation:** the marketing plan will establish the resource priorities required to achieve the planned goals. The budget allocation determines which resources of materials, equipment and labour including staff costs will be funded.

The marketing plan provides a basis for the allocation of resources and the allocation of budgets.

The marketing plan will identify activities to be carried out and should identify the resources required. The resources may be materials, equipment and labour or management time. Resources are always likely to be limited; therefore, the marketing plan provides an opportunity to consider priorities and those activities that are critical for the success of the organisation. Activities which are considered to be more important will receive a greater proportion of the resources.

Costs need to be calculated for each activity outlined in the plan and incorporated into the organisation's budgets. What is the cost of the internal marketing programme? What will that radio advertising cost? How much will the extra sales staff cost? What is the cost of that direct mail campaign?

The costs of all the activities should be incorporated into the marketing plan. Appropriate budgets should be allocated to the functional departments responsible for each aspect. Budget allocation requires strong negotiating skills, as politics within the organisation may conflict with the priorities set out in the marketing plan.

Responsibilities will need to be agreed and departments and individuals given authority to manage each delegated aspect of the master budget.

5 The marketing plan as a tool for performance measurement

The marketing plan provides a tool which can be used to measure performance or progress with marketing activities.

A good marketing plan will identify not only the strategies and activities but also the milestones or times when they should be achieved by. When the plan is implemented, the actual performance can be measured against the plan. Should the objectives not be achieved by the relevant milestones, corrective action can be taken to put the plan back on track.

The marketing plan will identify various performance measures or metrics. At the corporate level, financial measures such as net profit, earnings per share and return on capital employed will be used. At a marketing level, metrics such as sales, conversion of enquiries to orders and customer retention will be used. Objectives for all of these will be set out in the plan and the actual performance can be measured at regular intervals to ascertain whether the required performance is being achieved.

The measures of performance can be used to compare performance between one period and another, typically one year with another. However, the performance measures can also be used to compare the performance of the organisation with other organisations and provide a basis for benchmarking.

The National Health Service (NHS) has seven key principles:

1   The NHS provides a comprehensive service, available to all irrespective of gender, race, disability, age, sexual orientation, religion or belief

2   Access to NHS services is based on clinical need, not an individual's ability to pay

3   The NHS aspires to the highest standards of excellence and professionalism

4   NHS services must reflect the needs and preferences of patients, their families and their carers

5   The NHS works across organisational boundaries and in partnership with other organisations, in the interest of patients, local communities and the wider population

6   The NHS is committed to providing best value for taxpayers' money and the most effective, fair and sustainable use of finite resources

7   The NHS is accountable to the public, communities and patients it serves.

These form the basis of its marketing plan and shape the organisation's philosophy.

(NHS, 2012)

▶ Assessment tip

The role of the marketing plan covers a number of topics that combine to create the value proposition and delivery for an organisation. It is important to understand and be able to evaluate how each component contributes to the organisation's philosophy.

Summary

In this chapter, we have seen how the marketing plan provides a direction and focus for the organisation and provides a statement of intent. The inclusion of mission, vision and values further sets the focus of the marketing planning process around essential outcomes and key aspects of the organisation's activities. The marketing plan also provides a 'blueprint' for organisational operations and a means of measuring the performance.

The Chartered Institute of Marketing

- Recognise how the marketing plan is used as a means of conveying organisational purpose and future vision
- Understand the role of the marketing plan as a vehicle for setting direction and focus
- Appreciate the marketing plan as operational framework
- Use the marketing plan as a method of resource, budget allocation and performance measurement.

FURTHER READING

Doyle, P. (2002) *Marketing Management and Strategy*. Third edition. London, Prentice Hall.

Lynch, L (2006) *Corporate Strategy*. 4th edition. London, Prentice Hall.

Tutor2u (2012) Marketing resources. Tutor2u, http://tutor2u.net/sub_marketing.asp [Accessed on 19 June 2012]

REFERENCES

Airbus (2012) Company. Airbus, www.airbus.com/company [Accessed on 7 June 2012]

Bart, C. and Baetz, M. (1998) The relationship between mission statements and firm performance: An exploratory study. *Journal of Management Studies*, 35(6), pp823–53.

David, F.R. and David, F.R. (2003) It's time to redraft your mission statement. *Journal of Business Strategy*, 24(1), pp11–14.

Hamel, G. and Prahalad, C.K. (1989) Strategic intent. *Harvard Business Review*, 67(3), pp63–76.

IAG (2012) Annual Reports. IAG, www.iairgroup.com/phoenix.zhtml?c=240949&p=irol-reportsannual [Accessed on 20 June 2012]

Johnson, G. *et al* (2005) *Exploring Corporate Strategy*. 7th edition. Harlow, Prentice Hall

NHS (2012) NHS core principles. NHS, http://www.nhs.uk/NHSEngland/thenhs/about/Pages/nhscoreprinciples.aspx [Accessed on 7 June 2012]

Pearce, J. and David, F. (1987) Corporate mission statements: The bottom line. *Academy of Management Executive,* 1(2), pp109–15.

Wilson, R.M.S. and Gilligan, C. (2005) *Strategic Marketing Management*. 3rd edition. Oxford, Butterworth Heinemann

QUICK QUIZ

1 How does a mission statement set direction and focus for a) management and b) employees?

2 Select an organisation that you are familiar with. How could you use the marketing plan to allocate resources?

3 What criteria would you use to evaluate the marketing plan?

4 What are the critical issues in developing a marketing plan

5 How does business ethics impact on the marketing plan

Activity 3.1

Mission statements should clearly and succinctly describe the strategic aim and objectives of the organisation. The sentences in the statement should not be too long and they should explain the focus of the organisation. The mission statement should guide the actions of the organisation, spell out its overall goal, provide a path, and guide decision making. For each of the four organisations the mission statement should ultimately seeks to justify the organisation's reason for existing.

Activity 3.2

Use the mission statements from Activity 3.1 to develop the value statements for each of the organisations. Normally these are found in the organisation's annual report as it describes how the organisation provides value to these stakeholders, for example by offering specific types of products and/or services.

Activity 3.3

Ethical governance is an important contribution to the financial reporting for an organisation. Each of the organisations will describe in some detail how they embody ethical issues in the policies and procedures it adopts. Ethical issues become part of the behaviour and attitude of the organisation. For instance, British Airways places corporate responsibility at the heart of its business. It runs comprehensive programmes which are geared towards managing and minimising the environmental impact, supporting the communities, conservation projects and charities in the countries it flies to, encouraging its customers and suppliers to act responsibly and providing a working environment that motivates, develops and supports colleagues (www.iairgroup.com)

QUICK QUIZ ANSWERS

1   A mission statement provides a focal point and a sense of direction. Management understands the purpose of the organisation which shapes their attitude and the employees can understand the culture and the beliefs that are embedded within the organisation.

2   The marketing plan provides a basis for the allocation of resources and the allocation of budgets. It will identify activities to be carried out and should identify the resources required.

3   At the corporate level, financial measures such as net profit, earnings per share and return on capital employed will be used. At a marketing level, metrics such as sales, conversion of enquiries to orders and customer retention will be used.

4   Critical issues include time to develop new products, timing and speed of entry into new markets, timing and speed of response to competitor challenges, and timing of marketing communications.

5   Ethics will affect the mission and the objectives of organisations. This will mainly shape the response to issues of corporate social responsibility.

The Chartered Institute of Marketing

The relationship between corporate, business and marketing objectives at an operational level and the influences on objectives

Introduction

Having looked at the marketing plan as a means of conveying the vision and organisational purpose for the future, we will now look at how that vision can be translated into objectives.

Brassington and Pettit (2006, p949) emphasise that 'marketing strategy cannot be formulated in isolation. It has to reflect the objectives of the organisation and be compatible with the strategies pursued elsewhere in the organisation'.

Marketers must therefore look at the corporate goals and objectives before developing their own strategies.

We will see later that objectives are influenced by many internal and external influences. Developing clear objectives is critical to ensuring the overall effectiveness of the organisation. Objectives are developed at different levels within the organisation and we will see that these form a hierarchy whereby objectives at each level are linked.

Topic list

Identifying a hierarchy of objectives   (1)

Objectives at varying levels and timescales   (2)

The balanced scorecard   (3)

Consistency of plans with objectives   (4)

Recognition of environmentally driven marketing planning and the resource-based view of the firm   (5)

Internal influences on objectives   (6)

External influences on objectives   (7)

Drivers of organisational change   (8)

1.4	Evaluate the relationship between corporate, business and marketing objectives at an operational level and describe how they impact upon the activities associated with the marketing plan
	▪ Identifying a hierarchy of objectives
	▪ Objectives at varying levels and timescales
	▪ Different types of objectives: organisational, innovation, financial, market, relationship-focussed, societal, non-profit
	▪ Consistency of plans with objectives
	▪ Resource issues and constraints
1.5	Assess the external and internal influences on the formulation of objectives and specify the key environmental drivers of organisational change
	▪ Recognition of environmentally driven marketing planning and the resource-based view of the firm
	▪ Identify internal influences on objectives including objective setting process, corporate mission and strategy, culture, resources, capabilities
	▪ Identify external influences on objectives including economic conditions, markets, competition, industry life cycle, technological development
	▪ Identify drivers of organisational change including innovation, evolving consumer behaviour, globalisation, ethical consumption and corporate social responsibility, sustainability relationship management, stakeholder relations, globalisation
1.6	Critically evaluate the wider impact of external and internal environmental forces on the setting of objectives at different levels and the process of planning marketing
	▪ Macro-environment: political, cultural, social, economic, technological, legal, ecological, ethical
	▪ Micro-environment: market, customers, competitors, industry structure and dynamics, suppliers, intermediaries
	▪ Internal environment: capabilities in functional areas, assets and core competences, product and service portfolio, innovation, business relationships and strategic partnerships, current market position and past performance, dynamic capabilities, competitive advantage

1 Identifying a hierarchy of objectives

A key issue when setting objectives is to remember to ensure they are relevant to achieving the corporate vision and mission.

Objectives are not only developed across a range of key areas, they also exist at a number of levels within an organisation. Objectives should cascade down through an organisational structure, effectively forming a hierarchy. Objectives should be understood throughout the organisation and should be closely related to the organisation's resource capacity. The resource capacity will include the financial assets and facilities, human resources, production capacity, etc.

Setting objectives is an essential step in marketing planning and is central to developing effectiveness and competitive advantage.

Objectives are something you want to achieve. The objectives set should be SMART (see Table 4.1) if they are to be purposeful in directing the organisation towards corporate goals.

Table 4.1   SMART objectives

S	Specific	Should be succinct and provide clarity as to what is to be achieved
M	Measurable	Should identify targets that can be measured and monitored
A	Aspirational	Should be challenging but achievable, and should motivate staff
R	Realistic	Should be based on sound research. Should be achievable given the human, financial and other resources available
T	Time-bound	A timescale should be set for the achievement of the objective for performance monitoring

Corporate objectives

Organisations will set primary or corporate objectives. At the corporate level management will be concerned with the overall long-term profitability and objectives are usually expressed in financial terms. For example:

- To achieve a 15% return on equity
- To increase operating profits by 20%
- To achieve a return on investment of 25%
- To achieve a return of 20% on capital employed (ROCE)
- To achieve growth of 10% in earning per share (EPS).

Functional objectives

Objectives will be set for each functional area, such as operations, finance, human resources and marketing. Each functional objective developed for each function should be linked to the corporate objectives. Once the objectives have been developed, then strategies will be developed to achieve these objectives. For example:

Human resources:
- To reduce staff turnover by 15% over the next 2 years
- To increase training by 5%.

Finance:
- To reduce customer payment period by 12 days over the next 18 months
- To cut bad debts from 3% to 2% of turnover in next year.

Operations:
- To increase labour productivity by 10% over the next 2 years.

Marketing objectives

Marketing objectives need to be developed to support the corporate objectives and to ensure the corporate objectives are achieved.

These marketing objectives will be mainly concerned with products and markets. Therefore, it is likely that the typical marketing objectives will concentrate on:

- Increasing sales of existing products into existing markets
- Launching new products into existing markets
- Launching existing products into new markets
- Launching new products into new markets.

These aims need to be developed into quantifiable and measurable objectives. These should be SMART – note each of the examples below is specific and there is a target date by which to achieve the objective. All of them must relate to the overall corporate objectives.

- To increase sales by 15% by 2011
- To increase market share of product X by 10% by 2012
- To increase customer retention by 25% by 2012
- To increase the number of new products per year from 2 to 5 by 2012.

Cunard Line is one of the world's most recognised brand names in ocean travel, with a classic British heritage. For over a century and a half, the iconic ships of Cunard have been defining sophisticated ocean travel. They have always been the most famous ocean liners in the world. From fabled vessels of the past to her present royal court — Queen Mary 2, Queen Victoria and Queen Elizabeth — Cunard has carried guests across the great oceans and to the far points of the globe in unparalleled style. The corporate and marketing objectives for Cunard are aimed at their vision of providing memorable voyages and outstanding service to all of their guests.
(Cunard, 2012)

Operational or subsidiary objectives

These will be related to the marketing mix. These will tend to be objectives that are more tactical. This area will have objectives related to the product mix, pricing or distribution aspects of the marketing mix.

Each subsidiary objective should be developed with the higher level marketing objectives in mind.

The whole idea of the hierarchy of objectives is that the organisation integrates and works together as a whole – there needs to be synergy if corporate goals are to be achieved.

The fictitious garden and leisure group, 'Town and City Gardens', illustrates the hierarchy of objectives (Table 4.2).

The hierarchy should ensure that objectives are developed at each level that should be consistent with the objectives at the level above. It is also essential that strong co-ordination is developed between functional areas. Poor co-ordination between functional areas may result in conflict, which damages customer care.

Table 4.2   Typical hierarchy of objectives

	Objectives	Strategy
Corporate 20X9–20Y2 (over 3 years)	Increase operating profit by 25%	By increasing market share to 20% in regional market
Marketing 20X9–20Y2 (over 3 years)	Achieve 20% market share of regional garden and leisure market	By providing best range of products to key market segments
		By providing high service standards
		Promote effectively
Marketing mix		
Product	Provide wide range of products for key market segments	Upgrade centre facilities with restaurants and advice booths
Promotion	Create awareness of the garden and leisure centres	Re-launch centres after refurbishment
Physical evidence	Create an environment which conveys quality	Develop display gardens and professional signage
Service	Provide excellent service	Retrain staff

(Adapted from Drummond et al, 2008)

In larger organisations there may be a range of strategic business units (SBUs) operating below the corporate holding company. These SBUs add another level to the hierarchy. SBU objectives will be derived from the corporate holding company objectives and the objectives will then cascade down to the functional level. These are often termed Business Level Objectives.

The use of the balanced scorecard framework to setting objectives (outlined later) is another possible approach to ensuring a balance of objectives is achieved.

The Chartered Institute of Marketing

2 Objectives at varying levels and timescales

In today's marketing environment, it is becoming increasingly difficult to have a predetermined plan for the long term. The changing economic environment, shortening of product life cycles and dramatic advances in technology have made long-term planning difficult. Most organisations will prepare marketing plans for the medium term within a framework of less-detailed longer-term objectives or vision for the future (Table 4.3).

Long-term objectives are set for planning horizons of up to 5 years ahead. Shorter-term objectives are set which fit with the overall direction of the longer-term objectives. These short-term objectives are likely to be associated with driving operational activities.

Target and budgets will be set, based on the short-term objectives, for monitoring and control.

It is essential that the short-term objectives and the operational targets and budgets are closely linked with the long-term objectives.

Table 4.3   Planning timescale horizons

Typical planning horizons	
Short term	1–3 years (depending on sector)
Medium term	3–5 years
Long term	5 years and beyond

ACTIVITY 4.1

Select an organisation with which you are familiar and develop a set of objectives at different levels from corporate through to specific marketing outcomes over different timescales.

Objectives will vary from organisation to organisation. There will be differences between the different organisations that exist.

Organisations in the for-profit sector will set a range of financial objectives. These financial objectives will include:

- Operating profit
- Earnings per share
- Dividends per share
- Return on investment
- Return on capital employed
- Debt to equity.

Organisations may set organisational objectives which are related to markets. Typical objectives set include:

- Market share growth
- Market share maintenance
- Share of product market
- Share of market segment
- Establishing a market position in a new market.

4: The relationship between corporate, business and marketing objectives
at an operational level and the influences on objectives

43

Organisations increasingly need to innovate and learn. Typical objectives set in this area include:

- Number of new products introduced
- Products patented
- Time to market.

In the not-for-profit charitable sector objectives will reflect the desire to enhance the quality of lives. Typical objectives include:

- Raising funds
- Raising awareness
- Control of costs related to funds raised
- Number of clients supported
- Targeting key influencers.

THE REAL WORLD

The objectives of the charity 'Mencap', the leading voice of learning disability, are described below. Its aim is about valuing and supporting people with a learning disability, and their families and carers.

Mencap's vision of 'A world where people with a learning disability are valued equally, listened to and included' is supported by three aims. A selection of the objectives for each aim is shown below to illustrate how it is focussing on its vision.

1   To change society's attitude and culture

- Scope what a movement for change should look like, and develop and begin to implement a strategy to sign up individuals and organisations to it.

- Test and, if appropriate, develop a major integrated campaign aimed at transforming awareness of, and public attitudes towards, learning disability.

- Achieve a broader range of media coverage across a variety of outlets.

2   To influence people who shape policy and practice so that people with a learning disability and their families get the services and support they need.

- Develop and communicate our policy position in relation to education at all life stages.
- Develop new projects in support of strategic priorities and identify funding to meet 2012/13 fundraising targets.
- Better involve carers and people with a learning disability in informing Mencap's work.

3   To empower and directly support more individuals to live fulfilled lives.

- Meet growth targets for commissioned services to increase new business, grow financial contributions and reach more people.
- Strengthen advice and information services by:
  - developing a stronger multi-platform resource
  - reaching more people in the community through engagement with the expanded community-based advice team.

(Mencap, 2012)

This does make the measuring of achievement difficult, as marketers are used to dealing in measures such as units or money. However, charities and non-profit-making organisations start their marketing activities with a set of clear objectives.

Charities may also have commercial activities such as shops where funds are raised from the sale of goods donated. These charities will have a range of financial objectives related to those activities, as well as objectives related to the main purpose of the charity.

The Chartered
Institute of Marketing

3 The balanced scorecard

▶ Key term

Balanced scorecard: A performance metric used to identify and improve various internal functions and their resulting external outcomes. The balanced scorecard attempts to measure and provide feedback to organisations in order to assist in implementing strategies and objectives.

There is a link between the setting of objectives and the identification and setting of performance measures which will be needed for implementation, monitoring and control. The balanced scorecard (Kaplan and Norton, 1992) takes an approach which closely links objectives and performance measures.

Kaplan and Norton suggested that a balanced set of objectives should be prepared, with performance measures developed alongside at the same time.

Central to the balanced scorecard approach is the view that management should be able to look at the business from four key perspectives as shown in Table 4.4.

Traditional financial measures have encouraged a bias towards the short term. Research and development, customer service and training are often cut back to improve annual financial reports, with long-term consequences on profitability and growth.

The balanced scorecard provides managers with a more holistic view of the business than is provided by financial measures alone. Managers are required to develop clear objectives with performance measures. The process forces managers to understand the relationships between functional departments of the organisation, improving the prospect of consistency between objectives.

Table 4.4   Balanced scorecard perspectives

Customer perspective	How do customers see the business? Objectives and performance measures prepared from the customer's perspective (e.g. time, service, quality and performance) will be needed.
Internal perspective	What are the critical internal processes that will enable the organisation to meet customer needs?
Innovation and learning perspective	What is the innovation capability of the organisation? Is the organisation capable of learning?
Financial perspective	The view of the organisation from the shareholders' point of view.

Table 4.5 shows a range of objectives with associated measures using the balanced scorecard approach.

4 Consistency of plans with objectives

It is inevitable that organisations will experience conflicts when setting objectives. These problems are likely to be compounded when multiple objectives are set. For example, an organisation will always have to optimise its activities to satisfy objectives of maximising both sales and profitability at the same time. Likewise objectives of risk aversion with rapid growth are incompatible.

BPP
LEARNING MEDIA

4: The relationship between corporate, business and marketing objectives
at an operational level and the influences on objectives   **45**

Table 4.5   Measuring balanced scorecard perspectives

Strategic objectives	Strategic measures
Customer	
C.1 Value for money	– Customer ranking survey
C.2 Competitive price	– Pricing index
C.3 Customer satisfaction	– Customer satisfaction index
	– Mystery shopping rating
Internal	
I.1 Marketing	– Pioneer percentage of product portfolio
■ Product and service development	
■ Shape customer requirement	
I.2 Manufacturing	– Hours with customer on new work
■ Lower manufacturing cost	
■ Improve project management	– Total expenses per unit vs. competition
I.3 Logistics	– Safety incident index
■ Reduce delivery costs	– Delivered cost per unit
■ Inventory management	– Inventory level compared to plan and output rate
I.4 Quality	– Rework
Innovation and learning	
IL.1 Innovate products and services	– Percentage revenue from pioneer products
IL.2 Time to market	– Cycle time vs. industry norm
IL.3 Empowered workforce	– Staff attitude survey
IL.4 Access to strategic information	– Strategic information availability
IL.5 Continuous improvement	– Number of employee suggestions
Financial	
F.1 Return on capital	– ROCE
F.2 Cash flow	– Cash flow
F.3 Profitability	– Net margin
F.4 Profitability growth	– Volume growth rate vs. industry
F.5 Reliability of performance	– Profit forecast reliability
	– Sales backlog

(Adapted from Kaplan and Norton, 1992, 1993)

There are a range of strategic trade-offs facing organisations:

■ Profit margins versus competitive position
■ Profit goals versus non-profit goals
■ Growth versus stability
■ Short-term profitability versus long-term growth
■ Penetration of existing markets versus development of new markets
■ Growth versus stability
■ Risk avoidance versus risk taking.

These mean that the marketing planner must decide between the trade-offs if objectives are to provide useful goals.

There is a further challenge for the marketing planner. If plans are to be successfully executed, it is critical that the strategy and tactics outlined in the plan are consistent with the objectives set.

An objective related to raising quality standards would be inconsistent with marketing programmes including promotions and price reductions.

5 Recognition of environmentally driven marketing planning and the resource-based view of the firm

The foundation of any marketing plan is the organisation's mission and vision statement.

The mission statement will be based on careful analysis of existing and forecast environmental conditions and the resources, competences and technology of the organisation.

This matching of internal strengths and weaknesses with external opportunities and threats leads us to two views of the organisation:

- The market-orientation view – an outside-in perspective
- The resource-based view – an inside-out perspective.

Market orientation refers to the way the organisation implements the marketing concept. The marketing environments will be analysed, both macro and micro. The market will be analysed and competition identified. The customers' current and future needs will be analysed.

In the market-orientation view there is a deep knowledge of the competition from the point of view of the customer – effectively demonstrating the outside-in perspective. Without this understanding, the organisation is vulnerable to attack from new and unexpected sources of competition.

Market orientation emphasises responsiveness to market needs and superior performance related to market intelligence.

The marketing process is seen as cross-functional and not simply the domain of the marketing department. We should remember that an organisation's marketing orientation is not the exclusive responsibility of the marketing department; intelligence gathering should be the concern of all functional areas.

In contrast, the resource-based approach takes the view that superior performance is dependent on historically developed unique or distinctive resources.

The resource-based approach identifies the need for the organisation to develop capabilities that are unique to it. Resources are the organisational capabilities and competences that will lead to the development of competitive advantage if they match the opportunities available in the external environment.

Types of resources:

- **Technical resources**: These include the technology development and product development functions. This term covers access to research, information systems and processes as well as personal skills of staff.
- **Financial standing**: This covers the ability of the firm to attract capital and invest it to exploit opportunities. Firms are funded by a mix of debt and equity and the balance between these and the investment yields achieved are critical to the long-term well-being of the organisation. Financial standing will determine whether an organisation can raise capital and at what rate.
- **Managerial skills**: Firms require strategic management skills to succeed in their chosen environment. One reason that firms sometimes suffer when a 'shock' occurs in their environment is that the management skills required to assess the event, consider the options and take action are not up to the challenge. The recession of 2009 tested the managerial skills of many organisations.
- **Organisation**: The organisation has a range of organisational resources such as processes, systems, collective skills and a culture that can provide a strong basis for competitive advantage.

4: The relationship between corporate, business and marketing objectives
at an operational level and the influences on objectives

47

- **Information systems**: Information about the state of the environment and the organisation are crucial for making appropriate decisions. If an organisation is scanning its environment for opportunities and knows the availability and cost of specific resources, it will be in a stronger position to exploit this information over a competitor that does not have the information.

An alternative view of organisational competences is to link them to specific processes of the organisation – strategic operations or departmental competences.

For a resource to be considered a valuable capability or core competency, it needs to pass two tests:

- It should meet the needs of the business environment
- It should be difficult for the competition to reproduce.

In markets where products have become commodities, the skill in developing competitive advantage is derived from the organisation's ability to combine a series of capabilities, such as operational efficiency and speed of delivery.

The resource-based view emphasises the need for the organisation to exploit the distinctive capabilities it has. In contrast, the market-orientated view emphasises the need to be responsive to changes in the marketing environment.

6 Internal influences on objectives

There are a range of internal influences on the organisation that management will be aware of when setting objectives:

1 Internal stakeholder expectations

- **Shareholders** will be interested in the profitability of the organisation. They will expect to see rising profits each year. Institutions and individual shareholders also expect dividends to be paid and expect to see rising dividends per share over the years. Objectives and strategies will be watched to ensure the organisation is not engaging in high-risk projects

- **Employees** will be interested in job security and the potential for increased earnings

- **Trade Unions** will be interested in protecting the jobs, employment conditions and pay of their members

2 Management style

- Attitudes to risk will influence whether objectives are low risk or high risk
- Attitudes to growth will influence objectives, for example organic versus acquisition

3 Organisation culture

- Is the organisation responsive to change?
- Is there a culture of innovation?

4 Internal resources

- Financial: Poor cash flow will have an impact on objectives selected
- Staffing: A lack of skilled staff may encourage an objective of outsourcing.

The Chartered Institute of Marketing

7 External influences on objectives

The macro-economic environment

Political, economic, social and technological changes will all influence the objectives set by management. Some examples are as follows.

Political pressure has resulted in organisations setting objectives related to the environmental impact. The 'carbon footprint' energy-use objectives of all businesses, for example those related to reducing the use of plastic bags by supermarkets, are the result of political pressure.

The economic recession of 2011 is likely to have a profound impact on the setting of new objectives and the formulation of new strategies for the next one to five years. Therefore objectives related to survival, cash generation and cost reductions are likely to replace objectives for growth.

The micro-economic environment

Competition within influences the types of objectives set by management. Intense competition in the automobile manufacturing sector for example results in objectives aimed at maintaining or increasing market share. Some examples are as follows.

Customers' buying behaviour is changing with the impact of the internet and will influence the objectives set by management.

External stakeholders influence the objectives of organisations to varying degrees. These include:

- General public: The general public will have expectations of organisations and public opinion may influence the objectives.

- Pressure groups: Environmental pressure groups, such as Friends of the Earth or Greenpeace will lobby for changes in the objectives of organisations.

- Government and regulators: Expectations of government and regulators will influence objectives. The 2008–2009 credit crunch has resulted in regulators bringing pressure to bear on financial services organisations which are likely to influence future objectives, especially those related to risk.

REAL WORLD

Global oil companies and external stakeholders such as environmental pressure groups have had a turbulent relationship. Brent Spar was a North Sea oil storage and tanker loading buoy in the Brent oilfield, operated by Shell UK. With the completion of a pipeline connection to the oil terminal at Sullom Voe in Shetland, the storage facility had continued in use but was considered to be of no further value as of 1991. Greenpeace organised a worldwide, high-profile media campaign against this plan to dispose of it in deep Atlantic waters. Greenpeace activists occupied the Brent Spar for more than three weeks. In the face of public and political opposition in northern Europe (including a widespread boycott of Shell service stations, some physical attacks and an arson attack on a service station in Germany), Shell abandoned its plans to dispose of Brent Spar at sea – whilst continuing to stand by its claim that this was the safest option, both from an environmental and an industrial health and safety perspective.

4: The relationship between corporate, business and marketing objectives
at an operational level and the influences on objectives

49

8 Drivers of organisational change

All organisations are influenced by increasing levels of change. We can study change from two perspectives:

- **Cyclical change**: A variation that is repetitive and often predictable (seasonal variations or changes in business activity)

- **Evolutionary change**: A fundamental shift which is often sudden.

Whichever type of change occurs, it will have consequences on strategy formulation. Change should be seen as a natural consequence of the business environment and therefore should be an accepted part of strategic development.

Drummond *et al*. (2008) suggest that the following questions regarding change should be asked:

- What drives change?
- How does change impact on our markets?
- How does change impact on our business environment?
- What is the result of change on the organisation's strategy?

So, what are the key drivers of change?

The starting point should be the use of the PESTEL framework, which is a useful tool for examining the business environment. Changes are being driven by the following factors:

Political

- The changing political landscape of Eastern Europe
- Increasing power of economies such as China and India
- The enlargement of the European Union

Economic

- Downturn in the global economy
- Threats of inflation turning to threats of deflation
- Changes in the savings/debt ratio

Social

- Demographic trends such as falling birth rates, an ageing population and migration
- Greater social mobility
- Higher levels of education

Technological

- Convergence of technologies
- Growth of bio-technologies

Environmental

- Industry effects on climate change
- Reduced stocks of natural resources

Legal

- Trade restrictions and competition
- Safety standards and consumer protection.

Globalisation over the last 20 years has led to the emergence of trans-national segments of consumers with similar demands. Complex interactions now occur between organisations across the globe. Companies are changing business models and structures to take advantage of different costs of production in different locations and markets.

Corporate Social Responsibility (CSR) has emerged as an essential ingredient in business. CSR relates to actions which are above and beyond that required by law.

As well as all aspects of social responsibility towards their customers, organisations are also expected to be:

- Socially responsible towards the environment
- Socially responsible in employee relations
- Socially responsible towards the wider community.

Other dimensions of CSR include:

- Stakeholder relations: There is increasing pressure on organisations to engage more widely with stakeholders

- Ethical consumption: Consumers are increasingly concerned at the sourcing of products and wish to purchase from businesses that have ethical credentials

- Innovation: Shorter product life cycles have increased the pressure on organisations to place a greater emphasis on creativity and innovation.

Other drivers of organisational change include:

- Disintermediation: The growth of the internet has reduced the need for intermediaries

- Mass customisation: Customers can order bespoke products and these can be produced with similar efficiency to mass-produced goods (Table 4.6)

- Outsourcing and off-shoring: This has become common for many organisations as they pursue lower costs

- Fragmentation of media: Digital TV, proliferation of TV and internet channels

- Data mining: Increased information about customers available for segmentation and targeting customers

- Impending shortages of raw materials

- Increasing energy costs

- Increasing levels and costs of pollution

- Concerns over environmental change and global warming

- Increased cynicism over marketing.

What are the impacts of these changes?

- Demographic patterns mean traditional markets are becoming more challenging
- Consumer habits are changing
- Change is accompanied by intense competition
- Incremental growth rates of the past are likely to be replaced by more volatile patterns in future
- Shorter product life cycles will mean less time to recover investment in those products
- Greater difficulty predicting the future.

What are the results of these changes?

- Strategies of the past do not guarantee success in the future
- Markets will need to be redefined for the future
- New strategies will need to be developed to cope with the new circumstances.

ACTIVITY 4.2

Using the organisation selected in Activity 4.1 list the drivers of organisational change.

Organisations that are marketing-orientated, flexible and with an understanding of customer needs will survive. Many organisations will not survive as they do not have the capability to predict and cope with change.

4: The relationship between corporate, business and marketing objectives
at an operational level and the influences on objectives

51

Table 4.6   Drivers of consumer change

Changing demographics	■ Youthful elderly: better health and fitness and with more money than previous generations
	■ Ageing children: exposed to technology and media with strong brand awareness
	■ Changing family relationships: fewer defined life stages
	■ Smaller household size
Cash-rich/time-poor segment	■ More single households
	■ Over 70% of women work
The 24-hour society	■ Internet growth
	■ Home delivery
The search for greater value	■ Greater price awareness (driven by internet)
	■ Emphasis on quality in price/value relationship
Ethical consumerism	■ Fair trade
	■ Buyers with conscience
	■ Greater cynicism over marketing claims
Health and healthy lifestyles	■ Alcohol and tobacco health risks
	■ Low-sugar, low-fat products
	■ Fitness clubs

Such ability to be dynamic in response to change is a key factor in organisational success, and is one of the important aspects of internal capability that needs to be factored into the marketing planning process. This dimension of the internal environment, along with other organisational factors will be considered in more detail in the next section of this book.

> ▶ **Assessment tip**
>
> Typical exam questions will require candidates to critically discuss the relationship between corporate, business and marketing objectives at an operational level and the influences on objectives. This is a well-documented area of marketing and rich in relevant examples.

Summary

This chapter has considered the influences on the development of objectives, both internal and external. Objectives are developed at different levels of the organisation and for different time periods. The main drivers of organisational change are then examined and their effects on objectives and the marketing planning process are considered.

CHAPTER ROUNDUP

- Identify a hierarchy of objectives and objectives at varying levels and timescales
- Understand the balanced scorecard and consistency of plans with objectives
- Recognition of environmentally driven marketing planning and the resource-based view of the firm
- Evaluate internal and external influences on objectives and drivers of organisational change.

FURTHER READING

Doyle, P. (2002) *Marketing Management and Strategy*. 3rd Edition. London, Prentice Hall.

Lynch, L (2006) *Corporate Strategy*. 4th edition. London, Prentice Hall.

REFERENCES

Brassington, F. and Pettit, S. (2006) *Principles of Marketing*. 4th edition. Harlow, Pearson Education.

Cunard (2012) www.cunard.co.uk [Accessed on 19 June 2012]

Drummond, G. *et al* (2008) *Strategic Marketing Planning and Control*. 3rd edition. Oxford, Butterworth Heinemann.

Kaplan, R.S. and Norton, D.P. (1992) The Balanced Scorecard: Measures that Drive Performance. *Harvard Business Review*, 70(1).

Kaplan, R.S. and Norton, D.P. (1993) Putting the Balanced Scorecard to Work. *Harvard Business Review*, 71(5).

Mencap (2012) www.mencap.org.uk [Accessed on 19 June 2012]

QUICK QUIZ

1   What is meant by the hierarchy of objectives?

2   List three examples of objectives for a not-for-profit charity

3   What two perspectives have influenced change within organisations?

4   What are the key drivers of organisational change in a) the international passenger air travel industry, b) the food and grocery retail sector, c) the fashion clothing industry?

5   How has corporate social responsibility (CSR) emerged as an essential ingredient in business?

4: The relationship between corporate, business and marketing objectives
at an operational level and the influences on objectives

53

Activity 4.1

For the chosen organisation the organisational change will be based on cyclical change and evolutionary change. Cyclical change can occur from seasonal variations such as a distorted trading pattern with a higher proportion of sales in the last quarter of the calendar year. Evolutionary change can occur when an unpredictable external event, such as a sudden and detrimental change in currency exchange rates occurs.

Activity 4.2

The chosen organisation will have corporate objectives that will be concerned with the overall long-term profitability and the objectives are usually expressed in financial terms. Functional objectives will include those for marketing, operations, finance and human resources and will be based on timescales and will consider resource implications. The marketing outcomes will be mainly concerned with products and markets and these will depend on the organisation and its products and services.

QUICK QUIZ ANSWERS

1   A hierarchy of objectives is where objectives are not only developed across a range of key areas, they also exist at a number of levels within an organisation. The hierarchy should ensure that objectives are developed at each level that should be consistent with the objectives at the level above.

2   Typical examples include: number of clients supported, value of funds raised and raising awareness

3   Cyclical change and evolutionary change

4   Key drivers are those influences that have a fundamental impact on the organisation. For each of the three examples they could include:

   a) the international passenger air travel industry: aviation fuel price
   b) the food and grocery retail sector: disposable income of customers
   c) the fashion clothing industry: on-shelf availability in store.

5   Consumers are concerned about businesses being socially responsible towards the environment, with employee relations and responsible towards the wider community.

Section 1:

Senior examiner's comments

On completion of Section 1, students should have a detailed knowledge and understanding of:

- The role of the marketing function within organisations and how it interfaces with other organisational functions
- The purpose of marketing planning and the stages of the marketing planning process
- The different ways in which a marketing plan can contribute to an organisation
- The nature and relationship between organisational objectives at different levels
- The factors that influence the setting of objectives at different levels within organisations.

In addition students are expected to be able to apply this knowledge to practical marketing planning situations across a range of different organisational settings including consumer and business goods and services; profit- and non-profit-oriented organisations including the public sector; and large as well as small and medium-sized enterprises. Examples from local, national, international and global markets should be used to distinguish similarities and contrasts in marketing planning behaviour around the proposed models studied.

The critical requirement of the unit is the ability to examine and critically assess the implementation of marketing planning in practice, through recognition of how it is undertaken by different organisations. Furthermore, students need to be able to evaluate the validity of the marketing planning process as well as its constituent stages in directing organisations toward their goals, and apply the contribution of the plethora of concepts, models and frameworks employed.

Section 2: The marketing audit and strategic outcomes

Section 2 addresses the topic of the marketing audit as a platform for proposing strategic outcomes. The sourcing of information which can be analysed to offer alternative strategic directions for the organisation is critical to the planning process in marketing and forms the basis for the subsequent setting of objectives, strategy formulation and its implementation. This section specifically considers the practicalities of undertaking a marketing audit, the process of auditing the marketing environment and analysis of the internal and external organisational environments.

CHAPTER 5

The practicalities of undertaking a marketing audit

Introduction

This chapter looks at the practicalities of conducting a marketing audit, covering both the internal and external dimensions and its importance as part of the marketing planning process. In particular, we will identify the process of the audit and how it should be undertaken in practice.

Topic list

The marketing audit	1
What is an audit?	2
Frequency of an audit	3
Characteristics of an effective marketing audit	4

Syllabus reference

2.1	Critically evaluate the practicalities of undertaking a marketing audit including resource limitations and implications within the organisational context
	■ Conducting a marketing audit in practice
	■ Scope, timing and frequency
	■ Responsibility and objectivity
	■ Constraints and issues
2.2	Assess the concept of the organisation as an open system faced with changing environmental conditions and internal capabilities
	■ Complex and dynamic external environment
	■ Variability in organisational resource, asset and competence base
	■ Controllable and uncontrollable influences
	■ Responding to external and internal change
	■ Shaping strategy and plans proactively

1 The marketing audit

Having already looked at the main elements of the marketing planning process, we will now look at the foundation of marketing planning and plans, the marketing audit.

Kotler *et al.* (2008) suggests organisations continually need to ask themselves four key questions:

1. What business are we in?
2. What are we in business for?
3. Who are our customers?
4. What sort of business are we?

We will see later when we examine the concept of segmentation, how knowing the business we are in helps define future direction. Is Ryanair, for example, in the airline business or the transport business?

If you want to travel from London to Manchester, you can choose from the train, coach, car or aeroplane: so what business should Ryanair be in?

Clearly understanding why the organisation is in business gives it focus, and knowing exactly who its customers are enables it to concentrate on satisfying their needs. Who are the customers for a university? The students who are being taught, their parents who may be paying for them, the recipients of research services and the wider community, or potential employers?

THE REAL WORLD

Woolworths in the UK

For almost 100 years, it has offered everything for house and home, from kitchenware and tools, to haberdashery and toys.

Generations of teenagers popped in for CDs and some "pic 'n' mix" sweets on their way out.

However, nostalgia might not be enough to sell a brand which, in the past, had identified itself by value, convenience and reliability.

Giles Lury, brand consultant at The Value Engineers, believes that Woolworths' business model lacked clarity and vision, and this had an immediate impact on its brand.

'Woolworths had a great role as a generalist. But a lot of their market area moved to other suppliers. It tried to be a jack-of-all trades, but it lost out to those who were masters of one', he says.

The Chartered
Institute of Marketing

'Woolworths was left with no answers when faced with stiff competition from supermarkets and internet retailers,' adds Amy Frengley, senior consultant at Brandsmiths.

'Its original demographic has become much more sophisticated. Certainly they have new expectations, shaped in part by other retailers, as to what a store like Woolworths should be delivering even within the parameters of a low-price retailer'.

Woolworths closed its doors at the start of 2009.

(BBC, 2008)

'What sort of business are we in?' is therefore a crucial question. Porter's generic strategy model suggests an organisation has three positions it can take in the market: cost leadership, differentiation or focus. However it is possible to be stuck in the middle, which is to be avoided, as customers find it difficult to understand exactly what they can expect from the organisation. Woolworths found itself 'stuck in the middle' and paid the ultimate price by going into administration and eventually closing its stores in 2009.

The marketing audit has three purposes (Wilson and Gilligan, 2005):

- Identifying the organisation's current market position
- Understanding the environmental opportunities and threats it faces
- Clarifying the organisation's ability to cope with environmental demands.

2 What is an audit?

> ▶ **Key terms**
>
> **Micro environment:** Factors or elements in an organisation's immediate area of operations that affect its performance and decision-making freedom. These factors include competitors, customers, distribution channels, suppliers, and the general public.
>
> **Internal environment:** The conditions, entities, events, and factors within an organisation that influence its activities and choices, particularly the behavior of the employees. Factors that are frequently considered part of the internal environment include the organisation's mission statement, leadership styles, and its organisational culture.

The micro-environment comprises customers, competitors, suppliers, distributors, dealers and the public. These factors are also external to the organisation and are seen to be influenced in their behaviour by the wider external forces of the macro-environment. Assessing the micro-environment is critical to developing competitive marketing strategy that takes account of consumer behaviour, competitor activity and the role of intermediaries, as well as suppliers and the general public as stakeholders in the markets that the organisation is involved in.

The internal environment of the organisation must be audited to identify its current position and assess its particular competences and shortcomings in the light of the markets it serves and the competition that it is faced with.

A marketing audit is a systematic review and appraisal of the environment and the company's operations.

Kotler *et al* (2009, p865) suggest an audit is:

A comprehensive, systematic, independent and periodic examination of a company's or business unit's marketing environment, objectives, strategies and activities.

Organisations do not operate in a vacuum, but as part of a wider environment.

The audit is central to the planning process and supports the corporate and marketing decision-making process; it helps the organisation understand where it is now, where it wants to be and how it will get there. It is the key to the marketing planning process, particularly from the point of view of formulating strategies.

The marketing audit can be split into two parts: **internal** and **external**. According to Kotler and Keller (2006), it should comprise six components (Table 5.1).

The marketing environment audit relates to the external environment, and the remaining five components relate to the internal environment. Information on both external forces and internal capabilities are required if an organisation is going to develop effective marketing plans.

Table 5.1 Components of a marketing audit

Marketing environment	Analysis of the major macro-economic forces and trends together with actors in the micro-environment including customers, competitors, distributors and suppliers amongst others (see Figure 5.1)
Marketing strategy	Review of the organisation's marketing objectives and strategy to check on their suitability for the current conditions
Marketing organisation	Understanding the structural capability of the organisation and how well suited it is for the current or future conditions
Marketing systems	Evaluate the organisation's systems for analysis, planning and control of the marketing plan
Marketing productivity	How well are the individual components of the marketing plan performing and how cost-effective are they? Are alternative or more cost-effective methods available?
Marketing functions	Each element of the marketing mix should be evaluated

3 Frequency of an audit

The actual intervals which an audit should take place in will depend on the:

- Nature of the business being conducted
- Rate of environmental change taking place
- Duration or length of the organisation's planning cycle.

In a fast-moving market, such as technology, it is essential to ensure the organisation stays ahead of the competition and a frequent audit gives strength to the planning process. Equally the organisation's marketing environment may be changing rapidly, or unexpectedly; consider the severe economic changes which took place in 2008, for example. Organisations needed to have the structures in place to manage these difficulties, which had an impact on most business sectors.

Finally, most organisations will have an annual or rolling planning cycle, and the preparations for the planning cycle are usually the trigger to commence an audit.

Key areas within the organisation can then be reviewed on a flexible but timetabled basis.

When conducting an audit, most commentators would agree that a logical and consistent approach is more effective, as comparisons can be made with earlier audits to demonstrate improvements within the process. The generic stages are shown in Table 5.2.

Not all organisations conduct an audit, despite evidence to suggest that organisational performance is improved where an audit is conducted. Wilson and Gilligan (2005) suggest that those organisations that do not carry out audits tend to wait until things go wrong i.e. firefight rather than be proactive. This leads to a short-term reaction characterised by the rapid introduction and withdrawal of products.

Table 5.2   Stages of a marketing audit

1.Pre-audit	Here the scope or terms of reference of the audit are agreed and circulated
2.Information/data collection	The information to be collected is identified; this could include channel data, pricing, markets and market structure and the environment
3.Data analysis	Data which has been collected is now analysed. This will set out (for example) the industry standards and the organisation's own performance in relation to that standard
4.Recommendations	Recommendations arising from the data analysis are now made
5.Implementation programme	Findings/recommendations from the audit should be circulated to and implemented by key managers within the organisation

Firefighting (crisis management) may produce results for the organisation, but it does not address any fundamental problems which may be inherent within the organisation ie it simply masks them.

One of the benefits of conducting a regular audit is that problems can be identified at an early opportunity before they affect the entire organisation and eliminate the need for crisis management.

The 'top 10' most common findings from an audit (Kotler *et al.,* 2008) are illustrated in Table 5.3.

The findings or outcomes from undertaking a marketing audit need to be initially incorporated in a SWOT analysis (strengths, weaknesses, opportunities and threats), which forms part of the marketing planning process. It follows that the robustness of the audit will impact on the quality of the planning process.

Table 5.3   Findings from the marketing audit

Knowledge	Lack of knowledge relating to customer behaviour and attitudes
Segmentation	Failure to segment the market effectively
Marketing planning	Lack of effective marketing planning procedures
Price	Price reductions implemented rather than increasing volumes
Evaluation	Lack of market-based procedures for evaluating products
Company strengths	Often misunderstood through a lack of research
Short-term view	Short-term position taken on the role of promotion
Marketing is advertising	The position is held that marketing is simply about sales and advertising rather than building long-term positions for an organisation
Organisational structures	The marketing structures in place are not effective in delivering customer-focused marketing activities in an effective manner
Lack of investment	Insufficient investment is made to support the marketing function

Starbucks Marketing Audit

The US speciality coffee market continues to have an increasing number of firms looking to enter the market. Starbucks must be aware of competition on all levels and maintain its operational performance if it is to retain its status as the world's leading speciality coffee retailer. The company's focus on taste, quality and customer service is consistent with the market segment. The current product mix is in line with the industry and market forecast. Continual product review, particularly in non-food items, for additional sources of revenue is needed to increase sales. The current product line would be improved through a more regional perspective on consumer demand. The present pricing is competitive with other speciality coffee stores. The company has protected itself from volatile coffee prices and could use pricing advantage should the cost of its raw materials increase further.

(Oppapers, 2012)

ACTIVITY 5.1

For your own organisation or another that you know well, identify how often a marketing audit is carried out. Do you think changes should be made to the frequency, and why?

4 Characteristics of an effective marketing audit

Kotler and Keller (2006) identify that a marketing audit should be:

- **Comprehensive** – Covers all main marketing activities
- **Systematic** – Undertaken in an orderly structured manner
- **Independent** – Carried out by someone who will not be biased in their assessment of the situation
- **Periodic** – Undertaken at regular intervals, not just when there is a perceived marketing problem in the organisation.

Given the scale and depth of an effective audit, it is suggested that it is entrusted to a senior executive within the organisation. Often organisations will employ an internal audit team who will work with external auditors. The audit team, whether composed of internal or external staff, needs to be honest and rational in carrying out the audit if improvements to existing processes are to be made.

In conducting the audit, it is usually the senior management team who meet the auditors initially. Key members of staff will then be identified for interview as part of the process.

We have already noted not all organisations undertake an audit. This can be for a number of reasons including:

- Cost: it can be expensive to undertake an audit, especially if external auditors are used. Staff may need to be taken away from their regular duties to support the audit and this represents another cost
- Appointment of suitable auditors: selecting an auditor with the requisite skills may be difficult
- Auditors will want to examine the areas identified above in great detail, and this is disruptive for staff who still need to carry out their day-to-day duties effectively.

ACTIVITY 5.2

For the organisation selected in Activity 5.1 list the characteristics of an effective marketing audit.

The Chartered Institute of Marketing

Organisations are faced with an ever-changing marketing environment and need to have a comprehensive marketing information system in place to be able to effectively identify and track developments in the market to be able to take the necessary actions to improve their position. Trends can be categorised into opportunities or threats and an organisation will want to build on the identified opportunities while negating or minimising any threats.

Wilson and Gilligan (2005) suggest that an opportunity can be seen as any sector of the market in which the company would enjoy a competitive advantage. The opportunities can then be assessed according to their attractiveness and the company's probability of success in this area.

Similarly, threats can be categorised on the basis of the seriousness to the organisation and the probability of occurrence.

A company having assessed the opportunity and threats matrix will then establish a measure of the overall attractiveness of the market and four options exist, shown in Table 5.4.

Table 5.4   Market attractiveness options

Ideal	Numerous opportunities identified but few threats
Speculative	High numbers of opportunities and threats identified
Mature	Low numbers of opportunities and threats identified
Troubled	Numerous threats identified but few opportunities

However, the assessment does not rank the overall attractiveness of the market in any way and the company must undertake a strengths-and-weakness analysis which ranks a range of factors and maps them against current performance factors, together with a ranking of their importance. In this way, a company can focus on the areas where it has a fundamental strength which is regarded as important.

It is the case that, having conducted the analysis, a company will find there are too many potential opportunities to address.

The performance–importance matrix shown in Figure 5.1 will offer help.

Figure 5.1   The performance–importance matrix

	High	1. Concentrate efforts	2. Maintain efforts
Importance	Low	3. Low priority	4. Possible over-investment
		Low	High

Performance

Box 1 consists of factors which have been identified as important but where the company is performing less well. Therefore, the organisation should focus on strengthening those factors, which are currently perceived as weak.

Box 2 consists of factors which the company has identified as performing well in areas which are important and it needs to maintain this position.

Box 3 consists of factors which have low importance and where the performance is low.

Box 4 consists of factors which have low importance and where the performance is high.

Having reviewed its position in the matrix, the company needs to focus on the areas of opportunity when the company has strengths, or where it can prove cost-effective to acquire or develop new strengths.

Marketing audit report – Apple iPod

Apple Inc. was started in 1971 and since then it has always been improving and has become a well-known brand image. It has always been innovative, stylish, advanced, trendy, as well as simple in producing all its products. iPod is an excellent example which has simple looks but still is very stylish and a trend setter. It is the highest selling portable music player in the world with over 150 million units sold worldwide. iPod is the market leader in the product category of MP3 players and has created a niche for itself. The hype created by the teens, marketing and public relation strategies, and advertising has helped iPod gain the image and position of being 'cool' and the most-wanted device. A small survey was conducted to analyze the views of different people and consumers on Apple Inc. and iPod in particular.

The marketing audit of the iPod includes introduction of the company, situation analysis, product life cycle, market summary, SWOT analysis, product offering, competition, keys to success and critical issues, marketing strategies, marketing mix, and conclusion and recommendations. The iPod is currently in the middle of its growth and maturity stage. "Age demographics reveal that 14 per cent of people between 29-40 have iPods; as do 11 per cent of those between 41-50. Just 9 per cent of 18-28-year olds and 6 per cent of those aged between 51-59 have an Apple music player. Finally, 6 per cent of those 60-69 have them, while 1 per cent of those 70 and older have them." (Macworld, 2005). The SWOT analysis reveals Apple Inc. to be a very reputable company where people of all ages, gender, income, and race desire to own it. But the iPod series of Apple has incurred previous technical defaults but as a technology company iTunes can be used to download legal songs onto a variety of devices. And every day the world is changing and with it the technology is ever changing too.

Like any other technology-based product iPod is vulnerable and therefore has competitors. iPod has developed into a very successful brand from its inception around six years ago. iPod's competitors include Creative, SanDisk, Sony, Samsung, iRiver and Microsoft. The iPod is so well-ingrained in the market, that it has almost become unbeatable. This is because iPod has created a niche for itself, and has become a benchmark for music players. Consumers invariably end up comparing the other competitive products in the market to the iPod. Therefore, the competitors cannot afford to be simply good. They have to excel at uprooting iPod's solid position in the market, or simply leave.

(iBummed, 2009)

▶ **Assessment tip**

The audit is a key part of the marketing planning process. It is important to consider and present an evaluation of all internal and external aspects of the organisation, its stakeholders and the markets it services as part of the developed analysis.

Summary

This chapter has explored some of the practical issues of conducting a marketing audit. It recognises that not all companies undertake an audit and offers suggestions why this may be the case. Equally the important benefits of the audit to the planning process are identified ie where marketing opportunities and resources are assessed in relation to marketing objectives and the development of the plan to be implemented. It is an essential part of developing an overall marketing strategy and planning framework. Audits cover both the external (uncontrollable) elements as well as the internal (more controllable) elements. The audit needs to be conducted on a regular basis by a senior member of the company or by an external auditor who is objective. Areas for improvement can be identified and key areas can be prioritised and implemented.

CHAPTER ROUNDUP

- The scope, aim and definition of the marketing audit
- Frequency of an audit
- Characteristics of an effective marketing audit.

FURTHER READING

Doyle, P. (2002) *Marketing Management and Strategy*. 3rd Edition. London, Prentice Hall.

Kotler, P. *et al*. (2008) *Principles of Marketing*. 5th edition. Harlow, Financial Times/Prentice Hall.

REFERENCES

BBC (2008) Woolies brand loses its sparkle. BBC, http://news.bbc.co.uk/1/hi/business/7777361.stm [Accessed on 18 June 2012]

iBummed (2012) Marketing Audit Report – Apple ipod. iBummed, http://ibummed.com/uncategorized/marketing-audit-report-apple-ipod/ [Accessed on 19 June 2012]

Kotler, P. *et al* (2009) *Marketing Management*. London, Pearson education.

Kotler, P. and Keller, K.L. (2006) *Marketing Management*. 12th edition. Englewood Cliffs, NJ, Prentice Hall.

Oppapers (2012) The Coffee Shop. Oppapers, http://www.oppapers.com/essays/The-Coffee-Shop/1008939 [Accessed on 18 June 2012]

Porter, M. (1985) *Competitive Advantage: creating and sustaining superior advantage*. New York, The Free Press.

Wilson, R.M.S. and Gilligan, C. (2005) *Strategic Marketing Management: Planning, Implementation and Control*. Oxford, Butterworth-Heinemann.

QUICK QUIZ

1 Why should an organisation undertake a marketing audit?

2 Identify some of the practical constraints on performing effective marketing audits.

3 What are the consequences of not regularly undertaking an audit of the organisation?

4 What marketing information should be available for the purpose of the audit?

5 Who should be involved in undertaking the audit?

Activity 5.1

The frequency of undertaking an audit is based on the three issues of (i) nature of the business being conducted, (ii) the rate of environmental change taking place and (iii) the duration or length of the organisation's planning cycle. It is necessary to decide on the requirements of your organisation and then act accordingly. Crucially it is essential to ensure that your organisation stays ahead of the competition and a frequent audit gives strength to the planning process.

Activity 5.2

The list should be divided into the four headings of Comprehensive, Systematic, Independent and Periodic and each characteristic should be SMART to ensure academic rigour and consistency in approach. This will help to ensure that audits can be undertaken at regular intervals and comparisons made between them.

QUICK QUIZ ANSWERS

1   The organisation needs to understand the business or sector, the reason for its existence, who are its customers and stakeholders and its products and service provision.

2   Typical constraints are availability of information such as competitor performance, timescale to complete the audit and resources necessary to undertake the audit.

3   Organisations that do not carry out audits and tend to wait until things go wrong ie firefight rather than be proactive leads to a short-term reaction characterised by the rapid introduction and withdrawal of products. Firefighting (crisis management) may produce results for the organisation, but it does not address any fundamental problems which may be inherent within the organisation ie it simply masks them.

4   The information required is to effectively identify and track developments in the market or sector. Typical examples are trends that can be categorised into opportunities or threats to the organisation such as sales and cost data for products and service delivery. Alternatively it could be the length of time for new products or services to reach the market.

5   In conducting the audit, it is usually the senior management team who meet the auditors initially. Key members of staff will then be identified for interview as part of the process

CHAPTER 6

Auditing the market environment

Introduction

This chapter considers the structure of the marketing audit and how information can be gathered to fulfil the needs of the audit, taking account of both its external and internal dimensions. Key areas of the audit are identified within a framework for analysis that provides a basis for marketing planning relating to strategy development.

Topic list

Framework of external forces	1
Assessing the internal position	2
Structure of a marketing audit	3

2.3	Appraise the process of auditing the marketing environment and make recommendations for the utilisation of various approaches in a range of different organisational contexts and sectors
	▪ Past, current and future-oriented perspectives
	▪ Organising information for planning
	▪ Marketing audit structures, e.g. environment, strategy, organisation, systems, productivity and functions audits
	▪ External and internal sources of information
	▪ Organisational and sectoral constraints
	▪ Using models and frameworks to facilitate understanding

1 Framework of external forces

An organisation needs to be aware of the environment in which it operates and to do so effectively it has to consider a broad range of factors including:

- **Political issues** which may affect the company, not just in its home market, but any market it operates in. Political unrest and conflict, eg in unstable regimes with unsettled governments and terrorist attacks, may preclude opportunities for market entry.

- **Economic drivers** which may affect profitability. At the end of 2008, the euro approached parity with the pound sterling, which had a significant impact on the costs of imports and exports into and out of the UK.

- **Social and cultural considerations** which affect the nature and demand for products bought. Family and household composition have been constantly changing in modern society away from their conventional structure, which has implications for a range of products and services.

- **Technology** is developing rapidly and this will affect both the pattern of consumer demand and the way in which products and services are produced and made available in the market. The internet, for example, is changing purchasing behaviour and opening up new markets for businesses. Similarly it is used by organisations in offering their products in intermediary and distributor markets for business-to-business products and services.

- **Environment** factors are a concern of many consumers as they become more aware of the impact that producing goods may have on the environment and the future of the planet (eg pollution from intensive agriculture and increased car usage on climate change). How will these motives stand up in difficult economic conditions when disposable income is reduced?

- **Legalisation** may affect markets in terms of such measures as trade barriers and taxation. Further to this, it can affect individual consumer behaviour such as bans on smoking in public places or legislation to reduce risk in financial markets.

Collectively this is referred to as a PESTEL analysis. There are variations on the mnemonic, but this text will use PESTEL.

- Political
- Economic
- Social/cultural
- Technology
- Environment
- Legal.

The Chartered
Institute of Marketing

Organisations need to be active in understanding the importance of external forces. This became only too clear at the end of 2010 when a number of major high street names ceased trading (with the loss of many thousands of jobs) as a result of the severe economic conditions which confronted UK businesses. Names such as Dolcis, Borders, MFI and the Land of Leather all disappeared from the retail landscape. By comparison, supermarkets and value chains such as Primark gathered momentum as consumers traded down in the face of severe financial constraints. Weak economic data has led to financial markets factoring in a greater risk of a 'double dip' recession in developed economies beyond 2012. Looking forward, the most likely scenario is where global growth continues at a slow pace.

In terms of the micro-environment, organisations need to be able to respond rapidly to the external changes identified and while this is usually focussed on expanding the business it can equally apply to situations where survival of the business is the main objective.

A critical aspect of planning for marketing is being able to identify changes in key forces in the environment both now and into the future, and this may also have its roots in understanding the past when similar circumstances existed. In the current difficult economic conditions, it may be possible to predict consumer and competitive behaviour from previous downturns in economic demand and use these insights to assist in planning marketing. For instance, it may be possible to anticipate competitive moves such as international trade barriers, which may make it difficult to export, and possible shifts in consumption relating to necessity and luxury goods.

Organisations need to be able to collect and interpret information, and this is achieved through the process of environmental scanning, ie monitoring key information.

An organisation needs to be involved in two activities:

- Environmental analysis
- Environmental scanning.

Environmental analysis is the process of analysing, assessing and interpreting the information collected through the scanning process.

Environmental scanning is the physical process of collecting the data from the external environment for analysis and interpretation. In particular, it focuses on the wider horizons of the environment that may affect the organisation in its markets in the future and can be summarised as:

- Scanning the environment
- Monitoring
- Forecasting
- Assessment.

Drummond *et al.* (2008) identified five critical sources of external information, which has been adapted in Table 6.1.

This information can be collected as a result of formal searches, information collection in general, informal searches or conditional viewing, ie not an organised search, but when the organisation is sensitive to information on certain topics.

This information can be collected as a result of formal searches, information collection in general, informal searches or conditional viewing, ie not an organised search, but when the organisation is sensitive to information on certain topics.

Table 6.1   Sources of external information

Information area	Category
Market intelligence	■ Market potential; how big or profitable ■ Competitors and the industry: Competitor information and industry policy ■ Pricing strategies ■ Sales negotiations: Information on potential sales ■ Structural changes in the market e.g. mergers and acquisitions
Technical intelligence	■ Licensing and patents ■ New product processes and developing technology: Developing technology to be released into the market ■ Costs: Incurred by suppliers and competitors
Acquisition intelligence	■ Mergers, Joint ventures and acquisitions: Implications for the organization
Intelligence on broad issues	■ General conditions ■ Government actions and issues affecting the industry
Other intelligence	■ Suppliers and raw materials: Availability and continuity of supply ■ Resources available: People, equipment or premises

THE REAL WORLD

Tesco is the third largest food retailer in the world, operating around 2,318 stores and employing over 326,000 people. It provides online services through its subsidiary, Tesco.com. The UK is the company's largest market, where it operates under four banners of Extra, Superstore, Metro and Express. The company sells almost 40,000 different products, including clothing and other non-food lines.

Political factors

Operating in a globalised environment with stores around the globe, Tesco now operates in six countries in Europe in addition to the UK; the Republic of Ireland, Hungary, Czech Republic, Slovakia, Turkey and Poland. It also operates in Asia: in South Korea, Thailand, Malaysia, Japan and Taiwan. Tesco's performance is highly influenced by the political and legislative conditions of these countries, including the European Union (EU).

Economical factors

Economic factors are of concern to Tesco, because they are likely to influence demand, costs, prices and profits. One of the most influential factors on the economy is high unemployment levels, which decreases the effective demand for many goods, adversely affecting the demand required to produce such goods.

Social/cultural factors

Current trends indicate that British customers have moved towards 'one-stop' and 'bulk' shopping, which is due to a variety of social changes. Tesco have, therefore, increased the amount of non-food items available for sale. Demographic changes, such as the aging population, an increase in female workers and a decline in home meal preparation, mean that UK retailers are also focusing on added-value products and services.

Technological factors

Technology is a major macro-environmental variable which has influenced the development of many of the Tesco products. The new technologies benefit both customers and the company: customer satisfaction rises because goods are readily available, services can become more personalised and shopping more convenient

Environmental factors

There has been increased pressure on many companies and managers to acknowledge their responsibility to society, and act in a way which benefits society overall. Tesco's corporate social responsibility is concerned with the ways in which an organisation exceeds the minimum obligations to stakeholders specified through regulation and corporate governance.

Legal factors

Tesco offers consumers a price reduction on fuel purchases based on the amount spent on groceries at its stores. While prices are lowered on promoted goods, prices elsewhere in the store are raised to compensate.

(Ivory Research, 2012)

---

2 Assessing the internal position

▶ **Key term**

Internal forces: the competing forces generated from internal functions contesting for the available resources.

Understanding the internal environment is equally as important as the external environment for marketing planning and the key areas to be reviewed include:

Managerial functions

- Flexibility to change
- Level of innovation
- Ability to recruit and retain exceptional staff
- Responsiveness to change.

Competitive factors

- Barriers to market entry
- Selling and distribution costs
- Market share

Financial factors

- Ability to exit or enter markets
- Access to capital
- Financial liquidity

Technical factors

- Economies of scale
- Value added to product
- Availability/access to technology

Each of these areas should be audited and the components of the audit are shown in section 3.

ACTIVITY 6.1

For an organisation of your choice, identify the important internal areas of the audit for which information should be collected.

3 Structure of a marketing audit

An audit comprises six key components (Kotler and Keller, 2006):

- Marketing environment audit
- Marketing strategy audit
- Marketing organisation audit
- Marketing systems audit
- Marketing productivity audit
- Marketing functions audit.

We will look at each of the components in turn, remembering that each individual organisation will develop an audit questionnaire which is bespoke.

3.1 Marketing environment audit

(a) The macro-environment

This part of the audit examines the PESTEL factors.

- Political/legal

    - What political or legal changes are being planned nationally or internationally which may impact on marketing activity?

    - Are the levels of direct and indirect tax likely to remain stable?

    - Will changes in legislation affect the way products are advertised?

- Economic

    - Major developments in economic conditions: how will sales be affected?
    - Is inflation increasing or decreasing?
    - How much disposable income will customers have to make purchases?

- Social/cultural

    - What do customers think of our products?
    - What lifestyle changes are taking place?
    - How are customer values changing?

- Technology

    - How is technology changing purchase habits?
    - What new technology is being developed or trialled?
    - Main technological trends in the industry.

- Environmental

    - Implications regarding 'green' issues.
    - Alternatives to current environmental procedures.

(b) Task environment

- Markets

    - What trends are taking place, eg is the market consolidating through mergers or growing?

    - What are the key segments? How will they grow or contract?

    - What opportunities exist for market development?

    - Are any new markets expected to arise?

The Chartered
Institute of Marketing

- **Customers**
  - What are the needs and wants of our customers? Are we meeting them?
  - Do all the different customer segments purchase in the same way?

- **Competitors**
  - Who are the main competitors and what are their objectives?
  - What changes are likely to take place in the competitive landscape?
  - Will there be a change in competitor ranking, ie will the strongest competitor maintain that position or will another new or existing competitor emerge?

- **Distribution and dealers**
  - What are the main channels of distribution and how does the efficiency of each channel differ?
  - What new channels are being developed?

- **Suppliers**
  - Key trends emerging from suppliers and availability of supply
  - Are new suppliers coming into the market or are existing suppliers leaving?

- **Facilitators and marketing organisations**
  - How effective are the organisation's advertising agencies performing?
  - How are agencies utilising new technology?
  - What are the trends for distribution and warehousing costs?

- **Publics**
  - Where are the opportunities and threats for the organisation?

3.2 Marketing strategy audit

This section of the audit considers:

- Marketing objectives
- Strategy
  - Mission statement
    - ♦ Is the mission statement clearly stated in a marketing-orientated manner?
    - ♦ How realistic is the mission statement and is it compatible with the organisation's corporate and marketing objectives?
  - Marketing objectives and goals
    - ♦ Are the corporate goals clearly stated and do they guide the marketing objectives?
    - ♦ Are the objectives consistent with the organisation's position and capabilities in the market?
  - Strategy
    - ♦ Is the core strategy sound and will it achieve the objectives?
    - ♦ How clearly is the strategy stated?
    - ♦ Are there adequate controls to ensure effective monitoring?
    - ♦ Are the positioning, segmentation and targeting strategies clear and appropriate?
    - ♦ Are there sufficient resources to implement the plan?

3.3   Marketing organisation audit

Three aspects are evaluated:

- **Formal structure**

  - Is there a marketing director with the necessary authority for the company's marketing activities and customer satisfaction?

  - How well is the marketing function structured and how is it structured?

  - Are the current lines of authority adequate?

- **Functional efficiency**

  - How good is the communication between marketing and sales?
  - Any additional training or controls needed?

- **Interface efficiency**

  - Are there any identifiable problems between marketing and other functions?

3.4   Marketing systems audit

- **Marketing information system**

  - How effective is the marketing information system, does it provide accurate and timely information?

  - Can all key managers access the system easily?

  - Is the information clear?

- **Marketing planning system**

  - Is the system well designed and effective?
  - Is the system effective at forecasting sales and future trends?

- **Marketing control system**

  - Do the systems offer the organisation a complete picture of efficiency and control?
  - Are processes changed in the light of feedback or review?

- **New product development system (NPD)**

  - Does the company have an effective NPD process to develop new ideas?
  - Are new products effectively tested prior to market launch?
  - Is the rate of new product development acceptable?

3.5   Marketing productivity audit

- **Profitability analysis**

  - Are all the company's products analysed for profitability?
  - Are there scenarios for entering new markets or withdrawing from non-profitable markets?

- **Cost-effective analysis**

  - Do any of the marketing activities undertaken have excessive costs associated with them?
  - Who has responsibility for monitoring costs?

The Chartered
Institute of Marketing

3.6 Marketing function audit

- **Products and services**

    - What are the product line objectives?
    - How appropriate are the objectives?
    - Are there products which should be phased out?
    - How does the product line compare with the competition?
    - What products should be added or withdrawn?

- **Pricing objectives**

    - Are the pricing objectives, prices and strategies clear?
    - Are the pricing objectives appropriate?
    - Is price promotion used effectively?
    - How responsive is the market to price changes?
    - Are competitor prices monitored and reviewed?

- **Distribution**

    - Are the distribution strategies and objectives clear?
    - How effective are the various channel members?
    - Where does the balance of power lie with the channel?
    - How can the effectiveness of the channel be improved?

- **Promotional mix**

    - Are the organisation's advertising objectives sound?
    - Is the advertising effective?
    - What research is conducted prior to advertising?
    - How is the budget set?
    - Is the internet being used effectively?
    - Are the various promotional mix budgets adequate?

- **Sales force**

    - Are the sales team's objectives clear?
    - Is the team structured effectively?
    - How effective is the sales team when compared to the competition?
    - What is the rate of staff turnover?
    - Where does staff move to?
    - What do customers feel about the sales team?
    - Are challenging targets set?

(Adapted from Kotler and Keller, 2006).

THE REAL WORLD

The marketing audit is a fundamental part of the marketing planning process. It is conducted not only at the beginning of the process, but also at a series of points during the implementation of the plan. The marketing audit considers both internal and external influences on marketing planning, as well as a review of the plan itself. It is apparent that a marketing audit can be a complex process, but the aim is simple: it is only to identify those existing (external and internal) factors which will have a significant impact on the future plans of the company. It is clear that the basic material to be input to the marketing audit should be comprehensive. Accordingly, the best approach is to accumulate this material continuously, as and when it becomes available; since this avoids the otherwise heavy workload involved in collecting it as part of the regular, typically annual, planning process itself — when time is usually at a premium.

To give consistency to the finding of the audit and allow comparison with previous audits, organisations will often use a grading system based on Likert scale measures (eg ranking results on a 1–5 basis). This scale allows for a neutral position. Here, a '3' would be neutral and a '5' excellent, with '1' being unacceptable.

While many organisations operate without a formal or documented plan, Kotler *et al.* (2008) suggest that 'failing to plan means planning to fail'.

The process of formal planning allows a company to be clear on what it wants to achieve and how it intends to achieve those objectives. The argument for planning suggests and prepares for potential disruptions.

Companies usually set annual or long-range plans and the strategic plan gives direction to the marketing plan which contains the organisation's overall purpose for being in business along with its mission statement. This leads into SMART (specific, measurable, aspirational, realistic and time-bound) objectives being developed, which can be evaluated. The audit (external and internal) then allows information to be collected on the company, competitors, the markets and the operating environment. The resulting strengths and weaknesses are evaluated and action plans developed in order for a decision to be made on the product portfolio to be made available to customers.

ACTIVITY 6.2

For an organisation of your choice, identify the important external areas of the audit for which information should be collected.

The audit is the start point for the marketing plan as it is concerned with building and sharing an agreed and objective understanding through a systematic process of data collection and analysis.

▶ **Assessment tip**

Consider each element of the framework for external and internal forces and understand the structure of a marketing audit. Include real-life examples to demonstrate a wide understanding of each topic.

Summary

This chapter has considered the marketing audit structure covering the internal and external dimensions. It identifies the main areas of the audit and the key sources of information, and makes the link between the audit and the planning process.

The Chartered Institute of Marketing

CHAPTER ROUNDUP

- Framework of external forces
- Assessing the internal position
- Structure of a marketing audit.

FURTHER READING

Kotler, P. *et al* (2008) *Principles of Marketing*. 5th edition. Harlow, Financial Times/Prentice Hall.

REFERENCES

Drummond, G. *et al* (2008) *Strategic Marketing Planning and Control*. 3rd edition. Oxford, Butterworth Heinemann.

Ivory research (2012) www.ivoryresearch.com [Accessed on 19 June 2012]

Kotler, P. *et al* (2008) *Principles of Marketing*. 5th edition. Harlow, Financial Times/Prentice Hall.

Kotler, P. and Keller, K.L. (2006) *Marketing Management*. 12th edition. Englewood Cliffs, NJ, Prentice-Hall.

QUICK QUIZ

1. What is the critical aspect of planning for marketing?
2. Why do organisations need to be able to collect and interpret information?
3. What is environmental scanning?
4. What is the purpose of the marketing function audit?
5. How could an organisation give consistency to the findings of the audit?

ACTIVITY DEBRIEFS

Activity 6.1

It is important to list the internal forces. The internal environment of a business is that part over which you as a manager have control. The challenge of internal analysis is to identify, develop, and deploy resources, capabilities and core competences. Consideration of the following is required:

- Marketing
    - products/services
    - price/promotion
    - distribution/location
- People
    - management
    - farm hands
    - office staff/other
    - sales force

- Operations/facilities
  - implementation
  - facilities/equipment
- Management/efficiency
  - consider finances
  - profitability
  - debt position/capital structure
  - inventory/receivable management.

Activity 6.2

The list of external factors should include information using the PESTEL framework which clearly identifies the key issues confronting the organisation. For each topic there should be an understanding how it could affect the future marketing plan of the organisation. For instance if there has a trend of a challenging economic climate, how has the organisation adapted to that environment and what opportunities can be exploited from those changes?

QUICK QUIZ ANSWERS

1   A critical aspect of planning for marketing is being able to identify changes in key forces in the environment, both now and into the future.

2   Organisations need to be able to collect and interpret information, and this is achieved through the process of environmental scanning, ie monitoring key information.

3   Environmental scanning is the physical process of collecting the data from the external environment for analysis and interpretation.

4   The marketing function audit is to review the products and services, the pricing objectives, the distribution requirements, the promotional mix and the sales force needs.

5   To give consistency to the finding of the audit and allow comparison with previous audits, organisations will often use a grading system based on Likert scale measures (eg ranking results on a 1–5 basis).

The Chartered Institute of Marketing

CHAPTER 7

The external marketing environment

Introduction

Having identified the practicalities and structure associated with the marketing audit, this chapter assesses the nature of the external market, identifies the key drivers of change and introduces some models and frameworks to aid the understanding of the external environment. From this platform marketing opportunities can then be identified and a competitive position for the organisation established to enhance its standing in the market.

Topic list

The environment and marketing strategy   (1)

The nature of the marketing environment   (2)

The evolution of environmental analysis   (3)

Strategic group mapping   (4)

Competitive advantage   (5)

Marketing objectives, strategies and plans   (6)

2.4	Evaluate the external marketing environment through detailed analysis using a variety of marketing audit tools and techniques
	■ The evolving nature and extent of external environmental change
	■ Marketing intelligence and environmental scanning
	■ Macro- and micro-environmental analysis frameworks
	■ Gauging the impacts of external forces on marketing planning
	■ Identifying key external issues and assumptions
	■ External audit tools, eg PESTEL, Porter's Five Forces and strategic group mapping

1 The environment and marketing strategy

▶ **Key term**

Marketing strategy: is the long term plan to allow a company or organisation to focus its limited resources on the best opportunities to increase performance and thereby achieve a sustainable competitive advantage.

Marketing strategy is concerned with matching the demands of the environment with the capabilities of the organisation. This can be problematic as the environment in which an organisation operates can be complex, diverse and continually changing. Figure 7.1 reflects the complexity of the situation.

Wilson and Gilligan (2005) suggest that the environment can be considered under two headings:

■ The extent to which the environment affects strategy
■ Understanding how environmental pressures can be related to organisational capabilities.

However, we are warned not to just adopt a 'tick list' but develop a systematic approach.

We have briefly seen in the previous chapter that it is necessary for an organisation to scan and analyse the environment, and the various steps are outlined in Table 7.1.

Table 7.1 Scanning and analysing the environment

Scanning the environment	This is a general audit of the environment which identifies those factors which will influence the organisation. Trends and changes can be quickly acted upon
Monitoring	Monitoring changes and identifying opportunities and threats
Forecasting	Based on the available information, change may need to be made
Assessment	An assessment of the potential impact on the business needs to be made

Having completed the assessment, the firm's competitive position in the market can be established using strategic group analysis (see later) which highlights relative degrees of market power. Finally the opportunities and threats facing the organisation can be established, which will then form the basis for evaluating the organisation's strategic position.

The Chartered Institute of Marketing

2 The nature of the marketing environment

The marketing environment consists of the macro- and micro-environments and the organisation (internal) environment. However, in this chapter we will focus on the external influences on strategy, namely the macro- and micro-environments, represented by the two outside layers of Figure 7.1

Figure 7.1   Levels of the marketing environment

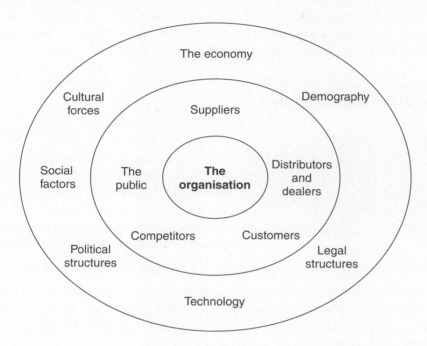

The macro-environment consists of the broader elements and is often referred to as the 'non-controllable' elements.

It is the micro-environment which is nearest to the organisation and the one it can have more control over. We have already seen that the micro-environment consists of customers, competitors, suppliers, distributors and dealers as well as the public. Collectively these elements are often referred to as the 'controllable' elements, yet it is recognised that not all elements are controllable, although it is possible to influence them.

We will explore each of these two environments in more detail shortly, but it should be clear that the environment is a significant determinant of strategy and organisational performance.

Often organisations will adopt a proactive stance to change the nature of the market.

THE REAL WORLD

In 2008 the difficult conditions facing the financial markets brought about the merger of two large financial services organisations in the UK. Lloyds TSB and HBOS merged to form one of the largest banks in the UK. In normal trading circumstances, the merger would not have been allowed, as it would have been seen as anti-competitive because of the market share enjoyed by both organisations, but a waiver of competition law to create Lloyds Banking Group enabled the creation of a high street lender with a potentially excessive share of the market. The Lloyds TSB-HBOS merger, arranged in the autumn of 2008, was designed to prevent UK taxpayers from owning the entirety of HBOS, the country's biggest mortgage lender.

While it achieved that objective, it left the taxpayer holding more than 40 per cent of a gargantuan bank with suspect loans and investments with a value worth billions of pounds. The new chief executive has already begun the process of selling just over 600 branches and addressing a funding gap (the bridge between loans and deposits) of more than £15bn.

While the pace of change in the environment can usually be identified with some certainty, it was clear that the deterioration in the UK economy in 2008 caught many organisations off guard. Debate will continue as to whether this was a 'one-off' situation brought about by a unique set of circumstances which originated in the USA and therefore could not have been expected, or if it was simply the scale of the situation which was not recognised. In either case, organisations will want to review their scanning processes for fitness of purpose to ensure that they are able to pick up signals of major changes in market conditions.

3 The evolution of environmental analysis

▶ **Key term**

Environmental analysis: is the study of all external factors that may affect an organisation or its marketing plan. Environmental analysis is a basic marketing function used to help marketers identify trends or outside forces that may impact upon the success or failure of a particular product.

Wilson and Gilligan (2005) suggest that the:

'potential significance of environmental changes highlights the need for a certain type of organisational structure and culture which is then reflected in both a balanced portfolio of products and an adaptive management style supported by a well-developed intelligence and information monitoring system'.

Without this approach, organisations have an increased risk of missing key trends in the market.

It is not just trading organisations that need to stay alert to market changes. The FSA (Financial Services Authority) is charged with regulating banks and other financial services organisations in the UK. However, it was challenged over its monitoring of Northern Rock, a bank which had to be taken into public ownership because it was no longer able to access funds to pay its customers.

As the financial crisis deepened in 2008, the government was forced to take other organisations into public ownership to retain confidence in the financial markets.

Diffenbach (1983) suggests that there are three stages in the evolution of corporate environmental analysis:

- **Appreciation**: looking beyond the short term and considering the wider PESTEL factors which constitute the business environment
- **Analysis**: finding reliable sources of data to develop trend analysis
- **Application**: real attempts are made to monitor the environment and assess the implications for change which are then translated into strategies and plans.

It has been suggested that there are three types of environmental monitoring processes:

- **Irregular systems** where the process is focused on reacting to a crisis, ie firefighting
- **Periodic models** where the irregular systems have been developed and are more systematic
- **Continuous models** where the periodic model has been developed and now looks towards the long term.

ACTIVITY 7.1

For an organisation of your choice, identify the firm's competitive position in the market.

The Chartered Institute of Marketing

3.1 PESTEL analysis

The macro-environment looks at the broad range of factors that can affect an organisation. Benefits of undertaking environmental analysis are wide, but include the following:

- **Resource effectiveness**. Changes to current resources can be planned for, increasing them to reflect a growing business, or reducing them when the market is contracting

- **Platform for change**. Understanding and reacting to external changes enables the organisation to evolve and respond to market conditions

- **Planning efficiency**. Understanding the organisation's strengths and weaknesses allows it to more effectively position itself in the market

- **External changes** can be planned in a controlled way

- **Competitor positions and strategies** can be understood and an effective response developed.

The roles of the PESTEL analysis (Table 7.2) are the key factors which affect the industry generally and the organisation in particular. Using the model an organisation can develop a systematic approach to analysing the external environment.

3.1.1 Political

Organisations which operate within their own country are generally well aware of the political structures that are in operation. However, in the UK, there is also the Scottish Parliament and the Welsh Assembly which need to be recognised. Equally, the EU is becoming important in many activities. Organisations that operate in Europe need to recognise the different political structures and implications.

With the increasing number of global businesses, the political dimension is important for many organisations and generates opportunities and threats in equal measures.

Issues to be considered include:

- Taxation
- Trade protection
- Stability of political systems.

3.1.2 Economic

Even if an organisation operates in the UK alone, it is not immune from the effects of economic conditions which are prevalent in other countries, both within and beyond Europe.

We have seen the effects on the UK economy of the housing market in the USA. Icelandic banks went 'bust' leaving investors having to take legal action to get their money back.

Countries go through economic cycles and the Labour government of 1997-2010 was keen to avoid the 'bust and bust' approach adopted by the previous Conservative government.

While economies across the globe go through the economic cycle illustrated in Figure 7.2, the difficulty is knowing the length of each stage of the cycle. Another key concern is the exchange rates of currencies. Many overseas organisations who had invested heavily in the UK were concerned at Britain's refusal to join the Euro, as this affected monetary exchange conditions and its influences on marketing such as price structures.

Issues to consider include:

- Spending patterns
- Consumer confidence

- Rates of exchange between different currencies
- Levels of direct and indirect taxation.

Figure 7.2   The economic cycle

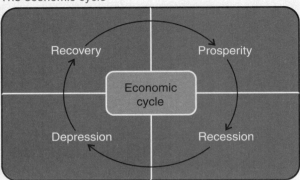

3.1.3 Social/cultural

The historic trend of better living standards has led to changes in the way we live, where we take our holidays and how we are educated. As the UK population is working to an older age of retirement, more people are paying taxes for longer and the more well off the country will therefore be. However, the increase in the number of people receiving a pension and the fact they are living longer is causing pressure on the pension funds of many organisations as well as the government.

Consider the way many of us buy music. Increasingly we download it from the internet rather than buying a CD.

Social issues to consider include:

- Demographics such as: age, social class
- Religious beliefs, culture, ethics.

Globalisation and the movement of people across continents have brought about some changes in cultural approaches (ie convergence), but nevertheless it is still an important consideration and covers:

- Language
- Religion
- Values
- Education
- Purchasing behaviour (finance, gambling, alcohol).

Organisations operating beyond their domestic market need to fully understand the markets through the process of research.

3.1.4 Technological

It can be argued that the pace of developing technology has never been faster. However, the role of technology and the benefits it delivers to the customer need to be clear. Often the effective use of technology can offer the organisation a competitive advantage.

Technology can affect both organisational and consumer behaviour, changing the way things are made and the way things are bought. It also affects behaviour in marketing channels: suppliers and intermediaries. For example, retailing has been revolutionised by online buying, but also through the way that manufacturers deal with their retailers in terms of stock ordering, delivery, payment, etc.

3.1.5 Environmental

There is growing awareness and concern for the environment. This has internal implications as well as political and legal considerations.

On the one hand, we can consider the environment from the perspective of climate change and the effects this is having on our weather systems. Ultimately this may have a major influence on (for example) where we take our holidays and the resulting impact that may have on certain countries.

We can also consider it from the perspective of protecting the world's scare resources and the effective use of them.

Finally there is the pollution aspect to consider; this can be in terms of the products manufactured or the use of resources in the manufacturing process.

3.1.6 Legal

Often linked with the political dimension, but can range from international law covering merger and acquisitions, to the concept of naming a product.

The amount and scope of legislation has been growing rapidly and covers areas such as honesty, decency and taste. Equally it is there to protect customers from the poor practices of some organisations as well as ensuring a certain standard of safety.

From an organisational perspective, some legislation prevents it from operating in certain countries or buying or merging with another organisation because it may be seen as anti-competitive or simply the law does not allow ownership by overseas companies.

3.2 Competitor analysis

Understanding the organisations that compete in the same market is an essential requirement. The competition can attack using a number of approaches and by understanding them the appropriate response can be generated.

Competitor analysis is central to any marketing strategy and to ignore the competition is to assume the organisation operates in a vacuum, which it clearly does not.

In undertaking an analysis of the competition, key considerations will include:

- Marketing capabilities: how effective is their advertising and how much money is available for this activity?

- Levels of innovation: how innovative is the competition and how is innovation delivered?

- Management: how skilled is the management team?

A more strategic review would consider:

- Who exactly is the competition?
- What are the objectives?
- What strategies are being pursued and what success is being enjoyed?
- What are the main strengths and weakness that have been identified?
- How is the competition likely to behave and how will they respond to offensive moves?

Table 7.2 Summary PESTEL analysis

PESTEL analysis
Political
▪ Taxation
▪ Stability of governments
▪ Protection of domestic markets from overseas companies
▪ Foreign trade agreements
▪ Environmental issues
▪ Monopoly controls
Economic
▪ Interest rates
▪ Inflation rates
▪ Economic cycle
▪ Unemployment
▪ Consumer confidence
Social
▪ Attitudes and values
▪ Culture
▪ Age profiles
▪ Social mobility
▪ Incomes
▪ Buying habits
Technology
▪ Rate of development of new technology
▪ Opening/closing of distribution channels
Environmental
▪ Green issues
▪ CSR
▪ Use of resources
▪ Pollution
▪ Climate change
Legal
▪ Restrictive practices
▪ Competition
▪ Safety
▪ Honesty

When we evaluate Porter's Five Forces model (Porter, 1980) we will see the importance of understanding the competition, but equally when we analyse and understand the competition we can build mechanisms to effectively compete against them, not just on price, but on a range of dimensions where a competitive advantage is held.

A competitor response profile will consider four dimensions, as indicated in Table 7.3 and Figure 7.3.

Table 7.3   Competitor response profiles

Current strategy	How is the business currently competing and what success is being achieved?
Capabilities	What strengths and weakness do the competitors have and what resources are available to them?
Assumptions	What assumptions do the competitors hold about themselves? How realistic are they and what is the basis of the assumptions?
Goals	What is it that drives each organisation and what are its goals?

Figure 7.3   Competitor's likely response profiles

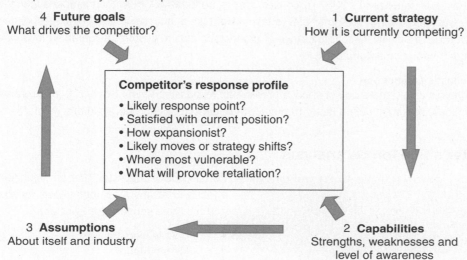

Having undertaken the analysis, the next step is to consider how the competition will respond to the broad changes and trends taking place in the market and, secondly, how it will respond to actions taken by the competition. To answer the questions it is necessary to understand why the company is vulnerable, ie where its strengths and weaknesses lie.

Davidson (1987) identified a list of factors that made an organisation vulnerable and the list below offers a broad range of factors to be considered:

Finance

- Lack of cash
- Low margins
- High distribution costs.

Resources

- Dated technology
- Staffing issues
- Old products.

Markets

- Focus on one market sector
- Reliance on one/small number of customers.

Kotler (2008) suggested that competitors will respond to change in different ways and grouped the range of change options into four categories:

- **Laid-back competitor**
  The laid-back competitor responds only slowly to change and may justify this on the basis of its loyal customer base, simply not recognising the changes taking place. Alternatively while the changes taking

place may be recognised, it may be the case that the company does not have the resources to deal with the situation. In any event the rational for this approach needs to be understood.

- **Selective competitor**
  Organisations may respond selectively to certain situations. It may never respond to price changes or sales promotions, but may react when a new product is introduced or an advertising campaign launched by a competitor.

- **Tiger competition**
  The tiger competitor will respond quickly and aggressively to any organisation which attempts to move onto its 'turf'. A supermarket will respond very quickly to another supermarket that enters its market.

  In the credit squeeze of 2008, Tesco was coming under attack from the cheaper supermarkets such as Aldi. Customers were moving to Aldi to take advantage of cheaper prices. Tesco responded by introducing a heavily discounted range of products to ensure customers remained loyal and were not tempted into competitor stores.

- **Stochastic competition**
  Stochastic competitors do not show a predictable response and will respond in different ways to different situations, making it very difficult to predict their behaviour and plan accordingly for it.

3.3 Porter's five forces analysis

▶ **Key term**

Porter's five forces analysis: determines the long run attractiveness of a market or market segment.

Porter (1980) suggested that an organisation should adopt a clear and meaningful basis for strategic thinking and his three generic strategies are:

- Cost leadership
- Differentiation
- Focus.

In other words, an organisation should understand its competitive stance and be clear what the organisation means to the customer. An organisation then needs to select the strategic approach which allows it to maximise its strengths recognising the competition. Porter then went on to suggest this could be done by taking into account five key factors (five forces).

The analysis that can be conducted is best completed at the SBU (strategic business unit) level and then aggregated up in order to provide a clear picture of the attractiveness of the industry to a particular organisation.

Understanding the 'forces' at work in a given segment of the market enables the organisation to decide whether to move into a particular segment.

The five forces are:

- Potential and new entrants and the threat of entry
- Substitute products
- Buyers and the power of buyers
- Suppliers and the power of suppliers
- Competitors and the nature of the competition.

Figure 7.4 shows the five forces model. However, before an analysis of each area is undertaken, the following checklist should be used to asses the strategic implications of the competitive structure of the industry:

- What is the likely threat of a new entrant coming into the market and where is it likely to come from?

- What and where are the potential substitute products that may be used and what is the likely impact on the organisation and the industry?

- Who are the suppliers to the organisation and what power do they have over the organisation?

- Who are the buyers and what power do they hold over the organisation?
- Who are the present and future competitors and how strong is or will be the competition?

Figure 7.4 Five forces model

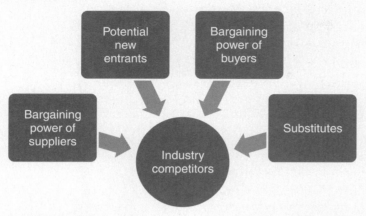

(Porter, 1980)

Taking each component in turn, Table 7.4 shows the five forces analysis of competition.

Table 7.4 Porter's five forces analysis of competition

Potential entrants

What is it that is stopping a potential new entrant from coming into the market? A key consideration will be the number of obstacles the organisation may encounter.

- The capital investment costs may be significant
- Economies of scale may be necessary to offset the entry costs and may not be achievable in the short term
- Access to distribution channels may be difficult and existing ones may need to be purchased or new ones developed
- Existing brands may have a loyal following and advertising costs to overcome this may be significant
- The existing competition may 'fight back' so making the market extremely competitive.

Buyers

Buyers can be powerful in markets where:

- A small number of buyers control a large share of the market and can exert pressure on the suppliers
- There is backward vertical integration, i.e. the buyer purchases from the supplier, removing the intermediary from the distribution channel
- The product lacks differentiation, which lowers the barriers to alternative sources of supply.

Substitutes

The threat of substitute products can arise in a number of ways:

- The new product may replace the old product: MP3 players replacing CD players

- Consumer substitution, ie when one product is in competition with another, eg a weekend at Alton Towers theme park or a holiday in Spain

- Using Tesco internet shopping rather than visiting the store.

Suppliers

The power that suppliers hold is liable to be strong when:

- Few suppliers control a large share of the market
- The supplier has a strong brand that people associate with
- The cost of switching suppliers is high and this will act as a deterrent.

Competitive rivalry

The intensity of the competition is affected by a range of factors:

- The size of the market sometimes organisations cannot grow any more without taking capacity out of the market. This has happened in the beer industry, where brewers have bought other brewers just to take capacity out of the market

- Markets with a dominant player and many smaller players are likely to be less competitive

- Competitors of equal size will make the market more competitive

- Where the market suffers from a high proportion of fixed costs, competition may be high as a result of price discounting to maintain volumes

- Are there high barriers to leave the market?

THE REAL WORLD

Bang & Olufsen

The differentiation strategy seeks competitive advantage in a broad range of market or industry segments.This strategy involves selecting one or more criteria used by buyers in a market - and then positioning the business uniquely to meet those criteria. This strategy is usually associated with charging a premium price for the product - often to reflect the higher production costs and extra value-added features provided for the consumer. Differentiation is about charging a premium price that more than covers the additional production costs, and about giving customers clear reasons to prefer the product over other, less-differentiated products.

Bang & Olufsen was founded in 1925 in Struer, Denmark. Bang & Olufsen a/s is world renowned for its distinctive range of quality audio, video and multimedia products that represent our vision: 'Courage to constantly question the ordinary in search of surprising, long-lasting experiences'. Bang & Olufsen employs over 2,000 staff members and had a turnover of DKK 2,762 million (ca. € 370 million) in the 2009/2010 financial year.

Bang & Olufsen manufactures a highly distinctive and exclusive range of televisions, music systems, loudspeakers, telephones, and multimedia products that combine technological excellence with emotional appeal. Bang & Olufsen products are sold by over 1,000 dealers in more than 100 countries, in an extensive network of retail stores. Approximately 70% of these stores are B1-stores, which exclusively sell Bang & Olufsen products. The B1 stores account for 82% of the total turnover.

The Chartered Institute of Marketing

Our vision

A vision is a way of expressing a company's state of mind and the highest ambition you are aiming at. The guiding principle - first laid down by the two founders Peter Bang and Svend Olufsen in the late 1920s - was stipulated in these words: "Enterprising is needed - a never-failing will to create only the best – to persistently find new ways of improvement". This vision has been passed on from one generation to the next and is today expressed by the following words:

Our values

To carry out such a vision, we have to establish a common platform from which we work and think. At Bang & Olufsen the values are expressed in four words of Excellence, Synthesis, Originality and Passion.

Excellence

We aspire to the highest in all we do, with care and attention applied to the smallest detail. The Bang & Olufsen brand is founded on substance and excellence, not "exclusive" only.

Synthesis

We possess the ability to balance and combine several apparently contradictory forces, and from that create something not previously seen or heard.

Originality

Predictability and the status quo are our enemies. We continuously transcend barriers and push ourselves to do that which seems impossible. This is what generates surprise and breaks new ground; this is how not previously thought ideas are created.

Passion

All human creative powers, all real creativity, and all extraordinary effort and energy require that we feel something out of the ordinary for what we do. Common for these feelings are enthusiasm, pride, and passion: for our company, our products, and our traditions.

The differentiation strategy is built on its core competences through experience, practise and development. At Bang & Olufsen we recognise the importance of identifying, cultivating and exploiting our strengths. They are the glue that binds us together as a company as well as the engine of new business development. The core competences provide the framework to sustain differentiation and to make the difference. Although we have many areas of expertise, we have identified eight, which we refer to as core competence areas: Picture, Sound, User Integration, System Integration, Moving Mechanics, Design, Materials and Finish, and Quality.

(Bang & Olufsen, 2012)

4 Strategic group mapping

▶ **Key term**

Strategic Group Mapping: an analysis technique that groups companies within an industry that have similar business models or similar combinations of strategies.

Having identified and analysed individual competitors in the market, it is then necessary to categorise the competition based on the strategies they are pursuing. The various competitors can be clustered together to see the competitive groups which have formed in the market as a whole.

Figure 7.5 represents three geographical distribution operations: local, regional and national, for heating oil companies.

X: represents a group of companies which offer industrial and domestic fuels nationally

Y: represents a group of companies which offers industrial fuels only and on a regional basis

Z: represents a group of companies offering domestic fuel on a local basis.

Figure 7.5   Strategic group map for fuels

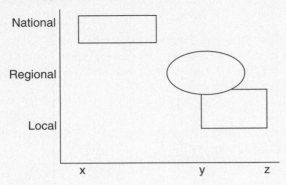

(Porter, 1980)

Complexity can be built into the grouping and so we could map all the various production options, (ie domestic and industrial fuel distributors, domestic only, industrial only) against the geographical distribution options. The various strategic groups' offering can then be established to understand their relative position.

A company which wants to enter the heating oil distribution market could use the strategic mapping exercise to identify where the main competition is and position itself accordingly. It should be noted that competition can still take place across the different strategic groups.

Similarly an organisation already in the market could use strategic mapping to develop competitive advantage for itself.

Various commentators have sought to identify the characteristics which can be used to define strategic groups and Table 7.5 highlights just some of the possible characteristics.

Table 7.5   Factors for defining strategic groups

Market share	Reputation
Product diversity	Distribution channels used
Market position	Geographic coverage
Market segments served	Product range
Branding	Size
Culture	Pricing

Figure 7.6   Strategic choice

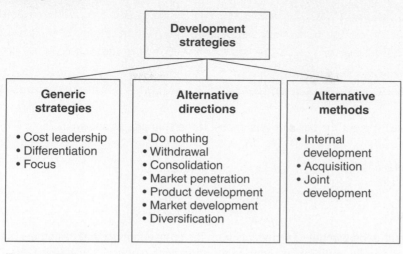

(Porter, 1980)

5 Competitive advantage

Competitive advantage (the process of identifying a fundamental and sustainable platform from which to compete with another or other organisations) is intrinsically linked with marketing strategy.

An organisation has a number of strategic choices available and we will explore Porter's approach in Figure 7.6.

An organisation needs to have a competitive advantage which can be used to base its strategic activity on, and which also supports the organisation's marketing programmes.

Porter suggests:

5.1 Cost Leadership

This does not mean the organisation must offer the cheapest products, but that it develops and maintains a low-cost base. Economies of scale will be a key feature. Overheads and other aspects of the business, such as marketing and purchasing, will be carefully monitored for cost efficiencies.

Table 7.6   Drivers of Cost Leadership

Infrastructure
The organisations' cost base is affected by a number of factors such as: <ul><li>Availability of skills. Many organisations located just outside major cities often find it difficult to recruit and retain staff because they prefer to work 'in the city'</li><li>Government grants or funding (both domestically and overseas, eg European loans) can affect location</li><li>Technology such as the internet is affecting the 'infrastructure' dimension by encouraging virtual locations and being able to establish a business in any location</li></ul>
Linkages and relationships
Here activities are linked together to produce cost savings. <ul><li>Airbus Industries share production across specialist contractors which produces cost savings</li><li>'Just-in-time' supply is an effective way of reducing stockholding costs and the need for large warehouses</li></ul>

Economies of scale

Economies of scale are usually regarded as the single biggest influence on the cost structure of an organisation.

- Larger volumes of production generate cost savings and efficiencies (often cited as a reason for globalisation)

- Bulk or volume purchase also drives cost reduction

Drummond *et al.* (2008) suggest the basic drivers of cost leadership are, as shown in Table 7.6:

- Infrastructure
- Linkages and relationships
- Economies of scale.

5.2 Differentiation

An organisation will want to differentiate its products from the competition so that customers have a clear reason for making the purchase, rather than choosing a competitor's product.

Customers will select a product on the basis of the value the product adds: confidence, status, etc.

The basic drivers of differentiation are:

- Product augmentation
- Product perception
- Product performance.

Table 7.7   Drivers of differentiation

Product augmentation

The basic product offering is enhanced by adding value-adding elements.

- The level of after-sales or technical service provided or the hours of staff availability
- Easy access to finance

Product perception

For many people or groups of people, the perception of the product is more important than the product itself.

- The Ford Galaxy and the Seat Alhambra are two versions of the same car made by different manufactures
- The brand Stella Artois is 'reassuring expensive', but may taste the same as other cheaper products

Product performance

The actual performance of the product will also improve the product in the mind of the consumer and will be evaluated relative to the products offered by the competition.

- Quality, durability and capability improve the performance of the product

5.3 Focus

Rather than concentrating on the mass market, the approach here is to 'focus' on a narrower approach. In other words, the organisation is concentrating its efforts on a smaller or niche segment. The organisation wants to develop specialist knowledge of the market.

The basic drivers of focus as illustrated in Table 7.8 are:

- Products and service specialism
- Geographic segmentation
- End-user focus.

Table 7.8   Drivers of focus

Products and service specialism
Highly differentiated, niche or premium products are developed
■ A narrow or single product line could be developed, e.g. Steinway pianos
Geographic segmentation
■ Production is based on the needs of the local market

End-user focus
Here the focus is on the specific needs of the end user and then looking at a segment; it may be more effective to develop a profile

Organisational focus should be one strategy, rather than trying to adopt different or mixing strategies. The effect of failing to adopt this approach is to become 'stuck in the middle' with the underlying principles of each approach being compromised.

Having identified the generic strategy, it needs to be developed into a specific competitive advantage which needs to be sustainable over the long term.

ACTIVITY 7.2

Consider a luxury garment company and suggest how it would seek to retain its customers.

To be sustainable, Drummond *et al.* (2008) suggest the advantage must be:

- Relevant to the current and future needs of the market
- Defensible, ie barriers to copying which are:
  - Skills-based
  - Asset-based

English universities are seeking to end Scotland's competitive advantage in attracting overseas students.

Universities UK are calling for the Scottish Executive's Fresh Talent visa scheme to be extended to England, Wales and Northern Ireland. The initiative, part of a drive to reverse population decline, allows overseas students a two-year visa extension if they study in Scotland.There were more than 2,000 successful applicants in the scheme's first year.

The vice chancellor of the University of Bedfordshire, Prof. Les Ebdon, confirmed that there was envy, especially in the north of England.

Speaking on behalf of Universities UK, he said the scheme offered a 'significant competitive advantage' and should be extended to the rest of the UK.

'After all, international students bring in some £3bn a year to the UK economy, so it is very important business,' he said. 'As far as immigration rules are concerned we are supposed to be one nation, we don't have devolved immigration rules.' 'It would be excellent to have the Fresh Talent scheme applied across the whole of the UK.' 'I know something like that will happen when the new immigration rules come into practice, but that could be a couple of years down the line.'

Unequal treatment

Boris Johnson, the Conservative higher education spokesman, described the situation as 'an anomaly'.

'Devolution was not intended to include immigration matters, and it is unjust to have an unequal visa treatment between Scotland and the rest of the country,' he said. 'I will be challenging Bill Rammell at the Universities UK annual conference to extend the Scottish visa regime to the rest of the United Kingdom.'

David Caldwell, the director of Universities Scotland, said it was understandable for the other UK universities to want to adopt the Fresh Talent initiative.'It is not an uneven playing field, it is just a very good scheme,' he told BBC Scotland. 'The important thing is that it does not just benefit Scottish universities, it benefits Scotland.' 'Scotland needs to attract talent if we are going to have a thriving, growing, knowledge-based economy and these international students that come to Scotland bring the country great benefits.'

He said Scotland would not lose out if the rest of the UK adopted a similar scheme, as there were an 'enormous' number of overseas students who were interested in studying abroad.

'I hope for the benefit of our English counterparts that they will get something like it as well,' he added. 'Scotland and England can both be winners.'

The Home Office has already watered down the Scottish advantage by introducing visa extensions for overseas postgraduate students in England.

They will be allowed to remain in the UK for 12 months without a work permit after completing their studies.

Higher Education Minister Bill Rammell said 'significant changes' had been made.

(Adapted from BBC, 2012)

6 Marketing objectives, strategies and plans

The marketing audit plays an important role in developing the marketing plan through a 'bottom-up' process which feeds it with key information about the organisation and the environment in which it operates.

Organisations need to ask themselves some important questions:

- Where is the business now?
- Where do we want it to be?
- How is it going to get there?
- How will we know when it is there?

Summary

This chapter has looked specifically at the external (macro and micro) environments and has highlighted the importance of marketing intelligence and environmental scanning.

Organisations do not operate in isolation within the market and must appreciate and respond to the changes taking place in order to maintain or improve their competitive position. Some changes need to be spotted well in advance and organisations that use audit tools such as PESTEL, Porter's Five Forces and strategic group mapping will be in a better position to respond to the external changes. Similarly, understanding the nature and basis on which the competition acts allows robust challenges and positioning to be established. Responses to changes made by the organisation's rivals can be identified and completion can take place beyond the basic concept of price and price changes.

CHAPTER ROUNDUP

- The environment and marketing strategy
- The nature of the marketing environment and the evolution of environmental analysis
- Strategic group mapping
- Competitive advantage
- Marketing objectives, strategies and plans

FURTHER READING

Diffenbach, J. (1983) Corporate Environmental Analysis in Large US Corporations. *Long Range Planning*, 16(3), pp107–116.

Wilson, M.S. and Gilligan, C. (2005) *Strategic Marketing Management*. 3rd edition. Oxford, Butterworth Heinemann.

REFERENCES

Bang & Olufsen (2012) www.bang-olufsen.com [Accessed on 20 March 2012]

BBC (2006) UK universities eye Fresh Talent. BBC, http://news.bbc.co.uk/1/hi/scotland/5341092.stm [Accessed on 23 March 2012]

Burberry (2012) uk.burberry.com [Accessed on 20 June 2012]

Diffenbach, J. (1983) Corporate Environmental Analysis in Large US Corporations. *Long Range Planning*, 16(3), pp107–116.

Drummond, G. *et al* (2008) *Strategic Marketing Planning and Control*. 3rd edition. Oxford, Butterworth Heinemann.

Wilson, M.S. and Gilligan, C. (2005) *Strategic Marketing Management*, 3rd edition. Oxford, Butterworth Heinemann.

QUICK QUIZ

1   When an organisation undertakes a competitor analysis, what are the three key considerations?

2   What are the four key components in a competitor response profile?

3   What are the key components of Porter's five forces analysis?

4   What do you understand by the term 'strategic group mapping'?

5   A consequence of not adopting one of the positions of Porter's Generic Strategies is that the organisation becomes 'stuck in the middle'; what are the potential consequences of this?

The Chartered Institute of Marketing

Activity 7.1

Using the various steps outlined below shows how each will be addressed. The important point is that there is a clear understanding what will be achieved from the analysis under each heading.

Scanning the environment	This is a general audit of the environment which identifies those factors which will influence the organisation. Trends and changes can be quickly acted upon
Monitoring	Monitoring changes and identifying opportunities and threats
Forecasting	Based on the available information, change may need to be made
Assessment	An assessment of the potential impact on the business needs to be made

Activity 7.2

A luxury company such as Burberry follows a focus strategy with a narrower approach to the market. Burberry is an internationally recognised luxury brand with a worldwide distribution network. The business concentrates its efforts on a smaller or niche segment. Burberry Group plc is a British luxury fashion house, manufacturing clothing, fragrance and fashion accessories. Its distinctive tartan pattern has become one of its most widely copied trademarks. Burberry is most famous for its iconic trench coat, which was invented by founder Thomas Burberry. Burberry has over 500 stores in over 50 countries. The core activities are product and marketing excellence which underpin this brand momentum. Developing and maintaining brand loyalty is the basis of customer retention. This is achieved through sustained research and development that enhances product innovation.

1   The three key considerations of competitor analysis are:

- **Marketing capabilities**: how effective is their advertising and how much money is available for this activity?
- **Levels of innovation**: how innovative is the competition and how is innovation delivered?
- **Management**: how skilled is the management team?

2   The four key components in a competitor response profile are current strategy, capabilities, assumptions and goals

3   The key components of Porter's five forces analysis are potential entrants, buyers, substitutes, suppliers and competitive rivalry

4   Having identified and analysed individual competitors in the market, it is then necessary to categorise the competition based on the strategies they are pursuing. The various competitors can be clustered together to see the competitive groups which have formed in the market as a whole.

5   The organisational focus should be on one strategy of either cost leadership, differentiation or focus rather than trying to adopt different or mixing strategies. The potential consequences of being 'stuck in the middle' are the effect of failing to adopt this approach and to become 'stuck in the middle' with the underlying principles of each approach being compromised.

CHAPTER 8

The internal marketing environment

Introduction

The internal marketing environment is equally as important as the external environment and helps the organisation to identify how effective the internal resources and structures are in achieving the organisation's stated objectives. In this chapter, we will be reviewing the frameworks which can be used for assessing the internal environment, examining the internal audit tools and considering the 'planning gap'.

Topic list

Internal change   1

Internal audit tools   2

Generating alternative strategic options   3

2.5	Assess the internal marketing environment of an organisation through an audit process using a range of evaluation processes and approaches
	■ The evolving nature and extent of internal organisational change
	■ Developing resource-based planning and strategy
	■ Internal environmental analysis frameworks
	■ Establishing the effects of organisational resources and capabilities on marketing planning
	■ Identifying key internal issues and assumptions
	■ Internal audit tools, eg product life cycle, portfolio models and the value chain
2.6	Utilise the planning gap as a means to identifying and assessing key marketing planning requirements to fulfil the organisation's marketing strategy
	■ Establishing objectives and the planning gap
	■ Generating alternative strategic options
	■ Filling the planning gap with new and existing strategies
	■ Evaluation of marketing opportunities and the achievement of competitive advantage
2.7	Assess the issues and constraints arising from the marketing audit and consider the consequences for the organisation in order to develop its marketing plan
	■ Prioritising issues and executing SWOT analysis
	■ Specifying marketing objectives, strategies and plans
	■ Consideration of timescales for implementation

1 Internal change

We have already looked at the components of the internal marketing audit. Now we will examine the evolving nature of organisational change.

Drummond *et al*. (2008) suggest that to establish an organisation's current and potential capabilities, its assets and competences should be established.

Organisational assets include:

- Financial, such as capital, liquidity and financial leverage
- Physical, which includes facilities and property
- Operational, such as plant and equipment
- People, ie employees and management
- Systems, such as marketing information systems.

Competences are the skills available to the organisation to enable it to use the assets identified above and are broken down into:

- **Strategic:** the management and strategic focus of the organisation

- **Functional:** the functional areas which manage the various activities (finance, marketing, human resources, etc) of the business

- **Operational:** responsible for the day-to-day operations of the organisation

- **Individual:** the individual skills and competences which employees have

- **Team competences:** how teams work together, both within and across business functions

- **Corporate-level competences:** skills which apply to the whole organisation.

The internal marketing environment determines what the organisation is capable of delivering to its customers. Change to the internal environment is often necessary and the starting point for any change emanates from the strategy and structure in place.

The Chartered Institute of Marketing

The McKinsey Seven 'S' framework looks at the organisation from a different perspective, identifying 'hard' and 'soft' shared values. Figure 8.1 shows the framework and reflects the concept that as each element is interlinked, a change in one area impacts on another area.

Figure 8.1   McKinsey seven 'S' framework

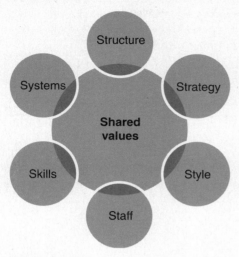

(Peters and Waterman, 1982)

- **Strategy** is the set of plans outlining how the organisation is going to achieve its objectives
- **Shared values** are the guiding principles which lead the organisation into behaving in a particular way
- **Structure** refers to how the organisation is structured functionally, ie who reports to whom
- **Skills** are the capabilities that the organisation has as a whole
- **Systems** are the processes and procedures which the organisation uses to meet customer needs
- **Style** is the management approach collectively used
- **Staff** are the people who constitute the organisation.

THE REAL WORLD

Telenor

'Telenor Group is the incumbent telecommunications company in Norway, with headquarters located at Fornebu, close to Oslo. Telenor Group is mostly an international wireless carrier with operations in Scandinavia, Eastern Europe and Asia, working predominantly under the Telenor brand. It is ranked as the sixth largest mobile phone operator in the world, with more than 172 million subscribers. In addition, it has extensive broadband and TV distribution operations in four Nordic Countries.'

Structure

Telenor is divided into a number of groupings: Asia, Center-Eastern European, Nordic, Finance, Communication and Corporate Responsibility, Human Resources, and Business Development and Research.

Strategy

As of August 5, 2010, two of Telenor strategies were to capture growth in three regions (Asia, Central-Eastern European and Nordic), and to undertake merger and acquisition (M&A) activities. These strategies were understandable, considering the condition of the economy (global financial crisis) and the commoditised telecommunication service (less average revenue per user).

2 Internal audit tools

When undertaking an audit, a number of tools can be utilised to analyse the situation of an organisation internally and provide information on which decisions relating to marketing strategy can be taken. We will consider a number of these separately below.

2.1 Product life cycle

Products are considered to have a finite life, which is referred to as the product life cycle (PLC) and the 'classic' view is shown in Figure 8.2. The PLC helps marketers to develop their marketing strategies as well as monitoring the progress of a product.

Marketers will want any newly launched product to have as long a life as possible in order to generate an acceptable level of profit after the costs of development have been covered.

It is difficult to predict the life of the product and consequently the shape of the PLC can vary as modifications or changes are made to the product throughout its life.

A fad – a temporary period of unusually high sales volumes driven by consumer enthusiasm and immediate product or brand popularity – will shorten the PLC.

Marketers will want to effectively manage each stage of the PLC and, while the concept receives criticism, it is undoubtedly a useful tool. As will be seen, each stage of the product's life will be monitored, so that strategies can be developed. Pricing, product features, promotion (repositioning, rebranding) and distribution strategies will be reviewed at each stage and adjustments made as necessary.

Figure 8.2   The PLC

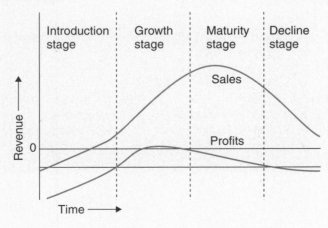

The Chartered
Institute of Marketing

Some organisations will find they have most of their products in the maturity stage and much time will be spent advertising the products, but with little thought being given to rebranding, repositioning or product modification. The changes made at this stage can be quite dramatic or subtle in delivery. For example, Mercedes Benz changed the shape of the headlights on its models to a 'teardrop' shape, which attracted new sales. The PLC in Figure 8.2 shows sales and revenue plotted against time.

The key stages of the PLC are as follows:

- **Introduction**

    Generally, it takes time for a product to be accepted and sales can be slow at this stage. Depending on the investment, profit can be negative. However, the role of the marketer is to raise the level of sales with the target audience and widen distribution into the market to develop the product through to the next stage. Depending on the marketing objectives, a skimming or penetration pricing strategy can be adopted. A skimming policy is a high initial price followed by downward adjustments. A penetration policy is a lower initial price to gain greater volume sales.

- **Growth**

    Sales start to rise quickly, possibly because there are now competitors in the market and more consumer awareness. The original product may be improved through the addition of new features to compete more effectively.

    Profit is starting to rise at this stage and promotional activity needs to focus on brand building to encourage customers to purchase with less focus on price.

    Brand building needs to be effective to encourage customers to buy from the organisation, rather than the competition, to build a strong position in the market and generate customer loyalty.

- **Maturity**

    Maturity tends to be the longest stage of the PLC, where sales now start to plateau and then fall. Profits come under pressure as the organisation focuses its marketing effort on countering competitive activity. However, the market becomes saturated and some of the weaker competitors will leave as profitability drops steeply. While many products at this stage remain unchanged, it is here that organisations develop enhanced versions of the product or launch new ones. Innovative use of the marketing mix can extend the maturity stage, ie prolong the life of the product, but eventually it will move into decline.

- **Decline**

    The decline stage can be a little unpredictable; sales can drop off dramatically, or follow a slow but steady downturn. The marketer has to decide on the most effective way of dealing with this by slowing down sales decline or by withdrawing marketing support and letting the product 'die', ie milking it.

    Depending on the product, there is always the possibility of repositioning it in the customer's mind or to develop new markets or customers.

THE REAL WORLD

Take for example Lucozade, which is the name for a range of energy and sports drinks. Originally a drink for people who were sick, designed to provide a source of energy, it was sold in glass bottle with an orange cellophane wrapper until 1983, when the slogan was changed from 'Lucozade aids recovery' to 'Lucozade replaces lost energy', along with a change in packaging. The glass bottle and wrapper was replaced with plastic. The rebranding was deemed a success as sales over a five-year period were reported as tripling. The brand still exists as a popular high-energy sports drink in a range of flavours, as well as the original.

The rapid development of technology increasingly forces manufacturers to consider letting the product die. We are currently seeing evidence of this in the 'demise' of video players and video tapes with CD players being replaced by MP3 players.

Organisations do need to understand that a failing product not only affects the organisation's profitability, but can diminish the brand in the consumer's mind if competitors are launching 'newer' or more advanced products.

ACTIVITY 8.1

For an organisation of your choice (this may be the one that you work for), analyse the portfolio of products that you produce in terms of the PLC stage that they currently 'fit' into. What are the implications for managing these products in future?

2.2 The BCG matrix

Developed by the Boston Consulting Group (BCG) in the 1970s, it is generally regarded as an important model of marketing and strategic planning. The model helps organisations to identify potential opportunities and problems associated with a product. It does this by categorising the organisation's products into four classifications.

The purpose of the BCG matrix is to help marketers develop their forward planning by suggesting strategies for the future development of the range: selectively invest in problem children; invest in and grow stars; maintain cash cows; and evaluate dogs removing them as necessary.

Many organisations, particularly those with large numbers of products, may find that they have a high percentage of dogs.

The BCG matrix (Figure 8.3) can operate at a number of levels including:

- Corporate
- Product
- SBU.

It is based on the principle that cash, not profits, drives a product from one box to another within the matrix and helps an organisation to develop its growth strategies based on two-dimensional variables:

- Relative market share
- Market growth rate.

Market share is measured against the product's nearest competitor, ie the degree of dominance the competitor enjoys, while market growth reflects the potential market opportunities and also indicates the organisation's likely cash needs.

The Chartered Institute of Marketing

Figure 8.3   BCG growth-share matrix

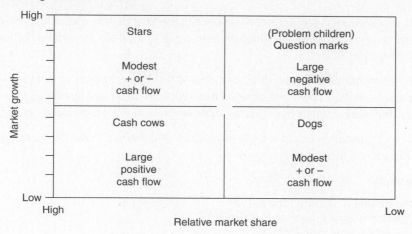

For each product, a circle can be plotted on the matrix to pictorially represent the relative value of sales in the category as well as likely cash flows.

The quadrants of the BCG matrix

- **Dog**

  A dog maintains a low market share in a low growth market and is likely to be cash neutral or consuming a modest amount of cash flow and resources.

  A dog may have been a solid performer, but has subsequently declined in terms of performance. Given its low market share and lack of growth potential, the organisation will generally want to remove the product from the portfolio, unless the cash flow is strong in which case the product could be harvested.

- **Stars**

  A star occupies a high growth share in a high growth market. It generally requires a substantial investment to support expansion, but it is cash neutral and therefore regarded as a potential investment for the future.

  Existing market share should be protected, or a larger share of new consumers should be sought.

- **Cash cows**

  A cash cow maintains a high market share in a low growth market. It generates cash which can be used to support other products.

  Market position or pricing should be maintained, or the profits used to invest in new products.

- **Problem child**

  Sometimes referred to as question marks, problem children will occupy a low market share of a high growth market. It consumes cash just to maintain its market share and requires cash to support product development.

  Strategies for a problem child include divesting, harvesting or removing from the portfolio. Looking externally, another strategy is to buy a smaller product from competitor in order to build a large market share.

2.3 GE matrix

Another tool available to marketers is the GE matrix which, like the BCG matrix, uses a two-dimensional approach. Both models can be used as an aid to future planning or to evaluate an existing portfolio or the current level of investment in an SBU.

The GE matrix uses two dimensions: industry attractiveness and business strengths. In contrast to the BCG matrix, these dimensions are broken down into other factors which are rated and combined into an index of industry attractiveness. Business strength also uses an index which is then ranked strong, average or weak.

To use the GE matrix, an organisation would identify key factors which would make the market attractive to it. These factors would include the following.

Industry attractiveness

- How large is the market now and in the future?
- What is the expected annual growth of the market?
- What are the expected profit margins?
- How easy is it to enter the market?
- What is the competition?

Business strengths

- Current market share
- Organisation's current rate of growth
- Ability to influence the market
- Available resources
- Current profit margins.

Having compiled its strengths and ranked them strong, weak or medium, the organisation can then map them across industry attractiveness. This will then produce a position on the matrix.

The positioning on the matrix then offers three potential strategic options.

Where the organisation has identified strong or medium business strengths and the industry has been medium to high attractiveness (indicated x in Figure 8.4), it should invest for growth.

Having identified a market with low to medium attractiveness, linked with medium to weak business strengths (indicated xx on the matrix), then the consensus would be to withdraw from the market or harvest.

The remaining positions, ie weak strengths linked with medium to low industry attractiveness (xxx) on the matrix, should be managed selectively. Careful consideration is needed here to establish the most appropriate strategy.

Figure 8.4   GE Matrix

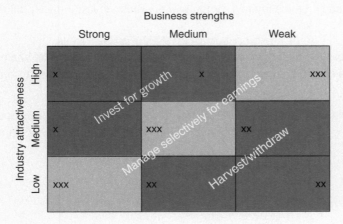

2.4 The value chain

The term 'value chain' was used by Michael Porter (1985). The value chain analysis describes the activities the organisation performs and links them to the organisation's competitive position.

Value chain analysis describes the activities within and around an organisation, and relates them to an analysis of the competitive strength of the organisation. Therefore, it evaluates the value each particular activity adds to the organisation's products or services. This idea was built upon the recognition that an organisation can be more than a random compilation of machinery, equipment, people and money. Only if these things are arranged into systems and systematic activities, will it become possible to produce something for which customers are willing to pay a price. Porter argues that the ability to perform particular activities and to manage the linkages between these activities is a source of competitive advantage.

Porter distinguishes between **primary activities** and **support activities**. Primary activities are directly concerned with the creation or delivery of a product or service. They can be grouped into five main areas: inbound logistics, operations, outbound logistics, marketing and sales, and service. Each of these primary activities is linked to support activities which help to improve their effectiveness or efficiency. There are four main areas of support activities: procurement, technology development (including R&D), human resource management and infrastructure (systems for planning, finance, quality, information management, etc.).

The basic model of Porter's value chain is given in Figure 8.5

Figure 8.5   The value chain

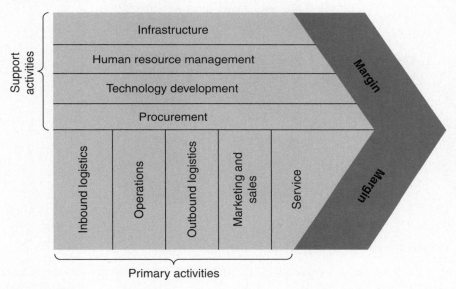

(Porter, 1985)

The term 'margin' implies that organisations realise a profit margin that depends on their ability to manage the linkages between all activities in the value chain. In other words, the organisation is able to deliver a product/service for which the customer is willing to pay more than the sum of the costs of all activities in the value chain.

These linkages are crucial for corporate success. The linkages are flows of information, goods and services, as well as systems and processes for adjusting activities.

Only if the marketing and sales function delivers sales forecasts for the next period to all other departments in time and with reliable accuracy, will procurement be able to order the necessary material for the correct date. And only if procurement does a good job and forwards order information to inbound logistics, will operations be able to schedule production in a way that guarantees the delivery of products in a timely and effective manner –

as pre-determined by marketing. To be successful, the linkages need to provide seamless cooperation and information flow between the value chain activities.

In most industries, it is unusual for a single company to perform all activities from product design, production of components and final assembly to delivery to the final user, by itself. Often, organisations are elements of a value system or supply chain. Hence, value chain analysis should cover the whole value system in which the organisation operates (Figure 8.6).

Within the whole value system, there is only a certain value of profit margin available. This is the difference between the final price the customer pays and the sum of all costs incurred with production and delivery of the product/service (eg raw material and energy). It depends on the structure of the value system, how this margin spreads across the suppliers, producers, distributors, customers and other elements of the value system. Each member of the system will use its market position and negotiating power to get a higher proportion of this margin. Nevertheless, members of a value system can co-operate to improve their efficiency and to reduce their costs in order to achieve a higher total margin to the benefit of all of them (eg by reducing stocks in a just-in-time system).

Figure 8.6   Relationships between value chains

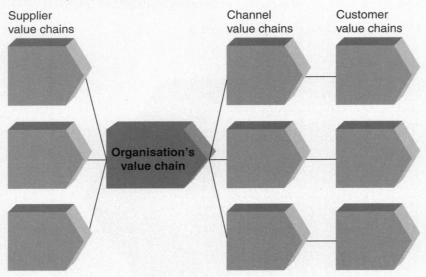

(Porter, 1985)

A typical value chain analysis can be performed in the following steps:

- Analysis of the organisation's value chain – in which costs are related to every single activity

- Analysis of customers' value chains – how does our product fit into their value chain

- Identification of potential cost advantages in comparison with competitors

- Identification of potential value added for the customer – how can our product add value to the customer's value chain (eg lower costs or higher performance) – where does the customer see such potential?

2.5 Gap analysis

The planning process requires an organisation to set objectives (where it wants to be) to be achieved in a specific time frame.

Organisations need to be able to monitor performance against objectives and while gap analysis should be conducted on a regular basis, it is an integral part of the marketing audit process. Gap analysis is a tool that helps companies compare actual performance with potential performance. At its core are two questions: 'Where

The Chartered Institute of Marketing

are we?' and 'Where do we want to be?' Figure 8.7 shows the situation for an organisation that sets itself a £60 million target, which was developed through the planning process from the corporate objectives.

However, sales are not as buoyant as originally forecast and there is a £30 million income gap in the plan (planning gap) identified. The organisation believes that it can reduce the gap by £15 million as result of introducing new strategies, which will now result in a £15 million gap.

Figure 8.7   The strategic planning gap

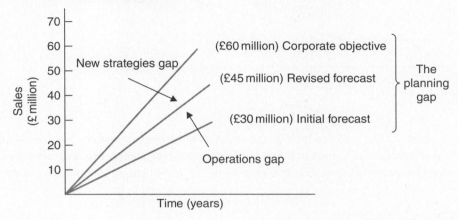

In reality, the marketing team would want to 'close the gap' and it can achieve this in a number of ways:

- Additional advertising
- Promotional pricing
- New distribution channels
- Product modification.

Of course, it may have been that the planning process was flawed and incorrect assumptions were made, leading to inflated corporate targets being incorporated into the plan and this can have serious consequences.

Equally, the most effective planning systems cannot take into consideration the 'unthinkable' and that is what happened in 9/11 when the world's aircraft stopped flying and the airline market collapsed overnight. In such circumstances, organisations may find the only option is to look at a cost-leadership approach and eliminate as many costs as it possibly can.

Organisations do not just plan for sales but can include a range of objectives in their plans and Figure 8.8 illustrates some of the variables, such as sales over a period of time which can be measured.

THE REAL WORLD

Cargill Magic, CG, is an ice cream well known in Sri Lanka and loved by the local population. CG was originally a retailer but has diversified into manufacturing and selling ice cream. Its performance has been suffering and the internal audit tools will aid its understanding of current activity. The gap analysis and PLC are shown below.

Gap analysis

Gap analysis is something which marketing managers need to monitor and consider in terms of filling the gap between corporate sales and financial objectives. The diversification of the business has diverted resource away from the retailing activity to selling to manufacturing product as illustrated in the diagram below.

Figure 8.8

Gap analysis

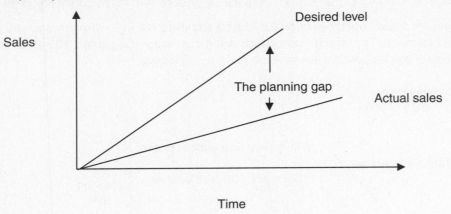

The gap can be closed by the business through the adoption of two main methods; modifying long-term strategic plans and with a short-to medium-term operational planning perspective. In general the methods for filling the gap relate to considering more appropriate marketing objectives, productivity or growth strategies.

2.6 The product life cycle

The product life cycle is a particularly useful concept that can be used to develop an appropriate marketing mix for the future period.

Figure 8.9

Stages of the product life cycle

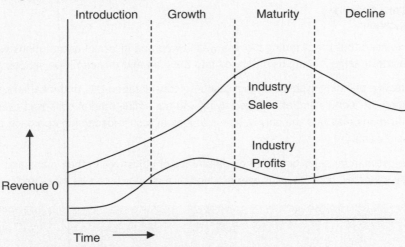

The different stages have the following characteristics:

Introductory Phase

- High investment in the promotional mix
- Secure few distribution channels
- Use price skimming method to raise revenue
- Basic product features

Growth Phase

- Still promote investment in promotions
- Consider providing extra features to product
- Reduce price to secure market share
- Use same distribution channels

Maturity Phase

- Promote brand image heavily
- Secure new distribution channels
- Price is inelastic in demand at this level
- Use selling as sales promotion – offers, discounts

Decline Phase

- Market share stable and then falling
- Hard selling required – investment into new product features or phase out
- Profits begin to fall
- Price needs to either remain constant or reduced

The usefulness of this concept is that you are able to consider these strategies at each stage reached by CG ice cream. It helps marketing decisions to be made about pricing, distribution etc. It also helps to identify an appropriate portfolio of products – ie need to consider that the range of ice cream needs to have mature products, newly developed products, etc to ensure that there is a healthy balance of products. Hence the entire product range can be plotted against each other and therefore showing where resources can be cut or invested.

2.7 SWOT analysis

SWOT analysis is the commonest structure for bringing together the strengths, weaknesses, opportunities and threats which have been identified as part of the audit.

Environmental factors relating to the internal and external position of an organisation need to be captured at all the various levels (typically the SBU) and categorised into strengths, weaknesses, opportunities or threats.

Having identified and categorised the various elements, an organisation will want to convert weaknesses and threats into strengths and opportunities (Figure 8.10).

Strengths and weaknesses are internally focused elements (but can be reflected externally) and opportunities and threats are externally focused.

A SWOT analysis will produce a wide range of information which the organisation needs to analyse and decide on a programme of actions which needs to be developed into a performance-importance matrix.

Opportunities need to be prioritised in terms of importance; threats similarly need to be ranked in terms of the seriousness of the threat.

Figure 8.10   SWOT analysis

Table 8.1 offers some examples of the contents of a SWOT analysis.

Table 8.1   Contents of a SWOT analysis

Strengths	Weaknesses
Strong brand awareness	High staff turnover
Experienced management team	Lack of investment funding
Innovative culture	Poor channel relationships
New technology	Excess product capacity
Opportunities	**Threats**
New distribution channels available	New players entering market
Dealer loyalty becoming important	Low margins in market
Demand for new products	Cost of new technology high
Internet/e-commerce initiatives	Competitive market

It can be the case that factors identified as a strength can also be a weakness. Take the example of a brand. An organisation may have a very strong brand with some consumers, but equally the brand in other sectors of the market may be viewed as large and uncaring.

SWOT analysis underpins decisions relating to the selection of strategies based on evaluation of various criteria, and these can be related to the target market segments that we can choose to focus upon with particular market offers. The link of this process into strategy and segmentation – targeting and positioning in particular – is made in the next chapter.

3 Generating alternative strategic options

In the previous chapter we identified options in terms of Porter's generic strategies, and we will now look at the alternative directions, in particular those derived from Ansoff's matrix. The matrix was developed in 1958 by Igor Ansoff and provides a linkage between the product and the market. Four strategic options are proposed for delivering a product to the market to ensure corporate goals are achieved.

Figure 8.11   Variance analysis in the planning process

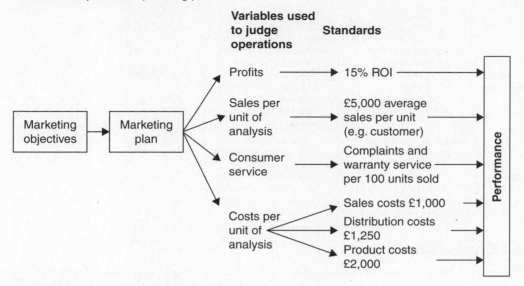

(Adapted from Luck and Ferrell, 1979)

The four strategic options are:

- Market penetration
- Market development
- Product development
- Diversification.

3.1 Market penetration

Market penetration occurs when an organisation seeks to sell its existing products into an existing market. It will often adopt an aggressive marketing campaign offering price promotions or other incentives to encourage product take-up.

Market penetration can generate additional business quickly; however, there will come a time when the market becomes saturated and other strategies need to be pursued. A market penetration strategy has the least risk associated with it.

3.2 Market development

Market development requires an organisation to offer an existing product to a new market. The new markets can include segments, distribution channels and overseas markets.

3.3 Product development

Product development requires a new product to be offered to an existing market. Organisations, through the PLC, for example, will be monitoring each product as it goes through the life cycle and will want to ensure it has a range of new products in development through its NPD process.

Figure 8.12 Ansoff's product market matrix

	Existing products	New products
Existing markets	**Market penetration** • Cross selling • Wins from competitors • Lower price • Advertise more	**Product development** • Modified or new products to existing markets, eg electronic banking services
New markets	**Market development** • Identifying new markets for existing products, eg joint ventures, geographic expansion	**Diversification** • Start or buy business outside current products and markets, eg portals, third party distribution channels

3.4 Diversification

This strategy requires not only a new product but also a new market and consequently this approach carries with it the highest level of risk.

Diversification can be 'related', ie have some connection with existing activities, or 'unrelated', where there is no connection with any existing activities. Clearly, diversification is moving an organisation into new territory, and as can be seen in Figure 8.12, it can involve the purchase of a new business. Of course with risk comes reward and diversification may be an essential strategy for some organisations.

Organisations should not pursue one approach at the expense of others. It is usually necessary to be pursuing two or more strategies at the same time if organisational objectives are to be achieved.

ACTIVITY 8.2

For your own organisation, or one you are familiar with, identify and explain a market penetration strategy, and a market development strategy.

THE REAL WORLD

Dell's diversification pays off

Dell, the world's second biggest PC-maker, has posted a 21% rise in third-quarter profits.

Texas-based Dell's financial results were broadly in line with IT analysts' expectations.

Dell said it made net profits of $677m in the three months to end-September.

Improved sales of servers and data storage systems for the commercial sector lifted revenue to $10.6bn from $9.14bn previous year, up 16%.

Smart strategy

Dell's latest financial results showed the benefits of its efforts to diversify its product range.

It has expanded into printers, data storage systems and cash registers in recent years.

In September, it announced plans to take the process a step further by launching its own digital music players and TVs.

Dell slashed PC prices in August in hopes of stimulating sales.

PC sales have remained sluggish worldwide for the past three years.

The Chartered Institute of Marketing

Dell specialises in selling inexpensive PCs by shipping direct to consumers, cutting out the retailer.

Price cutting by PC makers has pushed prices down 40% since 1997, according to analysts at investment bank Merrill Lynch.

Dell's third-quarter results were released ahead of schedule, coming shortly before the market closed. Its shares bounced upwards before dipping 3 cents to $35.64.

(Source: Adapted from BBC NEWS, 2003)

▶ **Assessment tip**

It is important to be able to understand and evaluate the relevance and limitations of each internal audit tool and apply them in a given context.

Summary

The internal marketing environment is equally as important as the external environment and helps the organisation to identify how effective the internal resources and structures are in achieving the organisation's stated objectives.

This chapter has reviewed a number of key frameworks which marketers can use to assess the internal environment, examining the internal audit tools and considering the 'planning gap'. Models like the BCG matrix help an organisation to ensure that it is maximising its cash flow through the careful management of the portfolio. The advantages and disadvantages of the model and other models have been discussed. However, the financial turmoil at the start of 2009 demonstrated the importance of retaining cash in the business.

Porter's value chain demonstrates the need for value to be added to a product, and the cost of the value-adding process should not exceed the additional income which can be generated. The concept of 'gap analysis' is examined and its importance to the organisation in ensuring that when, for example, sales are lower than planned at a given point, corrective and timely action can be taken. Ways of filling this gap are identified using combinations of products and markets. SWOT is then introduced as a basis for facilitating these decisions of selecting marketing strategies.

CHAPTER ROUNDUP

- Internal change
- Internal audit tools
  - Product life cycle
  - The BCG matrix
  - GE matrix
  - The value chain
  - Gap analysis
  - SWOT analysis
- Generating alternative strategic options

FURTHER READING

Hollensen, S. (2007) *Global Marketing*. London, Prentice Hall.

REFERENCES

BBC (2003) Dell's diversification pays off. BBC, http://news.bbc.co.uk/1/hi/business/3269299.stm [Accessed on 8 June 2012]

Craeser (2012) Strategy: McKinsey 7S Framework and Telenor Example. Craeser, http://craeser.wordpress.com/2010/03/23/strategy-mckinsey-7s-framework/ [Accessed on 20 March 2012)

Dibb, S. *et al.* (2006) *Marketing: Concepts and Strategies*. 5th edition. Boston, Houghton Mifflin.

Drummond, G. *et al.* (2008) *Strategic Marketing Planning and Control*. 3rd edition. Oxford, Butterworth Heinemann.

Luck, D.J. and Ferrell, O.C. (1979) *Marketing Strategy and Plans*. Englewood Cliffs, NJ, Prentice-Hall.

Peters, T. and Waterman, R. (1982) *In Search of Excellence: Lessons from American's Best-Run Companies*. NY, Warner Books.

Porter, M.E. (1985) *Competitive Advantage: Creating and Sustaining Superior Performance*. New York, Free Press.

QUICK QUIZ

1 Draw the GE matrix and explain the various components.
2 Explain the concept of the PLC. Of what value is it to marketers?
3 In the BCG matrix, what do you understand by the term 'star'? How should they be managed?
4 What do you understand by Porter's value chain analysis?
5 What is the purpose of 'gap analysis'?

Activity 8.1

Using the different PLC stages as headings, you should position each of the organisation's products. Then, for each product, predict where it will be in 12 months. This information is then used to determine how you will manage these products in the future.

Activity 8.2

The market penetration strategy will be used when your organisation wants to sell its existing products into an existing market. It will often adopt an be aggressive marketing campaign, offering price promotions or other incentives to encourage product take up. Give examples for your organisation.

Market development requires your organisation to offer an existing product to a new market. The new markets can include segments, distribution channels and overseas markets and you need to give relevant examples for your organisation.

QUICK QUIZ ANSWERS

1   See Figure 8.4

2   The PLC helps marketers to develop their marketing strategies as well as monitoring the progress of a product. Marketers will want any newly launched product to have as long a life as possible in order to generate an acceptable level of profit after the costs of development have been covered.

3   The term 'Star' occupies a high-growth share in a high-growth market. It generally requires a substantial investment to support expansion, but it is cash neutral and therefore regarded as a potential investment for the future. Existing market share should be protected, or a larger share of new consumers should be sought.

4   The value chain analysis describes the activities the organisation performs and links them to the organisation's competitive position.

5   Gap analysis is a tool that helps companies compare actual performance with potential performance. At its core are two questions: 'Where are we?' and 'Where do we want to be?'

Section 2:

Senior examiner's comments

On completion of Section 2, students should have a detailed knowledge and understanding of:

- The practical issues associated with undertaking a marketing audit
- The structure and content of a marketing audit
- The sources of information available for inclusion in the audit process
- The dimensions of the internal marketing audit and the identification of marketing opportunities
- The constituent components of the internal marketing environment
- The process of analysing audit information to generate strategic options.

An important factor in student success is the ability of applying the marketing audit process in different types of organisation and understanding the particular constraints that they may be faced with in each case. It is especially important that candidates are prepared for the information-gathering process that is involved in auditing the internal and external marketing environments, and how this can be analysed to form the foundation for marketing strategies and tactics. Being objective in analysis of audit material is critical to the formulation of effective strategies. Similarly, effective implementation of marketing plans needs to take account of the constraints on undertaking an audit in different situations and the timeliness and cost trade off of data availability in these scenarios.

Finally, students not only need a thorough understanding of audit tools and the contribution that each can make to analysis, but also be able to evaluate their use in the audit process. This also applies when bringing together information on both the internal and external situations of an organisation to provide a framework for generating strategies that provide the focus of a marketing plan.

Section 3: Creating marketing strategies through segmentation, targeting and positioning

In Section 3, marketing strategy formulation is approached through a detailed exposition of the segmentation, targeting and positioning approach. This provides the core of the marketing planning process which synthesises information from the audit in line with organisational goals and sets the strategy to define a detailed marketing programme that supports positioning in the markets targeted. Specific topics in the text relate to the process in defining marketing strategies, market segmentation techniques and evaluation, targeting approaches, and market positioning strategies. However, it is important to be cognisant of the holistic nature of this process, which should be addressed in an analytical manner drawing upon evidence to select appropriate target markets and formulate a complementary positioning for the identified customer groups.

CHAPTER 9

The role of marketing strategies and market segmentation

Introduction

The third section of the syllabus is focussed on segmentation, targeting and positioning (STP). Students will need to be able to critically evaluate strategic options within this stage of the marketing planning process and propose outcomes that relate to determining competitive strategy.

Of particular importance is the recognition that strategies need to be assessed in terms of their future contribution to the organisation's specific contextual objectives. In addition, students need to become familiar with the notion that both internal and external factors should contribute to any appraisal of the attractiveness of the value of alternative market segments.

Topic list

Marketing strategy   1

Market segmentation   2

Criteria for effective segmentation   3

3.1	Critically evaluate the role of marketing strategies and demonstrate how they can be used to develop competitive advantage, market share and growth
	▪ Marketing strategies for meeting marketing objectives through satisfying customer requirements ▪ Marketing strategies as product 'offers' providing benefits to customer segments ▪ Identifying customers and offers for future development
3.2	Assess the importance of market segmentation as a basis of selecting markets to achieve the organisation's business and marketing objectives via customer satisfaction
	▪ Defining local, national, international and global markets and their parameters ▪ Principle of market segmentation, targeting and positioning ▪ Benefits and costs of market segmentation ▪ Conditions for successful segmentation
3.3	Critically evaluate the different segmentation approaches available to organisations in different organisational contexts and sectors and make recommendations for their use
	▪ Segmentation variables for consumer markets ▪ Segmentation variables for business markets ▪ Profiling segments and defining customer types ▪ Critical evaluation of segmentation techniques ▪ Contemporary methods of segmentation such as relationship-based approaches and online behaviours

1 Marketing strategy

Marketing strategy addresses three separate aspects of marketing planning:

1. Customers
2. Competition
3. Internal issues

Dibb *et al*. (2006, p20) define marketing strategy as 'a strategy indicating the opportunities to pursue, specific targets, and the types of competitive advantages that are to be developed'.

A strategy requires clear objectives and focus aligned with the organisation's corporate goals.

A staged approach to marketing strategy development suggests the sequence of:

▪ Identifying mission, vision and corporate strategy of the organisation
▪ Undertaking opportunities, capabilities and resources analysis
▪ Scanning the environment for information relating to customer and competitor analysis
▪ Segmentation, targeting and positioning.

Looking at the sequence above, we have already addressed some of the issues, so in summary:

▪ A marketing opportunity is a set of circumstances and timings that allows an organisation to take actions towards reaching a target market.

How attractive the market is to an organisation will be determined by a number of forces and factors which will be determined by a strategic analysis of:

▪ External environment, through environmental scanning

▪ Internal analysis, identifying the relative competences and capabilities of the organisation

▪ The strengths, weakness, opportunities and threats faced now and in the future

▪ Customer analysis, to identify their needs and wants, so the organisation can understand them and respond to changing requirements.

For your own organisation or one you know well, identify what you believe to be the marketing opportunities available to it in the short, medium and long term.

2 Market segmentation

Organisations do not have finite resources and need to use the resources they do have in an effective manner. After all, a poorly targeted marketing programme not only affects sales but takes away financial resources which could have been better used, not just on other marketing programmes but on other divisions of the organisation.

We will be exploring the concept that, by identifying people or organisations that have similar needs and wants, marketers can be more effective by focussing resources and marketing programmes on those segments which have been identified as being more likely to make purchases.

Before we define what we mean by 'segmentation', we need to understand the term 'market' and the context in which it will be used.

Dibb *et al*. (2006) suggest that a market is 'an aggregate of people who, as individuals, or within organisations, have a need for certain products and the ability, willingness and authority to purchase such products'.

This is an important concept because we can divide the market into business (B2B) and consumer markets (B2C) that will have different requirements, which can be satisfied through effective segmentation.

The concept of segmentation was developed by Smith (1956) and has been defined by Dibb *et al*. (2006) as:

'The process of grouping customers in markets with some heterogeneity into smaller, more similar or homogeneous segments.'

They go on to define a market segment as:

'A group of individuals or organisations sharing one or more similar characteristics that cause them to have relatively similar product needs and buying characteristics.'

The concept of segmentation applies to both consumer and business (organisational) markets, and we will explore each separately. Although they enjoy similarities, there is the added complication in business markets that buying decisions, while being made by individuals, are usually made by the 'buying centre' or decision-making unit (DMU) where responsibility for different aspects of the process is given to specific people or functions. The stages of the STP process can be identified as follows.

Situational analysis

- Identify an organisation's current position, capabilities, objectives and constraints

Market segmentation

- Identify the segmentation variables and segment the market
- Develop profiles for each segment

Targeting

- Evaluate the potential and attractiveness of each segment
- Select the target market segment(s)

Product positioning

- Identify the position within each target segment
- Select and develop the appropriate positioning concepts

Marketing mix

- Develop the marketing mix strategy

2.1 Benefits of segmentation

Organisations may have different objectives depending on the market they are operating in. Charities will have different objectives from a private company. However, no organisation generally has the resources or appeal to be in every market.

Choices have to be made about which market or segment to operate in and equally where not to be.

Doyle (1994) offered organisations a number of benefits which accrue from segmenting a market and they are summarised below.

- A distinct marketing mix can be produced for each segment which gives it a specific solution for their requirements.

- Focussed communications through specific channels can be used, eg, trade rather than national press.

- Customer retention – It is far more expensive to recruit new customers than to retain existing ones, so by developing a specialism and understanding in specific segments, customers are more likely to stay with the organisation.

- Market leadership – Brand leaders in segments are generally very profitable.

- Profits – It is the desire of most organisations to make a surplus over costs which can be reinvested in the business.

- Segmentation also allows an organisation to differentiate itself and its products from the competition and therefore position itself clearly in the customer's mind through a different marketing approach for each segment.

2.2 Segmenting business markets

Business markets have:

- Macro- and micro-segments

Macro-segments are subgroups which share common characteristics with the whole market.

Micro-segments are based around different buying characteristics.

The Chartered Institute of Marketing

Micro-segmentation

Macro-segments can be divided into organisational characteristics and product applications characteristics (Tables 9.1 and 9.2).

Local authorities in the UK have generally made their own individual purchasing decisions. There is a growing trend in the sector to join with another local authority to combine not only purchasing power but expertise.

Table 9.1   Macro-segmentation of B2B markets

Organisational
Size of an organisation
The size of an organisation will often affect the purchasing process. Larger organisations will often have a formal purchasing procedure in place, not only to provide consistency but also to ensure the process is transparent to suppliers and other parties. The 'risk' (financial and reputational) associated with the purchase is another consideration.
Location
Often organisations specialise in local or specific geographical areas. This is evident in technology or retail parks.   Banks often locate their overseas offices in key financial locations across the globe.   Increasingly, some organisations only want to serve 'local' areas because of specialisation or environmental issues.
Usage
The level of product 'usage' is another way to segment the market. An organisation may want minimum purchase levels to make it effective to conduct business or it may introduce different price points depending on the level of purchase.
Product
Standard customer groupings
A standard industrial classification (SIC) code in the UK; all businesses are defined by SIC codes which identify legal status and industry sectors which can then be broken down into more detailed segments.
Specific application
Defining a specific product application and grouping the customers around that.

Table 9.2   SIC Codes as macro-segments

Example SIC codes
The agricultural sector is quite diverse and only a very specific segment may need to be targeted. SIC 01000 covers farming generally, but SIC 01330 covers fruit, nuts, beverage and spice crops, so quite specific.
01000
Agriculture, hunting and related service activities.
01100
Growing of crops, market gardening and horticulture.
01110
Growing of cereals and other crops not elsewhere classified.
01120
Growing of vegetables, horticultural specialities and nursery products.
01130
Growing of fruit, nuts, beverage and spice crops.

Within the broader macro-segmentation approach, it is possible to identify another subgroup or micro-segment. However, this can be quite specific and an organisation would generally have to explore a wide range of information sources to obtain the level of detail necessary.

Micro-segmentation

This approach relates to factors associated with the buying process in organisations, such as the DMU, purchasing strategy and relationships (Table 9.3).

2.3 Segmenting consumer markets

> **▶ Key term**
>
> **Segmentation variables:** characteristics of organisations, groups, and individuals which are used to divide a market into smaller units or segments. Some of these characteristics would be age, gender, geographic location, or psychological factors.

Figure 9.1 shows a range of segmentation variables for the consumer market.

It is generally the case that consumer markets are larger than business markets and can be subjective and variable.

The Chartered
Institute of Marketing

Figure 9.1   Approaches to segmenting consumer markets

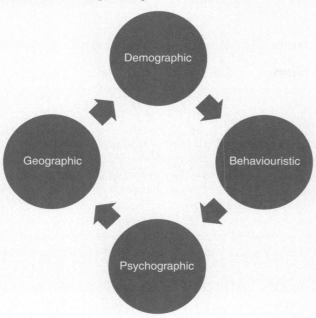

2.3.1 Geographic segmentation

This is a popular form of segmentation and can take into consideration markets beyond domestic boundaries. At its broadest, it can identify continents, regions, countries, which can be subdivided into cities, towns and villages.

Organisations which operate on a global or international basis often divide the operation into global regions to reflect the culture of a particular region.

Geographical segmentation is often used in conjunction with other forms of segmentation. Consider a UK-based company which operates internationally and is keen to standardise its products to take advantage of economies of scale. If it only segmented on the basis of geography, it would be unable to compete effectively with the local competition who are likely to be adopting a more robust form of segmentation. The additional segmentation approaches, to be adopted will depend on the organisation's marketing strategy.

Table 9.3   Micro-segmentation of B2B markets

Structure of DMU
The roles and responsibilities of the DMU.
Purchase decision process
Is a competitive tender needed?
Purchasing strategy
Does the organisation have one supplier for each product or multiple suppliers?
Buyer–seller relationships
Collaborative or adversarial approach?

On a more local basis, if an organisation wants to expand its business, it may want to establish a presence in major towns or cities where the size of the population within the catchment area is believed to be sufficient to operate a viable business.

Similarly an organisation may want to expand on a defined regional basis so that it can effectively control the business as a result of its local nature.

2.3.2 Demographic segmentation

Demographic segmentation takes into account a broad range of characteristics, which the marketer must clearly define. It provides a broad picture of the customer, enabling a finely targeted approach to be developed.

Car insurance companies can target the over-50s and offer cheaper insurance because the sector is generally considered to be safer. Similarly, other car insurance providers may actively avoid the under-21 age group because they are more likely to have an accident.

Some products are clearly tailored to the needs of the segment. Club 18–30 holidays are designed to appeal to that age group.

Clothing retailers aim at particular market segments, with some owning different retail brands for different target customer groups.

ACTIVITY 9.2

Consider the following high-street stores: Next, Marks & Spencer and Debenhams. What segments of the market do they appeal to?

Family life cycle segmentation assumes consumers will live their lives through a range of alternative scenarios and is shown in Figure 9.2. The cycle will continue until old age and retirement.

The Chartered
Institute of Marketing

Figure 9.2   Family life cycle groups

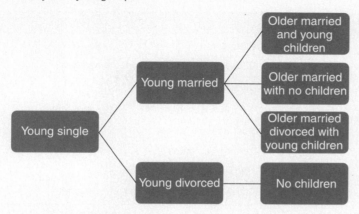

Banks offer a range of accounts to different age groups. Typically, young children are offered a savings account only. At around 12 years of age, the bank will offer an account which has immediate access through a debit card. At 18, for those going to university, a student account can be opened with greater financial flexibility reflecting the individual's situation.

The customer may then marry and want a home loan, followed by a saving account for their children. Understanding the family cycle and the customer's position within it, allows for a long-term relationship with the provider that offers different services products throughout the life cycle.

Geodemographic segmentation

Geodemographic segmentation combines demographic and geographic variables. It is an analysis of where people live and combines lifestyle data with location (postcode data).

ACORN

ACORN is a geodemographic tool used to identify and understand the UK population and the demand for products and services. Businesses use this information to improve their understanding of customers, target markets and determine where to locate operations.

Informed decisions can be made on where direct marketing and advertising campaigns will be most effective; where branches should be opened or closed; or where sites are located, including retail outlets, leisure facilities and public services.

ACORN categorises all 1.9 million UK postcodes, which have been described using over 125 demographic statistics within England, Scotland, Wales and Northern Ireland, and 287 lifestyle variables, making it the most powerful discriminator, giving a clearer understanding of clients and prospects.

People in similar areas are assumed to have similar demographics, lifestyles and buying behaviour (Table 9.4).

2.3.3 Psychographic segmentation

The previous segmentation strategies discussed have been reasonably straightforward to define and measure. Psychographic segmentation is more problematic because of its nature. It is sometimes referred to as lifestyle segmentation and perhaps this gives some clue as to its complexity.

Psychographic segmentation looks at variables such as beliefs, opinions, motives and aspirations, which collectively make 'lifestyle'. Psychographic data can be used on its own or in conjunction with other variables.

Such data is being increasingly used as it can be a better identifier of product usage. For example, some people would prefer to buy an organic wine, others a 'value for money' brand or supermarket special offer, while for some nothing less than vintage Bordeaux would be acceptable.

Table 9.4   ACORN classification (CACI)

Category	Group	Type
Wealthy achievers	Wealthy executives	01 – Affluent mature professionals, large houses
		02 – Affluent working families with mortgages
		03 – Villages with wealthy commuters
		04 – Well-off managers, larger houses
	Affluent greys	05 – Older affluent professionals
		06 – Farming communities
		07 – Old people, detached houses
		08 – Mature couples, smaller detached houses
	Flourishing families	09 – Larger families, prosperous suburbs
		10 – Well-off working families with mortgages
		11 – Well-off managers, detached houses
		12 – Large families and houses in rural areas
Urban prosperity	Prosperous professionals	13 – Well-off professionals, larger houses and converted flats
		14 – Older professionals in detached houses and apartments
	Educated urbanites	15 – Affluent urban professionals, flats
		16 – Prosperous young professionals, flats
		17 – Young educated workers, flats
		18 – Multi-ethnic young, converted flats
		19 – Suburban privately renting professionals
	Aspiring singles	20 – Student flats and cosmopolitan sharers
		21 – Singles and sharers, multi-ethnic areas
		22 – Low-income singles, small-rented flats
		23 – Student terraces
Comfortably off	Starting out	24 – Young couples, flats and terraces
		25 – White-collar singles/sharers, terraces
	Secure families	26 – Younger white-collar couples with mortgages
		27 – Middle income, home-owning areas
		28 – Working families with mortgages
		29 – Mature families in suburban semis
		30 – Established home-owning workers
		31 – Home-owning Asian family areas
	Settled suburbia	32 – Retired home owners
		33 – Middle income, older couples
		34 – Lower income people, semis
	Prudent pensioners	35 – Elderly singles, purpose built flats
		36 – Older people, flats

Category	Group	Type
Moderate means	Asian communities	37 – Crowded Asian terraces
		38 – Low-income Asian families
	Post-industrial families	39 – Skilled older family terraces
		40 – Young family workers
	Blue-collar roots	41 – Skilled workers, semis and terraces
		42 – Home-owning, terraces
		43 – Older rented terraces
Hard pressed	Struggling families	44 – Low-income larger families, semis
		45 – Older people, low income, small semis
		46 – Low income, routine jobs, unemployment
		47 – Low-rise terraced estates of poorly-off workers
		48 – Low incomes, high unemployment, single parents
		49 – Large families, many children, poorly educated
	Burdened singles	50 – Council flats, single elderly people
		51 – Council terraces, unemployment, many singles
		52 – Council flats, single parents, unemployment
	High-rise hardship	53 – Old people in high rise flats
		54 – Singles and single parents, high-rise estates
	Inner-city adversity	55 – Multi-ethnic, purpose-built estates
		56 – Multi-ethnic, crowded flats

Other examples include car purchase. What may have been a status purchase in the past may now take on a new dimension. Increasingly, segments of purchasers are interested in the car's fuel consumption, its CO_2 emissions as well as its performance and style.

2.3.4 Behavioural segmentation

The segmentation variables that have been considered have been customer-centric in order that the marketer develops as complete a profile as possible on each individual. Behavioural segmentation looks at building relationships with the individual.

Research by a major UK issuer of credit cards found that in the early stages of the relationship, the customer was wary about telephoning the card issuer if they had any concerns about the cards or how it should be used. The solution was to provide new customers with dedicated helpline number that identified them. The call centre staff, having been alerted to the status of the customer, was able to be more understanding of their situation.

Behavioural segmentation can be categorised into:

- End-use
- Benefits sought.

Increasing use is being made of behavioural segmentation, and we will look at two examples.

End-use

The purpose that the product will be used for dramatically changes the way the product is marketed.

Brands and products have been developed to reflect the use of the product.

A hotel may market itself as a conference venue during the week, reflecting the quality of the accommodation, the dedicated business centre within the hotel with access to administrative support, free internet access for delegates, photocopying and state-of-the-art IT equipment.

At weekends, where there are no conferences taking place, the emphasis may now be on the leisure facilities, the relaxing atmosphere and the quality of service.

A bank manufactures a loan product, which offers a fixed rate of interest and a fixed but variable repayment term. Interest rate is set at 7.9% APR, and the customer can select a repayment period of between one and seven years. The bank can market the loan in a variety of ways to reflect product usage.

- For customers looking to buy a car, it can be marketed as a car loan
- For general purposes, we can call it a personal loan
- For customers who have been overspending and need money to pay off other debts, it is now a consolidation loan.

Benefits sought

Consider the purchase of a pair of ladies jeans. Are the jeans being bought for weekend causal wear or are they simply something practical to wear while driving the car or sitting in the garden?

The purchase of convenience meals is increasing, but how should they be marketed? Are they for lazy people who cannot be bothered to cook for themselves? Or are they a quick and convenient alternative to spending time cooking, so that there is more time available for other more interesting activities. Finally, are convenience foods an alternative to a meal out or a takeaway?

Marks & Spencer ran a promotion offering a meal for two at £10, including a bottle of wine, positioning it as a 'good night in'.

Usage rate

Consumers use products at different rates; usage can be defined as light, medium and heavy. Understanding usage can lead to more effective marketing campaigns or, in some cases, migrating customers to more appropriate products.

Tesco monitors the usage of its internet shopping service. Regular customers typically make one purchase per week. If, after a certain period of time, no purchases are made, the customer receives an e-mail offering them some form of incentive to resume shopping. Otherwise, if customers change their purchasing habits, it is harder to encourage repeat purchase.

Loyalty

Customer loyalty can be a helpful segmentation variable, but brand loyalty can be fragile. Many organisations operate loyalty programmes or cards, but how many loyalty cards do we carry around with us?

It can be helpful for an organisation to understand whether customers are:

- Loyal to us
- Loyal to others
- Switchers.

Knowing which group a customer occupies allows them to be targeted.

The Chartered Institute of Marketing

Attitude

Customers may buy from an organisation for a number of reasons. The customer who buys electricity from a particular power company may not feel any loyalty or enthusiasm towards the company. Similarly, the credit card user who has a large credit balance on the card that attracts a high rate of interest is not going to feel as enthusiastic towards the organisation as the customer who pays off debt every month and sees the card as a great way to manage money effectively.

Buyer readiness

Customers go through various stages to make a purchase (awareness, interest, desire, action: AIDA) and organisations need to recognise and respond differently to the customers in the various stages of purchase.

2.3.5 International segmentation

Geographic segmentation is clearly an important part of international segmentation. Some of the world's largest organisations will have a physical presence in key world markets as well as operating in very many countries.

International segmentation benefits from a multi-variable approach, and it is not always distance from the home country that is important. France is the UK's nearest neighbour, but it could be argued that, culturally, the UK is closer to Hong Kong (an old UK colony), some 6,000 miles away.

All countries, even those grouped together regionally (eg Europe) can exhibit significant differences, not only in economic terms but culturally and politically. To address this, international segmentation requires world markets to be grouped into segments with distinct buying needs and behaviours.

For the UK, we have discussed ACORN as a way of segmenting consumers; Europe has similar tools including CCN EuroMOSAIC. Business segmentation uses SIC classification and the USA operates the North American Industrial Classification System (NAICS).

While geographic segmentation may be a good start point (acknowledging the problems mentioned earlier), it should also be recognised that incomes vary from country to country along with buying patterns, lifestyle, education and behaviour patterns.

Segments can be based around, for example, cultural dimensions; countries can be grouped together where the beliefs, values, religion and customers are similar; alternatively segments can be grouped together around political structures.

Another dimension to consider is that of global similarities. The Disney Channel targets young children and teenagers across the globe with the same films and TV programmes. Similarly MTV attracts the same teenage segment worldwide and brands such as Nike offer the same advertising messages worldwide: 'Just do It'.

Organisations like IKEA adopted an interesting approach to new markets. Generally regarded as a truly global company, IKEA targeted specific market segments, irrespective of the country in which they were located (intermarket segmentation). For example, young professionals and families would be similarly segmented in France, Italy, UK, etc.

We have looked at the different ways in which markets can be segmented. The point must be made that organisations, due to the levels and availability of high quality data, are moving away where possible from single variable segmentation to multi-variable segmentation, which will improve a company's competitive advantage.

Multi-variable segmentation, while having many advantages, such as being able to build a highly sophisticated profile on individuals and groups of individuals, also provides an organisation with a much wider range of segmentation options. As we will see later, effective segmentation relies on financial viability, ie when an organisation evaluates a segment it will want to know that it going to be financially rewarded. Therefore, a balance will need to be struck on the level of segmentation desirable with the income to be generated.

3 Criteria for effective segmentation

To even get attention, a segment must fulfil a number of criteria.

Measurable

The segment must be capable of being measured. This is usually a straightforward procedure with the data being available internally to the organisation or from external secondary sources. Primary data may need to be commissioned if insufficient data is available.

Accessible

Having identified the segment, has the organisation got the financial, or other resources to exploit the segment?

Substantial

The availability of data can lead an organisation to identify small segments, which in fact may be too small and therefore not cost effective. Segments can be aggregated to make them larger or ignored. Size is, of course, relative to the organisation undertaking the analysis.

Unique

The segment should be such that it can be specifically identified.

Appropriate

The segment should satisfy the organisation's mission, vision and objectives and support the brand values.

Stable

The future performance of the segment should be capable of being forecast with some degree of accuracy. Having invested in the segment, there is an expectation of future returns.

THE REAL WORLD

Attracting and retaining the right customers (relationship-based segmentation)

In unprecedented market conditions, balancing risk and reward is becoming critical in the financial services market. Lenders' attraction and retention strategies are being scrutinised by a multitude of stakeholders including the Bank of England, the Treasury and the FSA as well as ordinary investors and indeed the public at large. It is, therefore, essential that attraction and retention is optimised so as to maximise profitability, optimise operational costs and minimise risk, whilst carefully utilising resources and capital funding – all of course within the backdrop of TCF, Treating Customers Fairly.

Attracting and retaining customers over the long term can positively impact many factors and is the goal to sustaining a profitable mortgage book. Using the right methods that are focussed on customer retention will underpin this approach.

The use of data and technology

For a long time customers have been dealt with using the same standardised procedures and the effort required to attract their custom in terms of business volume has been relatively easy. Apart from the essential risk assessments, all customers had been treated to virtually the same service, processes, sales channels, products and more or less the same pricing. Up until now, many lenders have largely failed to build into their customer attraction strategies factors such as customer profitability, future potential and cross-sale propensity. But the recent financial turmoil from 2008 has caused most lenders to ask whether they had been targeting the right customers for their business.

Central to developing a targeted strategy is the availability of accurate, reliable and relevant data. Data goes out of date very quickly so it is imperative to keep it up to date so that informed decisions can be made that are based on valid data. And it here that significant advances in data collection and manipulation models have taken place that create the capacity to utilise it in the sales process in real-time. Thus the customer receives not only a better and more relevant product offering but it can be achieved using a single application process, which is both cheaper for the lender and more user-friendly for the customer.

The Chartered Institute of Marketing

Experian plc

One example is Experian plc, a leading global information services company, providing data and analytical tools to clients around the world. Its principal business activities are credit services, marketing solutions, decision analytics and interactive services. Experian has developed a suite of solutions focussing on the mortgage market; these utilise the breadth of Experian's data assets, including credit bureau data and the consumer dynamics data resource.

One element of this is a revolutionary tool which uses a series of scores, generated from real-time consumers' credit behaviours and activity, including external databases that monitor indebtedness, affordability, property indexing, profit forecasting and future opportunity modelling. The result is a tool that provides an effective mechanism to help lenders identify customers who present an attrition risk and take necessary retention activity if they have been identified as the right customer.

The future

Moving forward, a combination of data and technology will not only be essential for attracting and retaining, but will also play a key role in deciding how best to service customers to optimise profitability and operational efficiency. Multichannel distribution will become as much lender as customer driven.

(Experian, 2012)

▶ **Assessment tip**

Segmentation often gets limited attention but significantly contributes to an effective and successful marketing planning process. Attention should be given to the components of the different aspects of segmentation.

Summary

This chapter has introduced the role of marketing strategies in marketing planning and has focussed on the STP process. The benefits of segmentation have been outlined and the different variables, both the B2B and the B2C markets, have been explored. It should be appreciated that segmentation is complex and requires a detailed understanding of customers and customer behaviour. Some segmentation variables focus on market characteristics, whereas others are more concerned with product usage and buyer behaviour.

Increasingly sophisticated segmentation variables are combined to develop a detailed profile of segments which is then used to offer particular products to the customer in order to retain them and generate additional income. For most organisations, segmentation is an important strategy as it recognises that not all customers are equal and different approaches need to be adopted depending on value that each segment is worth to the organisation. Moreover, organisations do not have finite resources and, therefore, they must be used to their best advantage by identifying the most valuable segments to be targeted.

CHAPTER ROUNDUP

- Marketing strategy
- Market segmentation
- Benefits of segmentation
- Segmenting business and consumer markets
- Criteria for effective segmentation.

FURTHER READING

Sarabia-Sanchez, F. *et al.* (2012) Using values and shopping styles to identify fashion apparel segments. *International Journal of Retail & Distribution Management*, 40 (12) pp180-199.

REFERENCES

Debenhams (2012) www.debenhams.com [Accessed on 20 June 2012]

Dibb, S. *et al.* (2006) *Marketing: Concepts and Strategies*. 5th edition. Boston, Houghton Mifflin.

Doyle, P. (1994) *Marketing Management and Strategy*. Hemel Hempstead, Prentice Hall.

Experian (2012) Attracting and retaining the right customers. Experian, www.experian.co.uk/business-services/prospect-marketing.html [Accessed on 8 June 2012]

Gillete (2012) www.Gillette.com [Accessed on 20 June 2012]

Marks and Spencer (2012) www.marksandspencer.com/ [Accessed on 20 June 2012]

Next (2012) www.nextplc.co.uk [Accessed on 20 June 2012]

Smith, W. (1956) Product Differentiation and Market Segmentation as Alternative Marketing Strategies. *Journal of Marketing*, July, pp3–8.

Visa (2012) www.visa.co.uk [Accessed on 20 June 2012]

QUICK QUIZ

1. Give a definition of marketing strategy.
2. What do you understand by the term market segmentation?
3. What are the benefits of segmentation?
4. How can international markets be segmented?
5. What are the criteria for effective segmentation?

The Chartered Institute of Marketing

Activity 9.1

List the market opportunities under the separate headings of short, medium and long term. Be as opportunistic as possible and include all the different possibilities. Initially it is better to include all the possible opportunities in the list and then discount at a later stage. Quick hits should be included in the short term whereas those opportunities which need considerable attention would be considered long term.

The next step is to formulate a strategy based on the analysis and this will include establishing STP. This will be discussed in detail below; but by way of introduction from a strategic perspective, the following overview is provided.

Segmentation is the process of breaking down a large market into small manageable sub-divisions where the organisation can build up a detailed picture of the segment and offer it a specific marketing offering. Customers respond well to marketing approaches which they perceive address their needs. It could be argued that organisations that do not fully understand the needs of their customers will find it difficult to develop an effective marketing strategy.

Organisations having segmented a market will then pursue *targeting* one or more segments through marketing programmes. This is done on a priority basis, often based on the simple concept of which segment is going to be more profitable. For some not-for-profit sectors, priority can be on which sector(s) has the greatest needs or fulfil the most non-profit objectives. Effective targeting requires a number of decisions to be made on the best use of the marketing mix and whether the same mix needs to be used across each target segment.

An organisation then needs a clear *positioning* in the mind of the consumer and to develop a distinctive perceived location in the market relative to the competition, based on matching the product to the identified needs and wants of the customers.

Activity 9.2

The segments of the retail market are:

Next	Marks & Spencer	Debenhams
The Next retail chain was launched in February 1982 and the first store opened with an exclusive co-ordinated collection of stylish clothes, shoes and accessories for women. Collections for men, children and the home quickly followed. Next clothes are styled by its in-house design team to offer great style, quality and value for money with a contemporary fashion edge. Next trades from more than 500 stores in the UK and Eire and over 180 stores in more than 30 countries overseas.	Marks and Spencer is the number one provider of womenswear and lingerie in the UK, and is rapidly growing its market share in menswear, kidswear and home, due in part to its growing online business. Overall, the clothing and homeware sales account for 49% of its business. The other 51% of its business is in food, where its sell everything from fresh produce and groceries, to partly-prepared meals and ready meals.	Debenhams plc is a British retailer operating under a department store format in the UK, Ireland and Denmark, and franchise stores in other countries. The company was founded in the eighteenth century as a single store in London Debenhams has 153 stores across the UK and Ireland and a fully transactional website, reflecting Debenhams' commitment to offering its customers greater value, a wider choice and excellent service in womenswear, menswear, kidswear, beauty, home and furniture, and electrical.

(Next plc, Marks and Spencer, Debenhams, 2012)

QUICK QUIZ ANSWERS

1   A marketing strategy is as a strategy indicating the opportunities to pursue, specific targets, and the types of competitive advantages that are to be developed.

2   The process of grouping customers in markets with some heterogeneity into smaller, more similar or homogeneous segments.

3   Benefits include a distinct marketing mix can be produced for each segment, focussed communications, customer retention, market leadership, profit maximisation and product and market differentiation.

4   All countries, even those grouped together regionally (eg Europe) can exhibit significant differences, not only in economic terms but culturally and politically. To address this, international segmentation requires world markets to be grouped into segments with distinct buying needs and behaviours.

5   To even get attention, a segment must fulfil a number of criteria. These include measurable, accessible, substantial, unique, appropriate and stable

CHAPTER 10

Market targeting

Introduction

Having decided on a segmentation strategy in order to break the market down into more manageable and effective segments, the next stage in the process is to approach the target sub-markets with a distinctive approach.

A target market is recognised as a set of buyers sharing common needs or characteristics that the company decides to serve.

In an ideal world because each buyer has a unique requirement, a separate marketing mix would be designed for each. In reality, organisations generally target buyers broadly, narrowly or somewhere in the middle. This is known as **undifferentiated**, **concentrated** and **differentiated** targeting strategies (Figure 10.1).

Topic list

Targeting strategies	1
Alternative targeting approaches	2
Evaluating market segments	3

3.4	Assess the value of 'targeting' markets as an approach to achieving customer satisfaction, competitive advantage and retention
	▪ Focused effort and resource efficiency
	▪ Potential for achieving short-, medium- and long-term objectives
	▪ Potential for achieving competitive advantage
	▪ Scope for competitive advantage through distinctive positioning
3.5	Critically evaluate a range of targeting coverage strategies for different organisational contexts and sectors
	▪ Undifferentiated marketing
	▪ Differentiated marketing
	▪ Concentrated marketing
	▪ Customised marketing
3.6	Assess the attractiveness and value of selected market segments
	▪ External and internal criteria for evaluation: size, growth, profitability, relationship potential, competition, capabilities
	▪ Segment evaluation process: factor weighting and ranking of alternatives
	▪ Fit between potential and internal considerations

1 Targeting strategies

Figure 10.1 Targeting strategies

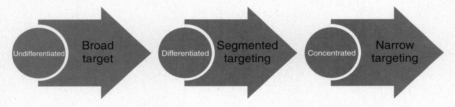

> ▶ **Key term**
>
> **Targeting strategies:** the selection of potential customers to whom a business wishes to sell products or services. The targeting strategy involves segmenting the market, choosing which segments of the market are appropriate, and determining the products that will be offered in each segment.

1.1 Undifferentiated

In an undifferentiated strategy, the organisation treats the whole market as being homogenous. No significant differences are perceived between the different buyers and so the organisation uses just one marketing mix to engage with the entire market.

Marketing mix ⟶ Market

Although this approach offers the advantages of cost and mass appeal, it clearly cannot suit the entire market, and it can be argued that sales will be lost. Competitors who have a more focussed approach could be stealing business away. It is an approach usually associated with low involvement in the purchase process.

Some commentators argue that an undifferentiated approach is rarely possible and examples such as the purchase of potatoes and salt are often citied.

No longer do we just buy a potato, we can choose from salad, baking, roasting, chipping or mashing. This makes the 'regular' or general purpose potatoes look like an inferior product.

Some organisations adopt an undifferentiated approach because they are small players in a small market.

1.2 Differentiated

Marketing mix 1 ⟶ Market segment 1

Marketing mix 2 ⟶ Market segment 2

Marketing mix 3 ⟶ Market segment 3

Marketing mix 4 ⟶ Market segment 4

A differentiated strategy requires an organisation to develop a different marketing mix for each segment. So, each of the market segments served by the organisation will receive a different offer.

Royal Bank of Scotland (RBS) operates a number of insurance brands including Tesco, Direct Line, Privilege, NatWest and Churchill. Each brand approaches the customer in a different way, to increase the appeal.

As organisations increasingly appeal to wider, more diverse and overseas markets, then the range of marketing mixes used has to be increased to reflect the needs of the customers.

Airlines will want to appeal to different classes of traveller, from economy to economy plus, through to business and first class.

Universities are differentiating the marketing mix to reflect the needs of undergraduate, postgraduate and professional students, which can then be grouped into EU and overseas students.

Cadburys, the chocolate manufacturer, bought Green and Black's, an upmarket and organic brand, to serve the needs of a growing market segment.

1.3 Concentrated

Marketing mix 1 ⟶ Market segment 1

In a concentrated strategy, the organisation concentrates on serving just one segment of the market, developing expertise and a highly detailed knowledge of the market in which just one marketing mix is used. The target market will see the organisation as the leader in the field, giving it advantages over other more general competitors.

Concentrated marketing works best in niche segments which tend, on average, to be small – so the mix tends to be highly focused.

- Rolls Royce, the car manufacturer, aims its vehicles in the affluent sector and does not compete with General Motors.

- Steinway pianos produce handmade pianos, which take over 12 months to build, and only focus on the concert hall and celebrity markets.

- Rolex, the watch manufacture, targets wealthy individuals and does not compete with Timex who produces an inexpensive and functional range of watches.

Although the advantages of a concentrated strategy may be clear, it can bring disadvantages in the sense that if the segment fails to perform, the organisation will not be able to move easily into another segment.

The growing appeal of the internet with low set-up cost will increasingly make concentrated marketing more appealing to organisations of all sizes, something which the larger organisations will be monitoring carefully.

Table 10.1 highlights the advantages and disadvantages of each of the strategies.

Table 10.1   Advantages and disadvantages of targeting strategies

Undifferentiated	
Advantages	**Disadvantages**
■ Economies of scale maximised ■ Cost of marketing and production minimised	■ Organisation may only be of general interest to the buyers, with few showing a particular interest ■ Buyers may prefer organisations specialising in their particular segment(s)
Concentrated	
Advantages	**Disadvantages**
■ Organisation gains detailed knowledge of the segment ■ Specialism can be very profitable	■ The organisation has a heavy dependency on one segment which may not be sustainable in the long term
Differentiated	
Advantages	**Disadvantages**
■ Organisation tailors the marketing mix to the needs of the segment	■ Additional costs incurred as a result of the differentiation process ■ Economies-of-scale opportunities lost ■ Organisational resources maybe spread thinly

THE REAL WORLD

Rolex Watches

Rolex SA was founded in 1905 by Hans Wilsdorf and his brother-in-law, Alfred Davis. Wilsdorf & Davis was the original name that later became the Rolex Watch Company. They originally imported Hermann Aegler's Swiss movements to England and placed them in quality cases made by Dennison and others. These early wristwatches were then sold to jewellers, who then put their own names on the dial. The company name Rolex was registered on 15 November 1915. Wilsdorf's desire was for the brand to be easily pronounceable in any language. The company name was officially changed to the Rolex Watch Company during 1919. It was later changed to Montres Rolex, SA and finally Rolex, SA.

Today Rolex manufactures watches and other accessories. It is generally considered a status symbol and a sign of significant wealth. It is the world's largest luxury watch brand and one of the world-leading global brands. The concentrated strategy adopted by Rolex has positioned the company as the number one premier brand for watches recognised in all parts of the world.

2 Alternative targeting approaches

In addition to the above strategies, the concept of **micro-marketing**, which refers to the practice of tailoring products and programmes to meet the needs of individuals and locations, may be considered as an alternative strategy.

Micro-marketing is about seeing an individual in every customer and not a customer in every individual, and includes local and individual marketing.

Micro-marketing is a form of target marketing in which companies tailor their marketing programmes to the needs and wants of a narrowly defined geographic, demographic, psychographic or behavioural segments.

The Chartered Institute of Marketing

Local marketing involves tailoring brands and promotions to the needs and wants of local customer groups.

'Tesco, the UK's leading food retailer, offers its customers a range of store formats for different locations, but within each of the formats, the store can carry an individual product range suited to local customer needs.

Tesco is an international retailer, and wherever it operates, it focuses on giving local customers what they want.

Store formats

It has four different store formats, each tailored to its customers' needs and one trial format called Homeplus.

Express (up to 3,000 sq ft)

Express stores offer customers great value, quality and fresh food close to where they live and work. Tesco opened its first Express store in 1994. They sell a range of up to 7,000 products including fresh produce, wines and spirits and in-store bakery.

Metro (approximately 7,000–15,000 sq ft)

Tesco opened the first Metro in 1992, bringing the convenience of Tesco to town and city-centre locations. Metros cater for thousands of busy customers each week and offer a tailored range of, mainly, food products, including ready meals and sandwiches.

Superstore (approximately 20,000–50,000 sq ft)

Tesco began opening Superstores in the 1970s and, during the 1980s and 1990s, built a national network, to which it is adding every year. There is an ongoing programme of extending and refreshing superstores to improve the overall experience for customers. In recent years, it has introduced a number of new non-food ranges into superstores, such as DVDs and books.

Extra (approximately 60,000 sq ft and above)

Since opening the first Extra in 1997, the one-stop destination store has proved extremely popular. Extra stores offer the widest range of food and non-food lines, ranging from electrical equipment to homewares, clothing, health and beauty, and seasonal items such as garden furniture.

Homeplus (approximately 35,000–50,000 sq ft)

Homeplus stores are dedicated to non-food, including clothing. These stores offer their widest range of non-food products in store, with more available through their Tesco Direct order and collection points. The latest, largest stores have Tesco Direct catalogue ranges on display, with most products available to take home instantly.

Understanding our customers

'Tesco Clubcard is a world-leading loyalty card scheme, with around 14 million active cardholders. Information provided by Clubcard enables us to better understand our customers and say 'thank you' for shopping with us. There are over 8 million unique coupon variations with each Clubcard mailing, making sure that everyone receives the kind of offer that is appropriate for them.'

(Tesco, 2012)

Individual marketing

Increased sophistication of marketing (see Tesco example above) offers organisations the opportunity to offer customers an 'individual' product.

For an automobile manufacturer of your choice, select just one model of car. Identify how many different options that 'one' model can be built with. Why do you think there are so many options?

The choice of which targeting strategy to use is influenced by a number of factors which are driven both internally and externally within the organisation.

- **Resources available** – It may be more effective for an organisation to utilise limited resources on developing one segment.

- **The nature of the market** – It may be homogeneous and therefore it may be more attractive to develop just one broad approach. However, as we will see in section 3, markets are increasingly being broken into much smaller segments, which may make this approach unwise in many and increasing circumstances.

- **The competition** – How is it targeting the market and is there the opportunity for a different approach?

- **Product life cycle stage** – At product launch stage, an organisation will often launch just one product variant and, as the competition enters the markets, other variants may be needed. Similarly, as the product reaches maturity, product variations can increase the life cycle.

Socially responsible consequences of target marketing

Social responsibility is concerned with an organisation's duty to maximise its positive impact and minimise its negative impact on society: customers, the environment and the wider community.

Targeted marketing, if planned and well executed, will enable an organisation to maximise revenue from the segment(s) and lead to greater customer satisfaction as their needs will have been met more effectively.

However, over the years, different market industry sectors have variously been accused of targeting vulnerable segments such as the elderly, infirm and children. Legislation has been introduced in the UK and overseas to ensure that target marketing is appropriate.

It is not just the vulnerable sectors which come in for criticism, sometimes boundaries are not clear. In the UK, the introduction of 'Alcopops' caused controversy; the drink came in a variety of sweet flavours such as blackcurrant and, although high in alcohol, didn't actually taste alcoholic. Arguments were founded on the fact that the drink had strong appeal to under 18s, although legally they could not buy it.

Advertisements for tobacco products, are now banned from TV in the UK and the ongoing issue of 'junk food' is being addressed through government awareness campaigns in a similar way to alcohol.

The internet as a new medium has yet to be fully regulated and organisations continue to use this medium to target special segments.

In conclusion, the issue which must be dealt with is *how*, and *what*, to target, ie the manner and the nature of the product involved, rather than *who* is being targeted.

Alcopops is a term that relates to certain flavoured alcoholic drinks, including:

- Malt beverages to which various fruit juices or other flavourings have been added
- Beverages containing wine to which ingredients such as fruit juice or other flavourings have been added
- Beverages containing distilled alcohol and added ingredients such as fruit juices or other flavourings.

The term Alcopops is a combination of the words 'alcohol' and 'pop', the drinks tend to be sweet and served in small bottles (typically 330 ml in Europe), contain between 4% and 7% alcohol by volume and are especially appealing to younger drinkers. The high sugar content and bright coloured drinks appeal to young adults but many Alcopops advertising campaigns have been criticised as trying to make the drink appeal to the targeted consumers of underage drinkers of alcoholic beverages.

3 Evaluating market segments

▸ **Key term**

Market segments: an identifiable group of individuals, families, businesses, or organisations sharing one or more characteristics or needs in an otherwise homogeneous market.

We have identified that markets can be 'oversegmented', which not only affects organisational profitability but also has the potential to confuse customers by trying to place them in a segment they cannot relate to or understand.

Banks often categorise business into turnover bands.

- Up to £1m (small)
- £1m to £10m (medium)
- £10m + (large)

Many businesses that had a turnover in excess of £1m felt they were a small business and could not relate to the banks' segmentation policy.

Decisions therefore need to be made as to which market segments to target, based upon some rationale.

To evaluate the potential of market segments, two issues are to be identified.

- The market attractiveness of the various segments
- The organisation's ability to meet the needs of the segments.

In addressing these issues, the competition, market factors and environmental considerations need to be taken into account.

3.1 The competition

- Bargaining power of the suppliers
- Bargaining power of the buyers
- Barriers to entry
- Likelihood of new entrants
- Cost of leaving the market.

You may remember the above considerations as Porter's five forces analysis. In addition, the strength, numbers and nature of the competition needs to be understood.

3.2 Market factors

- How big is the segment now and how big is it likely to be in the future?
- How will customers react to price changes, ie does the segment offer price elasticity or inelasticity?

- Are there seasonal patterns which will affect demand?

- Stage in the industry life cycle, declining industries will be short-lived and drain resources quickly. Conversely, new industries, eg telecoms, will be cash hungry at the outset with the potential for strong financial rewards in the longer term.

3.3 Environmental factors

These are based on a PESTEL analysis and could include the following.

- Political changes – What changes are likely, nationally and internationally? Increased levels of political risk will make certain segments less attractive.

- Economic – Will the reduced levels of credit and savings affect the market? The ageing nature of the UK population is encouraging growth in certain segments.

- Social – Lifestyle changes open up new markets.

- Technology – What substitute products will technological changes bring?

- Environmental – What changes will 'green' issues bring about and how will this affect competition within the segment?

- Legal – Are there any legal issues, which may affect the segment? The (brief) requirement for all homes to have a Home Information Pack (HIP) when the property is being sold opened up a new industry in the UK.

The shell directional policy matrix has been adapted to apply to market segmentation and the adapted matrix is shown in Figure 10.2.

The Shell Directional Policy Matrix is another refinement upon the BCG Matrix. Along the horizontal axis are *prospects for sector profitability*, and along the vertical axis is a *company's competitive capability.* The position of an organisation in any cell of the matrix implies different strategic decisions.

The axis shows two dimensions:

- Market attractiveness
- Strengths of the organisation in serving the segment.

Figure 10.2   Shell directional policy matrix

Market segment attractiveness

		Unattractive	Average	Attractive
Strengths (Current & potential company strengths in serving segment)	Weak	Strongly avoid	Avoid	Possibilities
	Average	Avoid	Possibilities	Secondary targets
	Strong	Possibilities	Secondary targets	Prime targets

The nine cells in the matrix indicate the various opportunities, so placing a segment in the appropriate cell provides a guide to the attractiveness of the segment.

The market attractiveness criteria can then be 'weighted' by the organisation relative to its importance as defined by the organisation (Table 10.2).

Table 10.2   Market attractiveness criteria

Criteria	Weighting (%)
Profit potential	60
Market growth rate	20
Market size	10
Strength of competition	10

The same process is used to identify the strengths of the organisation relevant to the sector (Table 10.3).

This process ensures that each organisation using the matrix adopts a unique approach and identifies the attractiveness from its own perspective. It therefore follows that different organisations will come to different conclusions about the attractiveness of particular market segments.

Table 10.3   Business strengths criteria

Criteria	Weighting (%)
Market share	60
Potential for differential advantage	20
Potential cost advantages	10
Brand image	10

Using the weighted approach will identify segments for priority and, in effect, acts as a screening process. The approach, while clearly identifying the key segments to target and avoid, allows the middle segments, ie possibilities, to be developed or ignored in accordance with their ranking.

ACTIVITY 10.2

How does each of the main supermarkets in your country segment their customers? What criteria do you think they use to evaluate target markets?

▶ **Assessment tip**

Target marketing is the application of theories and frameworks and therefore any assessment will require candidates to be able to demonstrate their understanding of the underlying knowledge in a particular context.

Summary

This chapter has explored the concept of market targeting, ie identifying a particular market segment and tailoring the marketing approach to the segment. The three different approaches of undifferentiated, differentiated and concentrated have been identified, illustrated and evaluated. The competitive environment is increasingly moving organisations towards adopting a more differentiated approach, recognising that not all customers have the same needs and wants and that competitive advantage can be gained through targeting. Customers are looking for specific solutions to their problems rather than having to work out for themselves whether a generic solution can be adapted to their needs. The ways in which alternative market segments may be evaluated for targeting is then considered, using a set of criteria based on external and internal factors.

CHAPTER ROUNDUP

- Targeting strategies
- Alternative targeting approaches
- Evaluating market segments

FURTHER READING

Hollensen, S. (2007) *Global Marketing.* 4th edition. Harlow, Prentice Hall.

Kotler, P. and Keller, K.L. (2006) *Marketing Management*. 12th edition. Englewood Cliffs, NJ, Prentice Hall.

Kotler, P. *et al* (2008) *Principles of Marketing*. 5th edition. Harlow, Financial Times/Prentice Hall.

REFERENCES

Tesco (2012) Our Strategy. Tesco, www.tescoplc.com/index.asp?pageid=12 [Accessed on 8 June 2012]

QUICK QUIZ

1   Explain how a company can identify attractive market segments.
2   What are the main advantages of a concentrated marketing strategy?
3   What impact do you think the internet will have on the choice of market strategy?
4   What do you understand by the term 'local' marketing?
5   What issues can arise as a result of socially responsible target marketing?

ACTIVITY DEBRIEFS

Activity 10.1

A typical example would be a mid-range compact saloon car such as BMW 3 series, Audi A4 or Mercedes Benz 'C' Class. Using information from the manufacturers' web sites, create a matrix of the different options for body type (saloon, coupe or estate) engine fuel and capacity, and external and internal features. The range will be quite wide, with the intention of allowing the customer to customise the base vehicle and give the chosen options their personal signature and individual design.

Activity 10.2

List the range of 'typical' customers, days and frequency of visit and the range of buying intentions (weekly shop, spontaneous purchase, end-of-week reward shop etc..). The chosen criteria will be used to measure the type and range of products purchased and the sales value for each visit. The retailer will gain a detailed understanding of their customers' purchasing intentions and behaviour patterns through the different days of the trading week.

The Chartered
Institute of Marketing

1   Attractiveness is based on profit potential, market growth rates, market size and strength of competition.

2   The main advantages are that the organisation gains detailed knowledge of the segment and that specialism can be very profitable.

3   The internet, with low set-up cost, will increasingly make concentrated marketing more appealing to organisations of all sizes, something which the larger organisations will be monitoring carefully.

4   Local marketing involves tailoring brands and promotions to the needs and wants of local customer groups. Micro-marketing is a form of target marketing in which companies tailor their marketing programmes to the needs and wants of a narrowly defined geographic, demographic, psychographic or behavioural segments.

5   Targeted marketing, if planned and well executed, will enable an organisation to maximise revenue from the segment(s) and lead to greater customer satisfaction as their needs will have been met more effectively.

CHAPTER 11

Marketing positioning

Introduction

Having segmented the market as part of its overall strategy, an organisation will then identify selected target segments within the market where it wants to compete for business. Then, as the final stage of the STP (segmentation, targeting, positioning) process, it will need to position itself very clearly in the minds of customers, so the organisation, its products or its brands will be selected rather than competitor offerings.

Topic list

Positioning   (1)

Brand positioning   (2)

Positioning alternatives   (3)

The marketing mix   (4)

3.7	Examine the concept of marketing positioning strategy and how it can be used to convey the organisation's value proposition
	■ Differential advantage, customer value and organisational benefits
	■ Consideration of alternative positioning strategies
	■ Relationship positioning strategies
	■ Competitive positioning strategies
	■ Selection of target markets and point of differentiation
	■ Positioning and perceptual maps
3.8	Critically evaluate positioning options and their implementation within the context of the organisation and its markets
	■ Criteria for effective positioning and competitive advantages
	■ Positioning and the marketing mix
	■ Positioning and repositioning in practice

1 Positioning

> ▶ **Key term**
>
> **Positioning:** designing an organisation's offering and image to occupy a distinctive place in the minds of the target market.

The organisation will want to develop and maintain a competitive (differential) advantage compared with the competition.

Differential advantage is an attribute of the brand, product, service or marketing mix that is desired by the targeted customer and provided by only one supplier. *(Dibb et al., 2006)*

An organisation needs to have a competitive or differential advantage over its rivals which can be actual or perceived by the customers, and this can be achieved through the organisation balancing the needs of the customer with the resources available.

Competitive positioning has been defined as 'the act of designing the company's offer and image so that they occupy a meaningful and distinctive position in the target customer's mind'. *(Kotler and Keller, 2006)*

To be successful, today's organisations needs to be market orientated, which requires them to strike a balance between customer and competitor focus. No longer can an organisation simply monitor the competition and then develop a response. Focus needs to be on understanding the needs of the customer and building profitable and long-lasting relationships through innovative strategies, which will deliver greater customer value than the competition is able to offer.

Positioning and competition can take place at the following levels:

■ Company
■ Product
■ Brand.

A supermarket can appeal to customers in a variety of ways: price, product range, freshness and so on. Customers will choose that particular supermarket because they know or believe it will meet their needs.

In the example of the supermarket, a customer would be making a choice based on the overall positioning of the organisation. But positioning can occur at product level; a customer looking to purchase a new TV may be evaluating a Samsung product against a Sony. Similarly, at brand level how does Coca-Cola position itself against Pepsi or Virgin Cola?

These considerations are important and can allow an organisation to move successfully into other markets.

Tesco has a slogan 'Every Little Helps' and, along with its strong brand name, this has helped it to move beyond food retailing into financial services, petrol, clothing, opticians and so on.

1.1 Criteria to create differentiation

It is the case that not all competitive differences will create strong competitive positions and Kotler and Keller (2006) suggest criteria which should be applied in an effort to create differentiation. Table 11.1 is based around these criteria.

Table 11.1 Criteria for differentiation

Importance	The point or points of difference should be readily appreciated and understood by the majority of customers
Profitability	The costs involved in developing the differentiation will be rewarded through being able to charge a price sufficient to repay the cost of investment and generate profits.
Distinctive	The product cannot be copied or performed better by others.
Superior	The difference must offer the customer a better way to receive the expected benefits.
Affordable	Customers can, and are willing to, pay for the product.
Communicable	The difference can easily be communicated and understood by customers.

In the Skoda example earlier, the car may appeal at the functional level, but be rejected at the emotional level.

Organisations can adopt a number of positioning characteristics which help to position the brand in the consumer's mind.

Perceptual maps are used to identify a consumer's perceptions of a product or brand and the position occupied in the market as measured by set criteria.

Competitive positioning has already been identified as the act of designing the company's offer and image so that they occupy a meaningful and distinctive position in the target customer's mind. For example, in the car market, Volvo may have an association with safety and Skoda may be associated with value-for-money.

Dibb *et al*. (2006) suggest that 'positioning' is not what is done to the product, but what is created in the mind of the consumer and therefore elements of the process are outside the control of the organisation. Skoda, in the above example, may score well when measured as value for money, but may not be purchased for social reasons, ie it is perceived as 'inferior'.

It has been argued that a brand operates at two levels:

- Functional, ie what the product does
- Emotional, ie what the product means.

Some airlines have a position statement on their web sites to help position the brand in a consumer's mind. Typical examples are:

Emirates Airlines – Hello Tommorow

Qantas Airline – Spirit of Australia

British Airways – The World's favourite airline

KLM – Royal Dutch Airlines

Delta Airlines - Great Expectations, Indeed

Flybe Airline – Book with confidence

EasyJet – Orange spirit

Ryanair – Cheap flights to Europe

Upshaw (1995) identified the following different types of positioning prompts (Table 11.2).

Table 11.2   Positioning prompts

Feature driven	The specific features of the product are used to differentiate it, eg bagless, cordless, wireless. Example: Apple's iPhone
Problem solution	Unique solution to the problem 'the product actually works'. Example: Domestos cleaning fluid
Target driven	The nature of the consumer identifies a place in the market, eg 'people like you'. Example: Kellogg's Special K Cereal
Competitive driven	A position taken against the competition is established, eg BA and Virgin.
Emotional	Charities often add emotion to their brand. Example: Oxfam aid and development agency
Benefit driven	The benefits to be gained from the product, eg Virgin Airlines' Business class offers a taxi to pick up from home or office.
Aspiration	Successful people use this brand. Example: Mercedes Benz cars
Value	Aldi or Asda, eg, use this positioning

2 Brand positioning

▶ **Key term**

Brand positioning: creating a brand offer in such a manner that it occupies a distinctive place and value in the target customer's mind.

Product positioning starts with the product and brand positioning 'starts with establishing a frame of reference, which signals to consumers the goal they can expect to receive by using a brand' (Yeshin, 2006). The frame of reference can often be other brands in the same category, eg Hugo Boss or Ted Baker. Alternatively, the frame can be in different sectors, e.g. Virgin trains and Easyjet where both offer travel solutions.

Kotler *et al.* (2008) suggested a brand could be positioned according to a range of associations (Table 11.3).

The Chartered
Institute of Marketing

Table 11.3   Brand associations

Attributes	Solvent free, no hydrogenate fat or GM ingredients
Benefits	Safety and durability
Occasion	Opening hours, Christmas, holidays, etc.
Users	Environmentally friendly
Activity	Sport or relaxation
Personality	Churchill Insurance
Origin	British heritage or German engineering
Symbol	Microsoft logo, NatWest logo
Product class	Morning goods, personal hygiene products
Competition	Positioned as 'Reassuringly Expensive' but not best-in-class in blind tasting sessions

Organisations need to decide carefully how they want to position their products compared to the competition. To aid the selection process (Jobber, 2007) identified four key factors critical to the process (Table 11.4).

Table 11.4   Positioning factors

Credence	Attributes used by the organisation to position the product must be credible, eg the BMW 3 Series Coupe with sports suspension offering 58.9 miles to a gallon of petrol is credible. Suggesting a Range Rover offers fuel efficiency would be difficult to justify.
Competitiveness	The product must offer benefits not provided by the competition. Tradition, prestige and superiority of Oxbridge colleges compared with other universities.
Consistency	Lloyds TSB has used 'with you for the journey' to demonstrate it wants to maintain a consistent positioning.
Clarity	Clear position: 'no nasty stuff' or 'it does what it says on the tin'.

THE REAL WORLD

Hugo Boss: International Fashion Brand

Hugo Boss, which specialises in menswear but includes womenswear, was founded in 1924 by Hugo Ferdinand Boss (1885–1948) with the company headquarters in Metzingen, Germany. The sales turnover was €1.729 billion in 2010 with 6,100 outlets in 110 countries and 9,940 employees (2011). Marzotto S.a.A separated their organisation into two different companies of Marzotto (textiles business) and Valentino Fashion Group (clothing business). The Valentino Fashion Group includes the brands of Marlboro Classics, Valentino SpA, Hugo Boss, Missoni, Lebole, Oxon, Portrait and Proenza Schouler. Hugo Boss is divided into separate brands that are targeted at specific segments in the fashion marketplace. These brands include

- **Boss Black** mature fashion for both business and social events
- **Boss Orange** aims to target the opposite audience with bright colours, metal-coloured clothing, and everyday items
- **Boss Selection** designed to be the premium label of the core brand
- **Boss Green** golf-oriented sport collection
- **Boss Kidswear** sport classic looks

(Hugo Boss, 2012)

2.1 Perceptual maps

Figure 11.1 represents a simple perceptual map of various airlines. The attributes identified through market research are price and perceived overall quality in this case, but a range of other attributes such as service standards or reliability could have been used.

Figure 11.1   Perceptual map of airlines

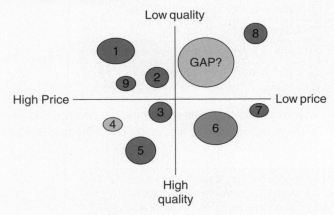

Each circle in the map shows the brand's perceived position mapped against two variables of quality and price. The size of each circle represents the relative market share held by the brand. We can see in the low price/high quality quadrant that two brands are competing and brand '6' has the higher market share.

Where the circles are located close together, customers see the brand as being similar when viewed against the two variables. Measurement against other attributes would show a different perception and therefore different relative position.

By positioning the brand in accordance with one of the criteria outlined above, the organisation is raising the customer's expectation of the nature of the product and offering. Failure to deliver on these promises will bring the inevitable consequences of failure.

The perceptual map shown is based on customer perception, but an alternative approach would be to develop the map based of the competition. This approach allows an organisation to develop a deeper understanding of the competition and form the basis of a strategy to attack or defend positions depending on the strength of the competition.

In the low price/low quality market only brand '8' is competing and there is potentially a gap in the market where an organisation may want to compete and it represents the ideal positioning, ie relatively low price, with relatively low quality.

ACTIVITY 11.1

For a market of your choice, develop a perceptual map showing the relative positioning of the competing brands based upon two key attributes on which customers distinguish between them. Identify whether there are any potential gaps in the market.

The Chartered Institute of Marketing

3 Positioning alternatives

Perceptual maps are based on research so the resultant map has validity and the organisation has confidence in the findings. However, Ries and Trout (1981) identified three alternative positioning approaches (Table 11.5):

- **Distinctive attributes**
- **Unoccupied positions**
- **Repositioning**

Table 11.5   Positioning approaches

Distinctive attributes	An organisation can seek to build on a current position and create a clear position for the brand. For example, John Lewis, the department store, is 'never knowingly undersold'.
Unoccupied positions	The perceptual map shown as Figure 11.1 suggests that the market has an opportunity for a relatively low-priced airline offering relatively low quality. This may be in the short-haul market, where passengers are focussed on price and not too bothered about quality.
Repositioning	As the product moves through its life cycle, physical changes may become necessary to extend its life, eg new features. Alternatively, it may be possible to reposition the brand in the minds of customers or potential customers by suggesting a new use, benefit or advantage.

Leeds College of Music

Leeds College of Music (LCM) is regarded as a dynamic and progressive institution. It boasts an impressive list of alumni and substantial performance facilities. Its mission statement is: " We aim to be the conservatoire of choice for forward-thinking musicians; renowned for the quality, distinctiveness and relevance of our provision, and the contribution that we make to the cultural life and economic prosperity of our city, our region and the wider world." For some time, there has been a disparity between LCM's reputation and its outward image. With strong competition coming from music conservatories and universities, it needs to achieve 'stand out' in a crowded market.

In 2005, Thompson Brand Partners created a distinctive brand identity which reflected the energy, ethos and experience of the institution.

In 2008, LCM topped the national league tables for having the biggest annual rise in UCAS applications.

On 1 August 2011, Leeds College of Music became a wholly owned subsidiary of Leeds City College, in a relationship which will offer a number of benefits to both colleges as well as students in the city. The alliance with Leeds City College will present Leeds College of Music with the benefits of shared resources and economies of scale and provide a secure financial future in today's uncertain funding climate.

Leeds College of Music will continue to offer its unique mix of conservatoire-style provision in Classical Music, Jazz, Music Production and Popular Music across Higher Education, Further Education and community courses, which complements Leeds City College's existing performance arts offer.

(LCM, 2012)

4 The marketing mix

As a result of developing the perceptual map, the organisation may need to change or fine tune its positioning in the market.

Brand positioning is not set in stone and can be changed. We have already mentioned Skoda and following its purchase by Volkswagen, it has been repositioned in the market very successfully.

If we look at our original perceptual map and now add in the ideal position of reasonable price and quality, we can see (Figure 11.1) some brands are some distance way from this position which may account for the 'gap' in the market. Brand 8 is considered to be of poor quality, which is reflected in the price.

While the importance of customer perception has been recognised, the marketing mix has a crucial part to play in the positioning process. In addition to the 4Ps identified in Table 11.6, the additional 3Ps of the marketing mix (physical evidence, processes and people) should also be considered as key aspects of positioning.

Table 11.6 The 4Ps and positioning

Product	• Are the features and benefits still relevant or do they need to be changed?
	• Does the branding reflect the product's position in the market?
	• Does the product's packaging and presentation reflect in the other aspects of the marketing mix?
	• Are there new products in the pipeline?
Price	• Is the price competitive and does it reflect the quality and desirability of the product?
	• Does the price reflect value for money?
Promotion	• Does the promotion reflect the positioning and pricing of the product?
	• Are the right communication channels being used?
Place	• Are the right distribution channels being used and do they reflect well on the product?
	• Is the channel structure right?

ACTIVITY 11.2

For each of the additional 3Ps of the extended marketing mix, suggest how they might affect brand positioning. Use real world examples to support your answers.

> ▸ **Assessment tip**
>
> It is important to understand the concept of positioning and brand and to be able recognise how they are closely related.

Summary

The focus in this chapter has been on positioning of organisations, products and brands which need to be supported in the market by an integrated and co-ordinated combination of marketing mix elements. Perceptual maps are a useful tool for comparing relative brand positioning and also for identifying gaps in the market where opportunities may exist. Pursuing these opportunities may provide strategic options for an organisation, which should be evaluated using appropriate internal and external criteria.

CHAPTER ROUNDUP

- Positioning
- Brand positioning
- Positioning alternatives.

FURTHER READING

Wigley, S. *et al* (2005) Product and brand: Critical success factors in the internationalisation of a fashion retailer. *International Journal of Retail & Distribution Management*, 33 (7), pp 531-544.

REFERENCES

Dibb, S. *et al* (2006) *Marketing: Concepts and Strategies*. 5th edition. Boston, Houghton Mifflin.

Hugo Boss (2012) www.hugoboss.com [Accessed on 20 June 2012]

Jobber, D. (2007) *Principles and Practice of Marketing*. 5th edition. Maidenhead, McGraw Hill.

Kotler, P *et al* (2008) *Principles of Marketing*. 5th edition. Harlow, Financial Times/Prentice Hall.

Kotler, P. and Keller, K.L. (2006) *Marketing Management*. 12th edition. Englewood Cliffs, N.J., Prentice Hall.

Laforet, S. (2010) *Managing Brands*. London, McGraw Hill.

Leeds College of Music (2012) www.lcm.ac.uk [Accessed on 20 June 2012]

Ries, A. and Trout, J. (1981) *Positioning: The Battle for Your Mind*. New York, McGraw Hill.

Yeshin, T. (2006) *Advertising*. New York, Thompson.

QUICK QUIZ

1 Distinguish between functional and emotional attributes of a brand. Use examples from a product or service market of your choice to illustrate this.

2 Explain the importance and use of perceptual maps in the positioning process.

3 Is positioning what is done to the product or what is created in the mind of the consumer?

4 Identify the three alternative positioning approaches.

5 At what three levels can positioning and competition take place?

The Chartered
Institute of Marketing

Activity 11.1

Using the two key attributes produce the perceptual map showing the competing brands. Keep the map so that it is easy to see each of those brands and their relative position to the focal brand. The gaps in the market can then be identified and discussed based on the two chosen key attributes.

Activity 11.2

Physical evidence

The clothes that the employee wears are part of the brand communication and help to position it for the benefit of the consumers. The look, style and quality of the clothing are all very important.

People

The attitude and behaviour of the staff are central to the perception of the brand. How they deal with customers, respond to complaints and portray the brand values in their interaction with the customer are extremely important.

Process

The processes the organisation utilises in administrating its transactions are important. Ease of use of payment, returns and customer relations procedures are important. And so too is the use of the organisation's web site including navigation and reliability of access to the different web pages and within the different functions.

QUICK QUIZ ANSWERS

1   A functional attribute relates to what the product does and its utility (such as a car transports from the starting point to the destination). An emotional attribute is linked to what the product means and connects to the individual's expressive values, such as style, looks and feelings in the journey.

2   Perceptual maps are a useful tool for comparing relative brand positioning and also for identifying gaps in the market where opportunities may exist.

3   In the mind of the consumer, according to Dibb *et al*. (2006).

4   They are distinctive attributes, unoccupied positions and repositioning.

5   They can take place at the level of company, product and brand.

Section 3:

Senior examiner's comments

On completion of Section 3, students should have a detailed knowledge and understanding of:

- The nature and purpose of marketing strategies
- The principle of market STP
- The different ways in which markets may be segmented and evaluation of these approaches
- The ways in which effective targeting may take place
- The positioning of products and services to meet customer requirements.

STP strategies are pivotal to marketing planning in practice as they focus marketing activity on defined audiences that have been selected to fulfil organisational objectives. Thus if students are to be successful in this unit, they need to be fully aware of the way in which strategies are defined in terms of target markets and product offers in different situations.

In order to achieve this, they need to be able to effectively segment markets using a range of variables, profile different customer types and determine an overall targeting strategy. Once segments have been defined in this way, students should gain practical insights into assessing the best markets to target using a set of evaluation criteria. Ultimately, they will be judged on their ability to develop a positioning statement based on target customer requirements using a coherent mix of marketing activities. This needs to be set against a competitive backdrop of gaining advantage over other providers in the same markets, and the way that strategies are based on differential advantage in providing customer value and achieving organisational benefits.

Examples of market segmentation strategy in practice are widely available, and students should also draw upon such activity within their own organisation to help better understand the process. Underpinning the approach that is adopted to understanding more about selecting and delivering offers to target markets should be practical analysis of internal capabilities of the organisation and the relative attractiveness of alternative segments.

Section 4: Adapting marketing planning in different contexts

Section 4 addresses implementing marketing planning in practice with a specific emphasis on differences in achieving this in a range of organisational and market settings. In particular, this section concentrates on organisational structures, responsibilities, timescales and budgets for implementation. Further it considers barriers to implementing marketing planning and plans and ways of addressing these. Contextual aspects of implementation are then considered including the nature of the customer or product, the markets served, and the characteristics of the organisation and the goals it sets out to achieve.

CHAPTER 12

Key dimensions of implementing marketing planning in practice

Introduction

This chapter covers the part of the syllabus which relates to the critical area of implementing marketing planning. We have seen how a marketing plan is researched, planned and structured. Strategies, marketing programmes and tactics will have been identified and evaluated, but we must now consider the very practical issues surrounding implementation.

Topic list

Implementation	1
Organisational structures, systems and processes	2
Forecasting and budgeting	3
Timescales and responsibilities	4
Managerial, organisational and cultural shortcomings	5
Monitoring and control mechanisms	6
Performance metrics	7
Contingency planning	8
Internal marketing	9

Syllabus reference

4.1	Assess the significance of the key dimensions of implementing marketing planning in practice
	■ Organisational structures, systems and processes ■ Forecasting and budgeting ■ Timescales and responsibilities
4.2	Critically evaluate the barriers and constraints to implementing marketing planning, and consider how they may be addressed by organisations
	■ Managerial, organisational, and cultural shortcomings ■ Planning inadequacies ■ Poor and inadequate organisational resource ■ Lack of innovation ■ Failure to integrate into corporate planning systems ■ Monitoring performance metrics and control mechanisms ■ Contingency planning ■ Internal marketing

1 Implementation

▶ **Key term**

Implementation: the managing process of carrying out and execution of the marketing plan.

In terms of strategy, planning is the easy part, and the real challenge is implementation. The process must be very carefully planned and managed. There are three key areas that are vital to implementation:

1. Communicating the marketing plan across the organisation
2. Specifying the required resources, finance, personnel and time
3. Changes to the organisational structure and culture.

A weakness of many marketing plans is the lack of implementation details, with the result that not all the planned activities are put into practice. A failure to identify the resources required and the time frame for the activities are typical omissions.

Marketing planning does not end when the marketing plan has been prepared. It is essential that all implementation details are attended to. Even then the process is not complete. The marketing plan document should continue to be updated on an ongoing basis.

Piercy (2002, p73) states that:

'Marketing strategy is all about finding new and better ways of looking at things (the customers) to get leverage for changing the way things are done (the marketing)'.

A marketing plan can be prepared with all the correct jargon, such as, competitive advantage, market penetration, segmentation, targeting and positioning. However, without implementation the plan will remain simply ideas on a piece of paper.

In terms of strategy, implementation is often the key determinant of success or failure. The history of corporate strategy is littered with examples of great plans but which were failures because of poor implementation. Therefore, implementation should be an integral part of any marketing strategy.

Never adopt a strategy you do not understand how to implement.

Implementation is critical to the success or failure of any venture and there are some key factors that influence this.

- Strong and committed leadership
- A marketing-orientated and customer-focussed culture
- An effective marketing structure
- Adequate resources – both financial and human
- Internal marketing
- Budgets, control and measurement systems.

If a strategy is to be successfully executed, it is important that each of these areas is planned and managed effectively.

1.1 Success factors

▶ **Key term**

Success factors: number of characteristics, conditions or variables that have an impact on achieving performance of the marketing plan.

Two dimensions determine the success of a strategy: the strategy itself and the ability to implement it. Bonoma (1984) examined both the appropriateness of strategy and the effectiveness of the skills to implement it (Table 12.1).

Table 12.1   Strategy implementation

Success	Appropriate strategy and strong ability to implement	Ideal situation. Few problems
Chance	Inappropriate or poor strategy, lacking detailed analysis, not building on existing strengths. Possibly saved by effective adaptation and execution	How inappropriate is the strategy. What adaptation is possible to the strategy. High risk
Problem	Appropriate strategy, poor implementation	Strength of strategic marketing plan dissipated by poor or inappropriate implementation
Failure	Inappropriate strategy. Lack of ability to implement	Is there any point struggling on with implementation. Quit and avoid further loss. Learn from the mistake

(Adapted from Bonoma, 1984)

There is some degree of subjectivity when defining appropriate or inappropriate strategies. Strategies are often labelled 'inappropriate' even when they have failed through poor implementation. Strategies are often labelled 'appropriate' despite being saved by adaptations in implementation or even luck!

Formulating an appropriate strategy has been covered in Section 3.

So what factors are needed for success? These are summarised in Table 12.2.

Table 12.2   Key strategy implementation factors

Key elements of implementation of plans and strategies	
Leadership	Skills
Strategy	Systems
Culture	Control
Structure	Resources

1.1.1 Leadership

The role of the leader is to get the best out of people. Many leaders reach their position based on technical skills which often creates problems. Leaders require effective *people skills* such as delegation and negotiation and a range of transferable management skills.

The role of leadership is to facilitate activities rather than do the work themselves.

Kotter (1990) suggests that leaders succeed by:

- Establishing direction and strategy
- Communicating it to those whose co-operation is needed
- Motivating and inspiring people.

The relative instability and unpredictability of the environment has influenced the emergence of a new concept of leadership, transformational as opposed to transactional leadership. The transformational leader motivates and inspires staff and ensures they understand the vision for the organisation. There is now emphasis on leadership to ensure that the organisation can adapt and succeed in a rapidly changing world.

Kouzes and Posner (2002) outline five characteristics of leadership:

- Challenging the process – Encourage others to develop ideas and take calculated risks
- Inspire a shared vision
- Enabling others to act – Encourage collaboration, co-operation, empowering others
- Modelling the way – Planning, reviewing progress and taking corrective action
- Clear about values and acting consistently with them.

Leaders need to adopt an appropriate style of management depending on the circumstances.

House (1996) suggests that the appropriate style depends on the characteristics of the subordinates and the work environment (Table 12.3).

Table 12.3   Leadership styles

Directive style	When task is ambiguous and staff lack flexibility
Supportive style	When tasks are repetitive, frustrating or unpleasant
Achievement-orientated style	Non-repetitive, sometimes ambiguous, challenging tasks which need pressure and encouragement to raise performance
Participative style	Non-repetitive and staff are confident in their ability to do the work

(Adapted from House, 1996)

1.1.2 Strategy

The potential strategy will need to be screened to ensure that it is appropriate to current circumstances. What is the basis of competitive advantage? Does it build on the strengths of the organisation? Are the weaknesses of the organisation addressed? What organisation changes are required to successfully deliver the strategy? How acceptable is the strategy to stakeholders?

Strategy should be an ongoing activity. Throughout the implementation stage, management will need to review and adapt. Strategic objectives should remain the same but changes may be required for the targets to be achieved.

1.1.3 Culture

Culture can be defined as the combination of shared values and beliefs that exist within an organisation. These are commonly observed and reinforced by corporate symbols such as logos. Great care must be exercised when implementing strategy.

A marketing planner or strategist must be sensitive to the shared values that exist within the organisation. A new strategy cannot be successfully executed without developing and maintaining support within the organisation. If the strategy goes against the dominant culture, there is a strong likelihood of failure. Restructuring, internal marketing and staff training will be required if the strategy is to be successfully implemented.

1.1.4 Structure

The structure of the organisation has two primary functions.

- It defines the lines of authority and levels of responsibility
- It provides a basis for communication.

There is a current trend towards flattened structures with more devolved authority and responsibility. It is important to consider how communication occurs, as structures can make senior management remote from customers and impede the flow of information and communication.

Multifunctional teams with a wide range of backgrounds can increase innovation, identify and solve operational problems and improve quality.

1.1.5 Skills

The appropriate skills mix is required to achieve any aim or objective. Successful implementation requires the following:

- Marketing/technical skills – Marketing research, design and R&D
- HRM skills – Selection, training and appraisal
- Project management skills – Forecasting, budgeting, resourcing and monitoring.

A range of both hard and soft skills is required. Implementing marketing strategy requires 'soft' human resource management skills as well as the 'hard' project management skills.

1.1.6 Systems

There are two groups of systems required for implementation.

- Forecasting
- Reporting.

These systems are essential for management decision making. The marketing information system (MKIS) will be essential for gathering marketing information and marketing decision making. The management information system (MIS) will cover areas such as finance, operations management, budgeting and monitoring.

1.1.7 Control

This is simply making sure what should happen actually does happen. The basic approach is to monitor and compare with some predetermined standard (a feedback loop) and take action if required. The business plan, the marketing plan, the budget or monthly targets are frequently used as targets.

1.1.8 Resources

A strategic marketing plan must be resourced. Resources usually relate mainly to finance and staff. Resources are normally budget-driven, although greater importance is now being given to the importance of time (time to market). Resources are often influenced more by internal politics than needs and the marketing planner should be aware of this influence.

Flexibility is essential and a sensible contingency should be built into the marketing plan to provide a buffer in case things do not go according to plan. Additional resources may be required during the implementation and the success of the strategy may well depend on having access to these, if conditions change.

2 Organisational structures, systems and processes

Having selected a strategy, the next important step is to select the structure that will deliver the corporate objectives in an efficient and effective way. It is important that the structure and the lines of communication within it are understood by all employees.

The structure of the organisation might be functional, territory or product based.

The functional organisation defines each of the functions with each having a management line of control.

For example, marketing is likely to be headed by a Director of Marketing and control will be exercised through a range of marketing specialisms including sales, market research, new product development and marketing communications. This will allow the marketing team to undertake the day-to-day marketing activities in an integrated way (Figure 12.1).

Figure 12.1   Functional organisational structure

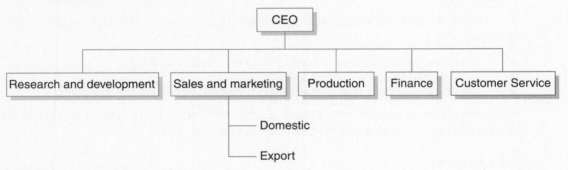

(Adapted from Hollensen, 2006)

The advantages of this type of structure are:

- Specialisation leads to efficiency
- Common interests promote good internal relations
- Clear career paths and professional development for employees.

The disadvantages of this type of structure are:

- Conflict over priorities
- Isolation from the wider aspects of the organisation.

2.1 The geographic or territory-based organisation

This is an effective structure where organisations trade regionally or internationally. This is a form of decentralised management. Business management functions, such as resourcing, budgeting and marketing, are devolved to each territory where local management has authority and responsibility to manage but still in line with the corporate goals and objectives.

This approach is typical of large organisations, operating in different regions or countries, especially where cultural differences make decentralised management sensible (Figure 12.2).

The Chartered Institute of Marketing

Figure 12.2   Territory organisational structure

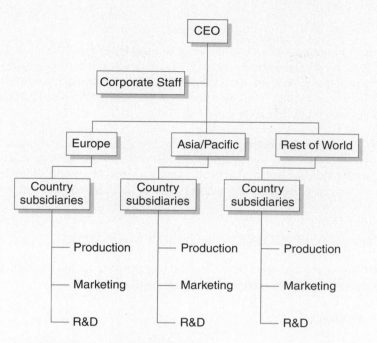

(Adapted from Hollensen, 2006)

The advantages of this type of structure are:

- Resources are pooled
- Co-ordination of different functional areas of management is improved
- Specialist staff can focus on the region.

The disadvantages of this type of structure are:

- There is a possibility that some products will be overlooked as there is no overall responsibility for specific products

- Efficiency depends on having a group of highly effective managers.

2.2 The product-based organisation

Major companies such as Philips and Unilever adopt a product-based structure where different brands and products are managed as separate business units.

THE REAL WORLD

Unilever

Unilever is a British / Dutch multinational consumer goods company with a diverse product range including foods, beverages, cleaning agents and personal care products. In terms of sales turnover, in 2011, it is ranked third in the world behind Procter & Gamble and Nestlé. Unilever has a wide portfolio of well-known own label household brands totalling approximately 400. Twenty five of these brands account for nearly three quarters of its total annual sales and it is the world's largest producer of ice cream. The business is grouped into Personal Care, Refreshments, Home Care and Foods.

The 2011 annual accounts stated that "Strong business performance is driven by our brands, people, and sustainability – which is increasingly giving us a true competitive advantage. We will invest in strengthening our brands so that they drive profitable growth as part of a sustainable business model: the more we sell, the more efficiently we can operate and, at the same time, by reducing the cost of running our business we can invest more in our brands, innovations, and advertising and promotions. This, in turn, enables us to sell more".

(Unilever, 2011)

In a product-based organisation, product managers have devolved responsibility for their particular brand and product and are expected to deliver in line with corporate expectations (Figure 12.3).

Figure 12.3   Product-based organisational structure

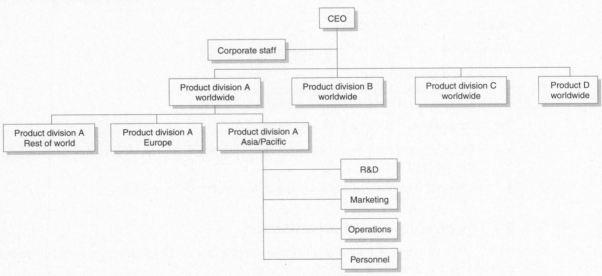

(Adapted from Hollensen, 2006)

Major advantages of this structure are:

- Decentralisation
- Motivated specialist divisional heads
- Products may be introduced and deleted, without effect on the rest of the organisation.

The disadvantages of this structure are:

- Co-ordination problems may arise
- Some products may be overlooked
- Bias when divisional heads move on into corporate management.

The Chartered
Institute of Marketing

2.3 The matrix organisation

Marketing has embraced more and more other business functions in order to develop a more integrated co-ordinated approach to achieve corporate goals. A matrix organisation incorporates many business functions. The real strength of this organisational structure is that it can respond to different political and economic environments because it combines the elements of product-based and territory management. For example, a product manager would have product responsibility worldwide for Product A, whereas geographic managers would be responsibility for all product lines including Product A. The management responsibilities overlap and this provides a good basis for decision making (Figure 12.4).

The major disadvantages of this structure are:

- The possibility of power struggles in this dual command structure
- The structure may collapse in times of crisis
- Communication can be complicated.

The organisational hierarchy determines what decisions people at each level can make. As an organisation grows, the hierarchy becomes more complex. At some point, a decision will need to be made on whether to centralise or to decentralise.

- **Centralisation**: when those at the top make most decisions, with managers at divisional level responsible for ensuring that the policies are carried out at the operating level

- **Decentralisation**: where a relatively large number of decisions are taken in the divisional or operating levels.

Figure 12.4   The matrix organisational structure

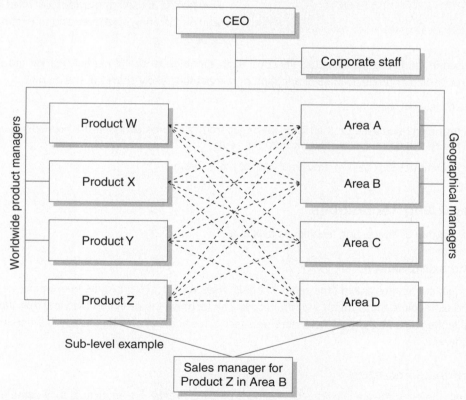

(Adapted from Hollensen, 2006)

A centralised approach provides management at corporate level with more control but decisions are usually slow. A decentralised approach to decision making provides quicker decision making and decisions are more likely to take account of local conditions.

The structures adopted reflect the history, management outlook and experience of the organisation. Strategy changes will have some effect on the organisation structure. The important thing to remember is the best organisational structure – the one that fits the external environment and the internal characteristics of the organisation.

Select an organisation of your choice. Go to the web site of the company and gather information about the structure of the organisation.

Which type of structure has the organisation adopted? What are the benefits of their approach? If the organisation has international operations, how are they represented in the structure? Has the organisation adopted a centralised or decentralised approach?

3 Forecasting and budgeting

▶ **Key term**

Forecasting and budgeting: forecasting is the use of historic data to determine the direction of future trends. Forecasting is used by companies to determine how to allocate their budgets for an upcoming period of time.

Forecasting is the process of using available information to develop one or more views of the future. There are a number of techniques which can be used independently or in combination to achieve this. Forecasting is used to provide quantified estimates on which marketing objectives and marketing plans can be based.

Forecasts used in marketing planning usually cover such variables as size of market, market growth, levels of demand for a particular product, rates of adoption or competitors' likely shares of the market.

There are two views of the future.

- The future will be based on the historical trends from the same period in the previous year
- The future will be radically different from the past.

Forecasting techniques can help to provide a view of the future.

3.1 Forecasting Techniques

There are a number of forecasting techniques available.

3.1.1 Trend extrapolation

This technique, sometimes called time series analysis, uses statistical techniques to examine past trends in markets and extrapolate those trends into the future. The technique is based on the view that the future will be incrementally the same as the past. Therefore, this technique is unsuitable for situations where the future is radically different.

3.1.2 Individual forecasting

An individual, ideally someone considered an expert, predicts events. The individual may come up with an accurate forecast, but this may be a personal judgement and provide a biased view of the world. This can be a high-risk method, therefore consensus forecasting may overcome the weakness.

3.1.3 Consensus forecasting

This uses a panel of experts who produce a judgement. One method is jury forecasting – they work together to produce a forecast on which they all agree. However, there is a danger of 'group think' with this approach. Members of the jury may influence each other resulting in an unrealistic forecast. The Delphi forecast attempts to overcome this weakness by using similar experts working independently of each other. It may employ a series of rounds in which each expert gives a view which is then fed back to other experts to be refined. It does not arrive at a single view and consensus is not required. Indeed difference can stimulate new ideas.

3.1.4 Scenario planning

This is the process of identifying a number of possible futures, instead of a single view of the future. It is usually used by a group of managers who define scenarios which they consider possible. They proceed through a series of set stages to identify relevant variables and critical issues. Models can be built to evaluate scenarios and the question of 'what if?' asked. A plan can then be developed with a range of alternatives considered suitable for the various scenarios.

THE REAL WORLD

Shell and scenario planning

Scenario planning may involve aspects of systems thinking, specifically the recognition that many factors may combine in complex ways to create sometime surprising futures (due to non-linear feedback loops). The method also allows the inclusion of factors that are difficult to formalise, such as novel insights about the future, deep shifts in values, unprecedented regulations or inventions. At Royal Dutch/Shell for example, scenario planning was viewed as changing mindsets about the exogenous part of the world, prior to formulating specific strategies.

Some analysts of the company publicly estimated that this planning process made their company the largest in the world. However, other observers of Shell's use of scenario planning have suggested that few if any significant long-term business advantages accrued to Shell from the use of scenario methodology. Whilst the intellectual robustness of Shell's long-term scenarios was seldom in doubt, their actual practical use was seen as being minimal.

(Schwartz, P., 1991)

3.2 Budgeting

▶ **Key term**

Budgeting: periodic estimate, usually annually of the income and expenditure for the organisation.

The processes of strategic development and budgeting are connected. The budgeting process translates marketing strategy into financial terms, which are the ways all plans are expressed, evaluated and controlled. A budget is the most common control mechanism and has the following purposes:

- Quantifying the plan
- Co-ordination of activities
- Identifying critical issues
- Assigning responsibility.

It should contain estimates for all the functional areas of the organisation. In marketing, this will mean the costs of sales, market research, advertising and other promotional expenditure. The budget is about resource allocation and financial and human resources will be essential for successful implementation. However, the marketing planner should remember budgeting is a political process and negotiation and bargaining will be necessary to obtain the required resources in order to achieve the objectives.

The budget is a financial plan outlined in quantitative terms for a set period, usually a year.

Common approaches to budgeting are:

- **Historic** – The organisation may simply base the budget on previous financial data, making adjustments for factors such as level of activity and inflation.

- **Zero-based** – These budgets are systematically re-evaluated, examining activities and benefits. Alternative ways of achieving the objectives are considered within the financial constraints.

- **Activity-related** – These budgets are based on measures of activity.

There are a number of other budgeting methods, which are shown in Table 12.4.

While organisations should be customer-driven, many organisations are budget-driven, with objectives related to time and budget.

Marketing planners should remember that budgets can be a key motivational tool, with targets being set and rewards being related to the achievement of targets contained in the budget.

Table 12.4   Budgeting methods

Incremental budgeting	Based on previous year with adjustment for growth and inflation
Objective and task	Budget is based on the estimate of what is needed to achieve the objectives. Clear definition of tasks and resources is necessary
Percentage of sales method	Based on a percentage of the previous year's sales being allocated to marketing
Competitive parity	This approach is based on spending the same percentage as others in the industry
Judgement methods	Managers are asked to use their judgement and experience to estimate the marketing costs to achieve different levels of sales
Experiment and test	The organisation may run an experiment in one area to test the effect of advertising to establish the level of advertising required to achieve a specified level of sales

Budgeting is critical for the measuring of the performance of the organisation and individuals. The budget provides the standard for measuring performance. This is achieved by comparing budgeted performance against actual performance (variance analysis).

4 Timescales and responsibilities

The marketing planning process begins with the audit of the marketing environment and preparation of the internal analysis. The marketing planning process should be ongoing. The co-ordination of the marketing planning process should be the responsibility of the marketing manager, who should obtain cross-functional support and input to the process.

The marketing function is responsible for identifying customers that the organisation can most effectively satisfy.

The Chartered Institute of Marketing

An effective MKIS is needed to provide an up-to-date and accurate information. Marketing intelligence and market research will be carried out or co-ordinated by marketing. Information will be gathered on consumer demand, competitor strategies and changes in the marketing environment. Data on its own has no meaning, so it will also be the responsibility of marketing to analyse and extract useful information for marketing and other organisation purposes.

If customer satisfaction is to be achieved, information on changing customer demand, preferences and tastes will need to be distributed throughout the organisation to functions requiring it. Information held by other functions will be useful to ascertain trends, eg sales and marketing will be responsible for gathering information. Marketing therefore holds a central position in organisations.

Marketing will be responsible for selecting the most appropriate marketing mix, the media and the messages with which to engage customers in order to achieve the organisational objectives.

Adopting a marketing orientation ensures that the whole organisation is committed to achieving organisational goals by continually satisfying consumer demands. Functional areas need to co-operate and co-ordinate activities towards customer satisfaction. Marketing staff play a key role in encouraging and developing a marketing orientation throughout the organisation. Internal marketing could be used to develop the required cultural changes and this will be the responsibility of marketing.

5 Managerial, organisational and cultural shortcomings

As already noted in Section 1, a range of barriers to effective marketing planning exist. The marketing planner must pay careful attention to these barriers, if marketing plans are to be implemented effectively.

The following are some of the key barriers.

Organisational barriers include:

- Managers' tendency to build empires will cause problems
- A focus on internal politics
- Failure to share information and ideas.

Lack of marketing competency within the organisation:

- Insufficient marketing skills
- Poor understanding of the marketing planning process
- Failure to see whole picture – obsession with individual products
- Poor grasp of marketing concept.

Lack of management time for effective marketing planning:

- Difficulty balancing day-to-day operations with strategic marketing planning.

5.1 Planning inadequacies

Too much short-term marketing

- Too much emphasis on a one-year time frame.
- No long-term vision

Marketing plans developed in isolation rather than on marketing analysis

- Lack of marketing intelligence system
- Poor sharing of marketing intelligence
- Insufficient analysis of competitors
- Poor understanding of the environment
- Insufficient understanding of customer behaviour

5.2 Failure to integrate into corporate planning system

In many organisations, whilst marketing plans may be prepared, the marketing planning process is not integrated across the organisation; possible reasons are as follows.

Isolation of marketing planning from other business areas

- Lack of involvement by different functional areas
- Lack of enthusiasm from non-marketing areas
- Limited power of marketers to co-ordinate different functional areas in process.

McDonald (2007) suggests a range of barriers to the implementation of strategic marketing planning.

Barriers to the implementation of marketing planning

- Weak support from the chief executive and top management
- Lack of a plan for planning
- Lack of line management support
- Confusion over planning terms
- Numbers in place of written objectives and strategies
- Too much detail, too far ahead
- Once-a-year ritual
- Separation of operational planning from strategic planning
- Delegation to a planner
- Failure to integrate marketing planning into total planning system.

In many organisations, the marketing plan or budget is simply an annual chore, something to do and get over as quickly as possible, rather than a meaningful and critical strategic process.

---

6 Monitoring and control mechanisms

> ▶ **Key term**
>
> **Monitoring and control:** the business activity to record, regulate, or control performance.

Monitoring and control is essential if the marketing plan is to be successfully executed. We need to monitor to ensure things are going according to plan and take corrective action if they are not.

Marketers are increasingly being pressurised by senior management to become more accountable for their activities and expenditure and are expected to monitor, control and evaluate activities.

- Monitoring and control has four key elements:
- Objective setting
- Setting performance standards
- Monitoring and evaluation of performance
- Reaction – Taking corrective action as required.

Monitoring and control involves setting standards, measurement, evaluation and monitoring, and aims to translate strategic plans into specific actions. They may include: financial measures, budgets, performance appraisal and benchmarking. These should be used to highlight where corrective action is necessary.

Effective monitoring and control systems should be flexible and should have the following attributes.

- Involvement – Staff are encouraged to participate (particularly relevant for a service organisation)
- Target setting should be quantifiable and achievable and be communicated in advance
- Recognise problems and not just symptoms
- Measure effectiveness and not just efficiency

The Chartered Institute of Marketing

- Management by exception – Take corrective action only if results fall outside tolerance zones (concentrate on the important issues)

- Should promote action – Not just detect problems.

Budgetary control involves financial control of the whole business through a system of budgets. There will be a master budget for the whole organisation, together with subsidiary budgets for each of the functions of the organisation, marketing, HR, etc. There will also be a cash budget to identify the cash implications of the various functional budgets and a capital budget for the major items of expenditure, such as new machinery.

Resources are scarce and costly, so it is important to have controls and measurements clearly identified in marketing plans. A marketing manager will be expected to compare actual figures against predetermined standards set out in the budget. Corrective action, if required, can then be taken and an investigation undertaken to establish precisely why the difference or variance has occurred.

6.1 Variance analysis

Variance analysis is used as part of the budgetary control process to identify movements of actual performance away from budget. The objective is to identify variances from budget on a regular basis so that corrective action can be taken.

A typical layout for an annual budget report is shown in Table 12.5.

Control systems need to be carefully designed. No system is perfect and no system is completely accurate. There are three problems of control systems, which must be remembered:

- They are costly – So the costs should not outweigh the benefits
- They stifle effort and creativity – The motivational effects need to be considered
- They promote attitudes of inspection – The focus on symptoms rather than problems.

Table 12.5   Annual budget report

	Budgeted	Actual	Variance under	Variance over
Sales	5,000	5,200		200
Direct labour	2,000	2,200		200
Direct materials	1,000	1,050		50
Royalties	500	450	50	
License fees	100	50	50	
Contribution	1,400	1,250	150	
Overheads	1,000	1,000		
Net income	400	250	150	

Care must be taken to avoid extensive bureaucratic systems which will often consume resources and take the focus away from the customer.

6.2 Benchmarking

A systematic and ongoing process of measuring and comparing an organisation's business processes and achievements against acknowledged process leaders and/or key competitors to facilitate improved performance.

Benchmarking is about the pursuit of continuous improvement. An organisation using benchmarking shows it is a learning organisation, willing to learn from mistakes and seeking to develop best practice.

There are three elements.

- **Competitor analysis:** Reviewing competitors' activities and identifying areas where the organisation can improve.

- **Best practice:** Investigating and analysing the best way to carry out activities. This may require going outside the industry to take a more innovative approach.

- **Performance standards:** Many industries publish industry standards, which can be used to compare an individual organisation's performance.

The whole process is about adaptation, identifying ideas and practices and adapting for the organisation. Typical areas that are benchmarked are customer service levels, logistics and time to market.

THE REAL WORLD

Rank Xerox and benchmarking

Rank Xerox, the document and imaging company which created the original market for copiers is known as the pioneer of benchmarking in Europe. Faced with severe competition from Japanese rivals who possessed superior imaging technology from their camera businesses, Rank Xerox developed the business process of benchmarking. Before the 1980's Rank Xerox had a near monopoly in its sector and particularly the lucrative European Market. The Japanese entrants provided an immediate and sustained high level of competition and forced Rank Xerox to undertake a thorough evaluation of its own business processes.

The results of this study gave a clear realisation that it was comprehensively uncompetitive in most aspects of its operation. Its Japanese rivals were selling machines for about what it cost Xerox to make them which could not be explained by differences in quality. The study found that, when compared with its Japanese rivals, the company had nine times more suppliers, was rejecting 10 times as many machines on the production line and taking twice as long to get products to market. Benchmarking also showed that productivity would need to grow 18 per cent per year over five years if it was to catch up with its rivals.

Rank Xerox saw benchmarking as helping it achieve two objectives. At a strategic level, by setting standards of performance it was able to match the process requirements to the product demands over the long term, while at an operational level it helped the company to understand the best practices and operations methods necessary to achieve its performance objectives.

---

7 Performance metrics

▶ **Key term**

Performance metrics: measures that are used to evaluate and improve the efficiency and effectiveness of business processes.

The objectives set by the organisation need to be supported by appropriate measures that can be used continuously to monitor performance against those objectives. Traditionally, measures have been financial, with the accountancy profession dominating the debate on how to measure performance.

Marketing does not have standardised techniques for measuring performance, consequently marketing expenditure and budgets may be allocated in an arbitrary way.

The performance measures selected have a strong influence on the behaviour of both management and employees. The measures selected will have an influence on what actually gets done.

It is important to understand that, on their own, metrics have little value or meaning; they need to be compared year-on-year (or period-on-period) – or against competitors, or industry averages. Only in this way can you tell if your situation is 'improving' or 'worsening'.

Financial performance is measured in terms of return on investment or profitability. **Gross profit** measures the profit margin and reflects changes in prices and costs. Intense competition may result in lower prices and a reduction in margin. The **net profit**, often referred to as the bottom line, will be influenced by the gross profit

margin and the overheads of the organisation. Measures such as **return on capital employed** and **return on investment** relate the profitability of the organisation to the financial resources employed to achieve that profit.

7.1 Profitability and return measures

- Gross margin $= \dfrac{\text{Gross profit}}{\text{Sales revenue}} \times 100$

- Net margin $= \dfrac{\text{Net profit}}{\text{Sales revenue}} \times 100$

- Return on capital employed (ROCE) $= \dfrac{\text{Net profit}}{\text{Capital employed}} \times 100$
  (where capital employed = total assets less current liabilities)

Although profitability is important, it is important to measure the long-term stability of the organisation. Those organisations with heavy borrowings carry a greater risk of failure than those with lower levels of debt. Those with higher levels of borrowing will find it harder to maintain interest payments and meet the terms of the finance when the economic environment is difficult.

7.2 Long-term solvency and stability measures

(a) Debt ratio $= \dfrac{\text{Total debt}}{\text{Total assets}}$

(b) Capital gearing $= \dfrac{\text{Long - term debt}}{\text{Total capital employed}}$

(c) Debt/equity ratio $= \dfrac{\text{Debt}}{\text{Ordinary share capital and reserves}}$

(d) Interest cover $= \dfrac{\text{Profit before interest and tax (PBIT)}}{\text{Interest charges}}$

(e) Cashflow ratio $= \dfrac{\text{Net cash inflow}}{\text{Total debts}}$

The ability to meet short-term liabilities is crucial to survival. Profitable businesses have failed where they have inadequate working capital or facilities in place and they have been unable to meet financial claims on time. Solvency and liquidity ratios are used to measure the ability to meet these short-term claims.

7.3 Short-term solvency and liquidity measures

(a) Current ratio $= \dfrac{\text{Current assets}}{\text{Current liabilities}}$

(b) Quick ratio $= \dfrac{\text{Current assets less stocks}}{\text{Current liabilities}}$

Various financial ratios are used to measure the efficiency of the organisation. How quickly does stock turn over? How long is stock left unsold? How quickly are payments from customers collected?

7.4 Efficiency measures

(a)   Stock turnover $= \dfrac{\text{Cost of sales}}{\text{Stock}}$ or $\dfrac{\text{Stock}}{\text{Cost of sales}} \times 365$

(b)   Debtors' turnover $= \dfrac{\text{Credit sales}}{\text{Trade debtors}}$ or $\dfrac{\text{Trade debtors}}{\text{Credit sales}} \times 365$

(c)   Creditors' turnover $= \dfrac{\text{Purchases}}{\text{Trade creditors}}$ or $\dfrac{\text{Trade creditors}}{\text{Purchases}} \times 365$

It is now becoming increasingly important for marketers to develop and use measures (metrics) that will measure the effectiveness of marketing alongside the traditional financial measures shown above. These metrics of brand equity, customer satisfaction, loyalty and retention and share of voice have been gradually adopted. However, many organisations still rely on the traditional financial measures.

7.5 Performance measures

There are three main areas that performance measures should cover:

- Efficiency
- Effectiveness
- Innovation or adaptability.

The efficiency measures in marketing show the ability of the organisation to utilise its asset base. Efficiency can be described as the ratio of outputs achieved compared to the inputs. Efficiency will mean different things to different organisations, but typical metrics used are given in Table 12.6.

Table 12.6   Efficiency metrics

Efficiency	
Capacity utilisation	Inventory levels
Sales turnover per employee	Conversion of enquiries to sales
Speed of delivery	

Efficiency is not enough. Every organisation needs to assess the *effectiveness* of its marketing strategies. Effectiveness measures the extent to which organisational goals and objectives are achieved – 'are we doing the right things'. The performance measures selected will vary from organisation to organisation and from industry to industry. Some of the typical measures used are given in Table 12.7.

Table 12.7   Effectiveness metrics

Effectiveness	
Number of customers	Number of new customers
Unit sales	Customer loyalty
Market share by volume	Customer complaints
Market share by segment	Customer loyalty
Relative value	Relative quality

The Chartered Institute of Marketing

If an organisation is to be successful, it will have to adapt to the changing environment. Innovation and adaptation will need to be high on the agenda. Typical metrics which are used to measure innovation are given in Table 12.8.

Table 12.8   Innovation metrics

Innovation	
Number of patents registered	New product success rates
Trade marks registered	Number of R&D projects
Percentage of sales from new products/services	Acquisition/introduction of new brands

Metrics can also be used to measure brand equity (Table 12.9).

Table 12.9   Brand equity metrics

Brand equity	
Purchase intent	Brand strength
Customer preference	Level of trust in the brand
Brand value	

The increase in online and digital marketing has led to the development of another range of performance metrics, which are given in Table 12.10.

Table 12.10   Online performance metrics

Online performance tracking	
Click-through rates	The number of times that users click on advertisement
Cost per click	The amount spent by the advertiser to generate one click through
Cost per lead	The amount spent by the advertiser to generate one lead
Cost per sale	The amount spent by the advertiser to generate one sale

Competitive conditions and the changing environment will require a combination of performance measures. The triple bottom line (TBL) approach uses a range of measures, social, environmental and financial, to judge success in the market place. The TBL is considered an approach which will provide a more balanced view of the overall performance of an organisation.

With the organisation used in Activity 12.1 and using the above framework of measures, select a range of metrics that would cover the financial, social and environmental performance of the organisation.

8 Contingency planning

Events in the real world rarely go according to plan. It is therefore essential that those preparing marketing plans consider the problems that might occur and make appropriate preparations to deal with them should the need arise.

Contingency planning is the opportunity to recognise different scenarios or series of events and to develop plans that involve different activities being taken at different times. The organisation must develop a capacity to adapt to new circumstances.

The organisation will need to set aside financial reserves and specific resources such as productive capacity.

Consideration should be given to developing contingencies covering a variety of scenarios such as the loss of a major contract, the loss of productive capacity through fire or flood, or delays in time to market.

Contingency planning should ensure that there is a prompt response to difficulties or delays in implementation or any unexpected events. Many organisations incorporate a contingency figure into the budget (say 5% or 10%)

9 Internal marketing

Internal marketing is the application of marketing internally within the organisation, with programmes of communication and guidance targeted at internal audiences to develop responsiveness and a unified sense of purpose among employees.

The implementation of a new corporate strategy may also require change within the organisation and the internal marketing plan will play a critical role in obtaining 'buy in' and a positive reaction from employees.

Marketing orientation can only be achieved when everybody in the organisation is customer focussed (both internal and external customers). Internal marketing again plays a fundamental role in helping to achieve this.

A number of internal cultural barriers may exist that can inhibit the development of a market-led orientation. These are:

- Fear of change
- Lack of time
- Poor communication
- Lack of understanding
- A cynical view of marketing.

Internal marketing is an approach that can be used to overcome these barriers. Internal marketing covers any planned effort to overcome resistance in an organisation to change and to ensure proper communication, motivation and training employees effectively to implement corporate and functional strategies and plans.

Internal marketing focuses on the relationship between the organisation and its employees. Berry and Parasuraman (1991) define the process in terms of viewing employees (or groups of employees) as internal customers.

The Chartered Institute of Marketing

9.1 Implementation

Successful implementation is reliant on three key skills:

- **Persuasion**
  - Present a shared vision
  - Sell the benefits
  - Communicate and train
  - Eliminate misconceptions
  - Gain acceptance by association
  - Support words with clear actions.

- **Negotiation**
  - Make the opening proposition high – allow room for negotiation
  - Trade concessions with different parties.

- **Politics**
  - Building coalitions
  - Take incremental steps
  - Invite the opposition in
  - Control the agenda.

The internal marketing plan provides a framework as follows:

- Vision, aims and objectives
- Internal marketing strategy
- Segmentation, targeting and positioning
- Marketing mix programme
- Implementation
- Monitoring and control.

9.2 Segmentation

Segmentation is the process of dividing groups into subgroups that have similar characteristics. Staff may be segmented by function, status, full-time/part-time or other segmentation variable.

An alternative approach is to segment according to the support for the strategy, as shown in Table 12.11.

Table 12.11   Segmenting internal markets

Segment 1	Segment 2	Segment 3
Influential supporter	Influential opposition	Non-involved supporter

Each group have different concerns and may require different training needs from other staff groups delivered through the internal marketing mix.

- **Product:** This is likely to be the process of change or the new strategy. It is useful to think of the job of each individual as an internal product, essential in delivering the overall strategy.

- **Promotion:** Communication is a key component of internal marketing. There needs to be a promotional campaign stressing the benefits of the change or new strategy. Discussion groups, presentations and newsletters, for example, could all be used to achieve awareness and get the change message across.

- **Place (or distribution):** How is the 'product' going to be delivered to the internal customer? Meetings, team briefings, seminars, magazine, notice boards and the intranet will be used.

- **Price:** This is a complex area. The costs of change and the cost of the communications can be calculated easily. However, the psychological cost of uncertainty and stress will be carried by the staff. These costs such as loss of status, change in work pattern, a change in income are costs that internal customers must pay as a result of accepting the plan.

▶ **Assessment tip**

Evaluating the key dimensions of implementing marketing planning in practice requires a thorough understanding of the underlying process and knowledge of each component.

Summary

This chapter has considered the key elements of implementation within the marketing planning process. These are critical to its ultimate success or failure. The preparation and delivery of marketing plans and new strategies will require appropriate structures and resources. Forecasting and budgeting, timings and responsibilities all need to be carefully determined to ensure that implementation is effective, and there are sometimes shortcomings in these areas. Measures will be required to monitor, control and assess the way in which the organisation performs against the targets set out in the plan. Internal marketing will be critical for communicating the changes required for the delivery of the strategy throughout the organisation, and in addressing the barriers that may exist that inhibit uptake of the plan.

 The Chartered Institute of Marketing

CHAPTER ROUNDUP

- Implementation
- Organisational structures, systems and processes
- Forecasting and budgeting
- Timescales and responsibilities
- Managerial, organisational and cultural shortcomings
- Monitoring and control mechanisms
- Performance metrics
- Contingency planning
- Internal marketing.

FURTHER READING

Business Link (2012) www.businesslink.gov.uk/bdotg [Accessed on 20 June 2012]

REFERENCES

Berry, L. and Parasuraman, A. (1961) *Marketing Services: Competing Through Quality*. New York, Free Press.

Bonoma, T (1984) Making your marketing strategies work. *Harvard Business Review*, 62 (2), pp69-76.

Dibb, S. *et al* (2006) *Marketing: Concepts and Strategies*. 5th edition. Boston, Houghton Mifflin.

Hollensen, S. (2006) *Marketing Planning, A Global Perspective*. London, McGraw Hill.

House, R.J. (1996) Path-Goal Theory of Leadership: Lessons, Legacy and a Reformulation. *Leadership Quarterly*, 7(3), pp323–352.

Kotler, J. *et al* (2008) *Principals of Marketing*. 5th Edition. London, Prentice-Hall.

Kouzes, J. and Posner, B. (2002) *The Leadership Challenge*. 3rd edition. San Francisco, Jossey-Bass.

McDonald, M. (2007) *Marketing Plans How to Prepare Them, How to Use Them*. 6th edition. Oxford, Butterworth Heinemann.

Piercy, N. (2002) *Market Led Strategic Change*. 3rd edition. Oxford, Butterworth Heinemann.

Schwartz, P. (1991) *The Art of the Long View*. New York, Doubleday.

Unilever (2011). www.unilever.co.uk [Accessed on 25 March 2012)

QUICK QUIZ

1   Why are marketing measures now considered to be an important aspect of a company's performance?
2   What factors are needed for formulating success within an appropriate strategy?
3   What are the barriers to the implementation of an internal marketing programme?
4   What is the benefit of using variance analysis?
5   List four financial measures.

Activity 12.1

This exercise will help to identify the range of different structures within an organisation. Use published company reports to gain the information and refer to the Chairman's statement for the year to understand how the organisation has performed within its organisational structure. Often the company report will refer to how the organisation adapted to the external environment and describe any changes that it made within the organisation.

Activity 12.2

The activity requires you to list the different measures, both hard and soft, to select a range of metrics that would cover the financial, social and environmental performance. You should be able to understand how each metric contributes to the overall performance of the organisation. When selecting performance measures the following should be considered:

- Is the measure suitable for the required purpose?
- Is the measure acceptable to key functions and stakeholders?
- Is it feasible, given resource constraints?
- Can the measure be used for benchmarking?

Financial measures will continue to be important because of reporting requirements. However, it is likely that marketing measures will become increasingly important for determining organisational performance and strategic, environmental and ethical health.

QUICK QUIZ ANSWERS

1   It is now becoming increasingly important for marketers to develop and use measures (metrics) that will measure the effectiveness of marketing alongside the traditional financial measures. These metrics of brand equity, customer satisfaction, loyalty and retention and share of voice have been gradually adopted.

2   The success factors include leadership, culture, structure, skills, systems, control measures and resources

3   A number of internal cultural barriers may exist that can inhibit the development of a market-led orientation. These are fear of change, lack of time, poor communication, lack of understanding and a cynical view of marketing.

4   Variance analysis is used as part of the budgetary control process to identify movements of *actual* performance away from *budget*.

5   Financial measure include:

   i.   Profitability and return measures
   ii.   Long-term solvency and stability measures
   iii.   Short-term solvency and liquidity measures
   iv.   Efficiency measures.

CHAPTER 13

Approaches to implementing the process of marketing planning

Introduction

This chapter looks at marketing planning and the implementation of marketing plans in a range of different contexts. Marketing planning is commonly associated with large FMCG (fast-moving consumer goods) organisations, with strong brands and large budgets. The process of marketing planning and the benefits from it are applicable to a wide range of organisations, whether domestic or international, large or small and for profit or not-for-profit.

Topic list

Marketing planning for FMCG	1
Marketing planning in B2B markets	2
Marketing planning for services	3
Marketing planning in SMEs	4
Marketing planning for not-for-profit organisations	5
The international and global dimension of marketing planning	6
Marketing planning for the virtual marketplace	7

4.3	Propose and justify approaches to implementing the process of marketing planning in different contextual settings
	■ Marketing planning for different stakeholder groups
	■ Planning in consumer and business-to-business markets
	■ Services marketing planning
	■ Issues of marketing planning in large and small organisations
	■ Internal marketing segmentation
	■ Marketing planning in non-profit organisations
	■ The international and global dimension of marketing planning
	■ Marketing planning in highly competitive markets
	■ Facilitating relationship-based marketing planning and customer retention
	■ Planning marketing in the virtual marketplace

1 Marketing planning for FMCG

▶ **Key term**

Fast moving consumer goods (FMCG): frequently purchased essential and non-essential products.

The FMCG market is particularly competitive. In the UK, a FMCG company developing a new brand will be selling not only in the domestic markets but also across Europe and much of the world. Therefore, there must be a more global vision in the development of new products and brand strategies.

Consistent quality will be important for success and the brand name can be critical. Considerable financial resources will be essential, since establishing a brand may take several years and require a heavy expenditure on product development as well as marketing communications.

FMCG packaged goods organisations must take a multilingual approach or a non-verbal approach or must be prepared for the high expenditure of packaging products in a number of different languages. The FMCG market is particularly competitive with major players fighting for market share, therefore appropriate products and brand strategies are required.

FMCG organisations selling packaged goods must consider whether they are going to use product names and brand names and whether they should be used independently or combined.

Where there is a relationship between product and brand names, marketing can develop an integrated approach with marketing communication messages developing associations between product and brand. Messages that are related to quality help to reduce price sensitivity and develop a competitive position.

Where there are successful products and strong brand associations, organisations will find it easier to introduce new products or extend existing product lines. However, there are also many benefits associated with keeping products and brands separate.

- It provides greater flexibility for packaging and promotions

- When an organisation is test marketing a new product, there is less risk of being damaged by the failure of that product

- The failure of a product will be less likely to damage the brand.

The success of any FMCG product is based on the success of a well planned and integrated marketing mix. The product and the brand play an important part, but we should not forget the other elements of the marketing mix and how they contribute to the success of FMCG organisations.

The Chartered Institute of Marketing

Cathedral City is Dairy Crest's leading brand of Cheddar cheese and the most popular brand in the UK. It is produced from a 25-year-old recipe at Davidstow in Cornwall. Dairy Crest bought the brand from Mendip Foods Ltd in 1995. According to Dairy Crest, Cathedral City was worth £16m in 1996 with a current market value of £192.3m and leads the category against Pilgrims Choice, Seriously Strong Cheddar and Wyke Farms, which collectively Dairy Crest claims is worth £186.5m.

In 2007, Dairy Crest announced an integrated marketing campaign designed to drive growth for Cathedral City, which it has called 'The Big Cheese Tease'. From 2009 Cathedral City Cheese is advertised with the line "Mature, yet Mellow". In 2010 Dairy Crest invested £10m in the re-launch of its Cathedral City cheese brand, supported by updated packaging and a new marketing campaign.

The TV ads were launched with a new strapline - "The Nation's Favourite" - which features on packaging but has not previously been heavily pushed in its advertising. The TV ad will be supported by posters, with an initial launch investment of £1.9m. Activity will include on-pack promotions, radio and press ads, instore, direct mail, social media and PR activity, plus a new website.

1.1 The marketing mix for FMCG organisations

1.1.1 Place

In terms of place, an organisation must consider whether its strategy will be:

- Intensive
- Selective
- Exclusive.

FMCG organisations will mostly adopt an intensive distribution strategy. This means that the products will be widely available and will be seen in many outlets. Chocolate bars are found in supermarkets, petrol stations, newsagents, leisure centres, DIY stores and garden centres, and at airports and railway stations. Ice cream, soft drinks and paper tissues are further examples of products where an intensive distribution strategy has been adopted.

Intensive distribution is based on the idea that market coverage is more important than the types of stores selling the product. The expansion of the range of goods sold by DIY stores and garden centres illustrates the intensive distribution strategies adopted by major confectionery, ice-cream and clothing companies.

1.1.2 Price

Pricing in the FMCG sector is a very difficult element to manage as a consequence of the intense competition in these markets. Major FMCG organisations are constantly striving to attain an increased market share. Price skimming is less likely to be found in these markets than others you will be studying. FMCG organisations are highly responsive to market demands and consumer needs in terms of price, but also need to take account of brand positioning.

1.1.3 Promotion

The most common communications used by FMCGs are advertising and sales promotion. High levels of expenditure are made by FMCG organisations on marketing communications each year.

In the FMCG markets, the main elements of the marketing communications mix are:

- Packaging
- Point of purchase
- Merchandising
- Direct mail (competitions and money-off coupons)
- Web sites

- Advertising
- Sponsorship
- Corporate identity
- Public relations
- Product placement
- Trade promotions.

FMCG organisations use a variety of tools to communicate and develop their brands with retailers, customers and other stakeholders. The aim is to introduce the organisation and their brands to their audiences and to engage with them, stimulating them to make a succession of purchases over the long term. These organisations use a variety of media and messages, some being informational and some emotional, to engage with their audiences.

This is a market characterised by price and non-price competition and constant promotional battles. Common sights are 'Buy one, get one free', 'Three for the price of two', 'Extra 10% free' and 'Extra reward points'.

A major development has been the introduction of rewards schemes operated by the major supermarkets to develop customer loyalty and repeat purchases.

ACTIVITY 13.1

Select a FMCG company of your choice. How does this company use marketing communications to engage with its audience? You will find some of the FMCG web sites have examples of previous award-winning campaigns.

2 Marketing planning in B2B markets

▶ **Key term**

Business-to-Business (B2B): a transaction that occurs between one company to another company and therefore does not include the consumer.

Marketing in B2B markets presents a range of different challenges to those to be found in B2C markets. It is therefore useful to understand the differences between these two market types (Table 13.1).

There are various terms used to describe B2B markets; a frequently used one is **organisational markets** and marketing within this context is often termed **industrial marketing.**

Table 13.1   Major differences between B2B and B2C markets

Characteristic	B2C	B2B
Nature of demand	Primary demand	Derived or joint demand
Nature of buyer	Purchase by individual/family	Group decision
Seller emphasis	Immediate satisfaction	Economic needs
Customer needs	Groups with similar needs	Each customer has different needs

The Chartered Institute of Marketing

Characteristic	B2C	B2B
Purchase motivation	Individual or family need	Multiple buying influences Support company operations
Time effects	Short-term relationship	Long-term relationship
Products	Lower technical detail	Technically sophisticated
Price decisions	Price generally fixed. Discounts important	Price determined before purchase. Terms important
Place decisions	Large numbers of small buyers	Limited number of large buyers
Customer service	Less important	Critical for success
Legal factors	Contracts only on major purchases	Contractual arrangements
Environmental arrangements	Impact on demand is direct	Sales impact both directly and indirectly through derived demand

An organisational market is where buyers within an organisation buy on behalf of the organisations they work for. Typical products handled in these organisational markets are plant and machinery, computers, raw materials, components and stationery.

Organisational markets include manufacturers, hospitals, hotels, wholesalers and retailers as well as government departments.

B2B or organisational buying behaviour is influenced by a range of factors:

- Finance available
- Purpose of the purchase
- The size and volume of purchase
- The buying situation
- The level of risk
- Delivery lead times
- Supply and demand
- Competitive offerings
- The time frame for decision making
- Organisational objectives
- Conditions of purchase
- Credit terms
- Contract terms
- Demand inelasticities
- Individual relationships
- Environmental factors
- Packaging
- PESTEL factors.

One of the most important factors the marketing planner must take into account is derived demand. The demand in B2B markets will be derived from the demand in consumer markets. Increases in demand for consumer products will be followed by demand for capital goods, to produce more consumer goods (plant and machinery for instance) and increased demand for materials and components. For example, demand for

electrical components such as microchips will be determined by demand for end-user products such as computers, mobile phones and MP3 players.

A downturn in economic activity, such as the 2009 recession, will have a big impact on organisational markets where demand in that market depends on the demand in other markets.

The objectives and motivations of buyers in organisational markets are going to be very different from typical buyers in consumer markets. Their function and objectives will revolve around the organisation and its customers.

These buyers are better informed, more technically minded, more rational and generally more demanding than typical consumer purchasers.

However, marketing planners should be aware that sometimes they have their own personal goals and agendas.

The organisational buyer will be most frequently interested in the overall value proposition, because they are responsible for obtaining the best deals for the organisation. The key considerations in relation to the value proposition are quality, delivery, service, the range of products available and price.

You should expect the buyer to demand significant amounts of information, technical specification and performance specification and require access to a range of staff for advice before they will make an (informed) decision. They will also have researched the competition and will be aware of other options, prices and alternatives.

2.1 The buying and decision-making process in organisational markets

The organisational markets have a decision-making unit or buying centre. The roles of a typical decision-making unit for the organisational markets is shown in Table 13.2.

Decisions can have far-reaching consequences, which will have implications for years to come. History and previous experience of the organisation will be a key influence on the choice of supplier in B2B markets.

Table 13.2 The decision-making unit (buying centre)

User	The person who actually uses the product
Influencer	Typical influencers will be users, R&D staff, accountants
Decider	Individual buyer, management team, tendering committee
Buyer	The person who will handle the sourcing, information seeking and negotiations
Gatekeeper	Usually secretarial and administrative staff who handle the flow of information through the organisation

There are two approaches to managing suppliers as indicated in Table 13.3.

The approach adopted tends to reflect a number of factors such as market structure and, in particular, the culture and objectives of the businesses involved.

Table 13.3   Approaches to managing suppliers

Adversarial	Collaborative
Multiple suppliers	Few suppliers
Regular price quotations requested	Long-term relationships
Little co-operation	Partnerships
Infrequent use of marketing communications	Frequent use of marketing communications
Ad hoc approach to operations	Integrated approach to operations
Quality	Quality designed in
Emphasis on lowest price	Emphasis on the value proposition

Market segmentation

Segmentation will help to serve to specific markets more thoroughly and is as important in organisational markets as consumer markets.

Segmentation criteria will include:

- Type of industry
- Size of company
- Type of product or service
- Type of buyer
- Location.

In order to target customers, it will be useful to know the people involved in the buying process and the nature of the benefits they are seeking.

The marketing mix for organisational markets

- **Product.** The type of product will be wide ranging and can involve complex technical specifications (eg customised machinery) or, alternatively, simple raw materials such as screws and nails. The nature of the product depends on what the customer wants, which will affect buying behaviour and aspects of how it is provided, such as service – which we will explore later.

- **Place.** There is likely to be a wide distributor network similar to the wholesaler-to-retailer network found in consumer markets. These need to be incentivised and supported.

- **Price.** Pricing will be based on a variety of methods and will be subject to negotiations and sometimes tenders. Reliability of supply is a key component and, therefore, switching of suppliers is less likely than in consumer markets.

- **Promotion.** Promotion in B2B markets is very different to promoting consumer products; whilst advertising will be necessary, more emphasis will be placed on direct marketing and personal selling, backed up with sales literature.

3 Marketing planning for services

There are major differences between the marketing of goods and the marketing of services. However, there is one common factor; consumers purchase goods and services for the benefits that each provides.

Marketing planners are faced with a variety of challenges relating to the characteristics of services, the gap between expectations and what is delivered, and the different views on what constitutes a quality service.

The UK and European service sector is growing rapidly. In the UK, over two-thirds of the workforce is engaged in the tertiary sector which provides services to its consumers in a wide range of activities such as utilities, education and so on. An economic slow down, such as the current recession, will slow the growth of services but, in the long term, the sector is expected to grow further.

One of the main reasons for the growth of the services sector is the changing lifestyles of the population. Economic growth has created demand for more services and consumers spend more on financial services, travel and leisure services than ever before. People may enjoy a standard of living greater than previous generations, but they are time poor. Therefore, more people are buying services such as takeaway meals, landscape gardening, home maintenance and cleaning in order to provide quality time with their families. Changes in society have led to changes in lifestyles and new services have emerged to fulfil all sorts of new needs.

In order to successfully deliver any form of service, it is important to understand what implementation means in practice.

An intangible product involving a deed, a performance or an effort that cannot be physically possessed.
Dibb *et al.* (2006)

Services are usually divided into two main sectors, consumer services and business services, as shown in Table 13.4.

Table 13.4   Consumer and business services

Consumer services	Financial services
	Professional services
	Personal services, eg hairdressing
	Education
	Health
	Leisure
	Tourism
Business services	Accountancy
	Advertising
	Market research
	Banking
	Consultancy services
	Transport
	Recruitment services

Consumer services can be provided by both not-for-profit organisations (health, education, charities and the government) and by profit-making organisations (insurance, banking, entertainment and hairdressing).

The Chartered Institute of Marketing

3.1 Services characteristics

Whether customers buy goods or services, they purchase for the benefits each provides. However, there are differences between goods and services which the marketing planner must be aware of. Services have five main characteristics:

- **Intangibility**
- **Inseparability of production and consumption**
- **Perishability**
- **Heterogeneity**
- **Lack of ownership.**

Let us examine each of these characteristics in turn.

3.1.1 Intangibility

Services are intangible because there is no physical product. There is no physical substance, nothing to see, touch, taste or smell before purchase.

The major challenge for a service provider is to ensure that the service is analysed and the extent of the intangible elements assessed. Tangible elements can then be added to aid the understanding and expectations of the customer. Insurance organisations offer insurance; therefore, they are covering potential losses, providing security and peace of mind. To overcome the intangibility of this service, they provide quality documentation.

Services are provided on one occasion only. The service provided at the supermarket check out, at the bank or by a driving instructor will never be delivered in exactly the same way twice.

3.1.2 Inseparability

An important distinction exists between products bought and used many times by a customer and services which are consumed as they are purchased. For instance: having a haircut means it is not possible for anyone else to have the same haircut and stylist at the same time.

Inseparability has important implications for the service provider. The involvement of the customer in the production and the delivery service means that the service provider must take great care in what is being provided.

3.1.3 Perishability

Services are perishable because they are produced and consumed at the same time. Goods can be produced and stored to be used later or sold later. Services cannot be stored and consumed at a later date.

For example, if you consider an aircraft flight, if you do not take up your seat and it is not booked by anyone else, it cannot be used again. That flight has gone for ever.

Perishability and fluctuations in demand can affect the sales revenue and profitability of organisations. The airline seat not taken, the hotel room empty, the dental appointment not kept–all represent time and revenue lost.

Organisations have responded to this problem in different ways. In health care, missed dental appointments may be charged for. Last-minute discount deals for holidays and hotel rooms have become available as more organisations attempt to get some revenue rather than none in these circumstances.

3.1.4 Heterogeneity

Sometimes referred to as variability, heterogeneity means that the service is different. The service can be provided several thousand times, but each time there will be variances in the service delivery. It is highly unlikely customers will ever receive exactly the same service delivery and quality twice. A service cannot be produced, quality assured and boxed, like products. It is extremely difficult to determine the quality and level of service because services are produced as they are consumed.

This is a major challenge in the marketing of business services. There is no guarantee the service will be as marketed, because of the variability of human nature and behaviour – or simply human error.

3.1.5 Lack of ownership

Services do not result in the transfer of ownership. When we use the services of a rail company, we are transported from one place to another but no transfer of ownership takes place. On arriving at our destination, the only evidence of the service may be part of our ticket. This lack of ownership is a characteristic of many services such as banking, insurance, air travel and medical care. However, retailing is a service and in this case, ownership of tangible goods is transferred. The lack of ownership and the intangible nature of services may lessen the perceived value of a service. The provision of symbolic tangible items are often provided to overcome the problem. Examples would be theatre programmes and quality folders for insurance policies.

According to Mudie and Cottam (1999), service organisations need to understand and recognise the importance of the first law of services, which states:

Satisfaction = Perception – Expectation

In services marketing, we need to understand the behaviour and perceptions before and after the event. This is essential to ascertain whether the service exceeds, equals or fails to meet expectations. However, as individual perceptions and interpretations will differ, the result of using the above formula can be quite subjective. Yet, measuring customer perceptions is essential for adopting the correct marketing mix and pursuing continuous improvement in services.

3.2 The service marketing mix

The marketer has the traditional elements of the marketing mix, referred to as the 4Ps, available. These are product, price, place and promotion. To these we can add a further 3Ps, physical evidence, people and processes. It is these last three elements of the services marketing mix that gives the opportunity to establish a high-quality service.

3.2.1 Product

The lack of tangibility poses a challenge to the marketing planner. Think benefits; stress the psychological rather than the physical aspects.

3.2.2 Price

Price might be set according to demand, for example, rail and electricity prices reflect differences in demand and varying off peak charges are set.

The price charged for a service will frequently be based around the service value proposition, with some influence from the proportion of intangibility and market forces.

The marketing planner should remember that price will provide a perception of quality.

3.2.3 Place

Physical evidence can play an important part in the case of place. Restaurants, leisure facilities and clubs are examples where physical evidence plays a major part.

Services might deliver to the customer, e.g. Ocado, the home delivery service of grocery retailers Waitrose.

The element of place has changed rapidly with the growth of the Internet with many services being of a virtual nature. Here, the physical evidence will be provided by the quality of the customer experience in the use of the website.

The Chartered Institute of Marketing

3.2.4 Promotion

The greater the level of intangibility, the more difficult it is to promote.

Positioning, with its relationship with core values will need to be carefully considered when planning the promotional activities.

'Don't promise what you cannot deliver'

3.2.5 Physical evidence – the physical environment

The physical evidence element of the marketing mix relates to the place where the services are prepared and/or delivered. In the example of a restaurant service, the actual restaurant where the meal is both delivered and consumed will be the physical environment.

When establishing the marketing mix for services, the physical environment will play a major role in establishing the quality perception of the service and the organisation.

The physical environment can be portrayed through staff uniforms, interior design and relaxing surroundings. Well-known brands such as Harvester and David Lloyd Leisure have made significant investment in high-quality surroundings to convey consistency and guaranteed service in support of the brand.

3.2.6 People

One of the big challenges in planning the service marketing mix is the element of human nature. The people element is seen as critical to the delivery of a quality service with good customer care.

Managing the people element of the marketing mix requires strong interpersonal skills, leadership, team management, training and an effective internal marketing programme. The role of staff, their contribution and value to the service process needs to be communicated. The people aspect of the mix should include the following:

- Professional recruitment – Search for attitude, then train for skills
- Investing in staff and training – Organisational training as well as product/service knowledge
- Empowerment of staff – Staff to make a full contribution
- Internal marketing – Communications with, and motivating, staff
- Authority to make decisions – Ability to make fast decisions related to service delivery.

3.2.7 Process

Process is about developing ways of delivering the service that will add value to the customer experience. It is important for organisations to develop systems that allow service providers to provide a seamless passage through the customer service experience.

Processes will be essential to the customer experience, but they should be discrete or invisible. The customer requires the whole experience to be a positive one. The processes should be managed with the customers in mind. What are their expectations, their needs and wants? Processes should be designed to deliver all elements of the service to the customer with the minimum of trouble or delay.

The process of booking a holiday or a flight may involve a considerable number of stages from advice, through to the booking, payment and finally to receipt of tickets. Every step must be considered and viewed from the customer experience.

Select a service organisation of your choice. Identify and illustrate the importance of each of the extended mix elements, (physical evidence, people and processes) in the effective delivery of its services to its customers.

3.3 Key components of designing a services mix

In addition to the importance of the 7Ps of the services marketing mix, we should consider the design elements of the service mix.

Mudie and Cottam (1999) suggested service design principles should be considered, which are shown in Table 13.5.

Table 13.5   Principles of service design

Customer contact	How much contact is there between organisation and customer during service?
Service mix	How many service offerings will there be? What is the service portfolio?
Location	Should the service go to the customer or the customer to the service?
Design	Design extend to interior design, uniforms, logos and literature
Technology	What technology is required to deliver the service? Is it reliable? What will be the customer experience?
Employees	Effective delivery will depend on the right employees, training, culture and internal marketing supported by adequate resources
Structure	The structure will influence the organisational culture and establishes the chain of command and the communication channels
Information	A good MIS system is essential for maintaining the appropriate levels of information to support service delivery. A good MKIS system will be essential to understanding customer expectations
Demand	Demand will affect the standards of delivery, therefore plan for peaks (add contingency)
Procedures	Analyse the procedures, understand what procedures are essential for excellence in service delivery
Control	Continuous improvement will only be achieved through monitoring and control and learning

People, physical evidence and processes are critical to the delivery of exceptional service quality.

It will always be difficult for a service organisation to deliver 100% quality. However, service organisations should always consider:

- Customers' expectations
- Service specifications
- Employee performance
- Managing customer service expectations.

The SERVQUAL (Parasuraman *et al.*, 1985) model can be used to measure quality within the service sector. It looks at five key factors:

- **Reliability** – The ability to perform the service dependably and accurately
- **Responsiveness** – Response to customers and prompt service
- **Assurance** – Knowledge and courtesy of employees, ability to inspire trust and confidence
- **Empathy** – Caring, individual attention to customers
- **Tangibles** – Physical facilities, quality of equipment, appearance of personnel.

SERVQUAL measures the gap between customer and management perceptions of quality.

The gaps are as follows:

Gap 1 – Consumers' expectations compared to managers' perceptions of consumer expectations

Gap 2 – Managers' perceptions of consumers' expectations compared to service quality specifications actually set

Gap 3 – Service quality specifications compared to actual service delivery

Gap 4 – Actual service delivery compared to external communications about the service

Gap 5 – Resources

Service quality is based on the three key service elements of the marketing mix: people, physical evidence and processes. Analysing the performance in these key areas, using SERVQUAL, will help the organisation to understand their position from a customer perspective and a competitive perspective. Quality can be used as a useful tool for competitive advantage.

Developing a quality culture will require the organisation to look at the following key areas within an organisation.

- Leadership
- Values
- Rewards
- Empowerment of employees
- Development of a learning organisation.

To be able to continuously improve the level of service offered, monitoring and evaluation processes could be used, some of which are shown in Table 13.6.

Table 13.6   Methods of monitoring customer service

Customer satisfaction surveys	Performance appraisals
Mystery shopper survey	Employee discussions
Evaluation of complaints	Observation of customers

4 Marketing planning in SMEs

4.1 What is an SME?

In 1996, the European Commission adopted the definitions of SMEs, which are shown in Table 13.7.

Table 13.7   Definitions of SMEs

	Micro-enterprise	Small	Medium-sized
Number of employees (max)	10	50	250
Turnover (million euros) (max)	n/a	7	40
Balance sheet total (million euros) (max)	n/a	5	27

The term 'small and medium enterprises' covers a wide range of businesses from sole trader enterprises through to businesses with sales of several million.

It is widely accepted that SMEs have different characteristics from larger companies. Schollhammer and Kuriloff (1979) summarised these as:

- Scope of operations
- Scale of operations
- Ownership
- Independence
- Management style.

Entrepreneurial characteristics and activities impact on marketing activities in SMEs. This entrepreneurial marketing has a distinctive marketing style, which is often characterised as shown in Table 13.8.

Table 13.8   Characteristics of entrepreneurial marketing

The stage of development of the firm	Young firms will have simple marketing whereas the mature SME may have quite sophisticated marketing
Size of the firm	The stage of development, the size of the firm and limited resources will restrict marketing activity
Informal	SMEs do not have formal structures or communication structures
Simplistic and erratic	The influence of the entrepreneur, the size and lack of resources means *ad hoc* marketing takes place
Reactive	Reactive rather than proactive. Marketing tends to react to competitors' activity
Opportunistic	SME advantage is ability to react quickly to new opportunities, innovations and seize opportunities as they occur
Short term	SMEs decision making is mostly short term

The Chartered
Institute of Marketing

These characteristics, once recognised and understood, should be exploited in the preparation of marketing plans.

A business plan is essential for businesses applying for loans and grants or seeking outside investors; this is the only time many SMEs engage in planning activities. Many entrepreneurs object to preparing plans because they feel their time is better spent actively pursuing their business interests. The marketing plan is an integral part of any business plan. Marketing planning is basically a logical sequence of activities which lead to the setting of marketing objectives and the formulation of plans for achieving them. In major companies, there is usually a systemised management process followed in the preparation of plans, but in SMEs the process is quite often informal.

- Identifying things the business was not aware of
- Identifying the strengths and weaknesses of the business
- Identifying opportunities and threats
- Identifying critical success factors
- Setting out clear objectives.

In many small businesses, the failure to research the market and prepare business and marketing plans results in a failure to achieve sales targets, poor profitability and cash flow problems. The business failure rate among SMEs is high, with many failing in the first five years. A real understanding of the market and an effective marketing strategy is essential for the survival and growth of SMEs.

It is advisable for both the business plan and the marketing plan to be monitored on regular basis to establish whether targets and objectives are being achieved and to take corrective action if not.

SMEs, however, are often constrained in their marketing by limitations of financial resources and also the skills of marketing. Yet it is important, whenever possible, to see expenditure on planning marketing as an *investment* in the future of the business rather than a *cost*.

4.2 The marketing mix for SMEs

4.2.1 Place

Many small and medium-sized manufacturing businesses concentrate on design and manufacture. Therefore, they rely on distributors to promote and sell products. These distributors will need to be incentivised to motivate them to work effectively for the businesses.

4.2.2 Price

These markets are often sensitive to price changes. Price wars and discounting can be a threat to SMEs, particularly those which do not have substantial financial resources. Attention to the breakeven point is essential to those businesses and close attention to profit margins is critical. Where discounts are necessary, these should be for regular customers or to encourage larger orders.

4.2.3 Promotion

Sales promotion in SMEs involves generating an awareness of the company and its products. Close communication with customers and potential customers is essential. Limited budgets will require close attention to the effectiveness of promotions.

Typical forms of promotion used by SMEs are:

- Yellow pages
- Direct marketing
- Internet
- Exhibitions
- Magazines

- Local radio
- Direct selling.

5 Marketing planning for not-for-profit organisations

▶ **Key term**

Not-for-profit organisation: An organisation whose prime goal is non-economic. However, it may undertake profit-making activities in pursuit of that prime goal.

The major difference between profit-making and non-profit-making organisations is the aims and objectives they pursue. The objective of commercial profit-making organisations is to maximise the profits and therefore the wealth of the owners or shareholders. Not-for-profit organisations, like charities, have aims and objectives such as... 'To serve the needs of clients'.

Marketing planning is as important to charities and other not-for-profit organisations as it is to major commercial ventures. The board or trustees of a charity or other not-for-profit organisation is composed of professionals who are responsible for the strategy and the effectiveness of the organisation in meeting its prime goals. The board will set the objectives, develop strategy, utilise the resources, allocate funds and oversee any commercial profit-making activities the charity may develop.

There are many different sources of funds for not-for-profit organisations. Government grants, lottery funds, trust funds, donations and corporate funds from major companies are among the most usual.

THE REAL WORLD

The British Red Cross helps those left in need by major emergencies of all types, aims to help build more resilient communities, provides essential health and social care to those most vulnerable to everyday crisis and will support the International Red Cross and Red Crescent Movement to meet growing humanitarian needs around the world.

The aim of the British Red Cross is to prepare the organisation for the challenges of the future through making volunteering and working for us the best experience possible, ensuring key people and groups know about our work, making sure our organisation operates as effectively as it can and continues to raise the essential funds we need for our work.

The marketing plan will support a number of activities including emergency response and recovery, helping communities to prepare for and withstand disasters, providing support health and social care activity, and maximising our net income as cost-effectively as possible.

(Red Cross, 2012)

The organisations may also receive the profits from profit-making activities such as charity shops.

Charities

The objectives of charities will reflect the constitution of the charity, with many having the objective of 'improving lives'. Objectives are likely to include creating awareness, generation of funds, whereas another might be to generate those funds at a lower cost of administration.

The strategy should include the charity considering how it can retain some form of competitive advantage over other similar organisations. This should be considered not only in terms of funds raised, but also in terms of attracting support from volunteers.

Marketing segmentation and targeting

Marketing segmentation consists of closely targeting individuals who are able to support the charity in various ways.

The Chartered Institute of Marketing

The key target audiences are:

- **Donors** – Those who provide funds or other support
- **Clients** – Those who are the users of the charitable donations
- **Volunteers** – Those who give time and effort to support the charity.

Charity marketing usually has to offer some benefit, hence the flag days – where the donor gets a flag – as physical evidence of the support given by the donation.

The marketing mix

- **Product**

  This is the benefit the charity provides to donors, which may be just a feeling of well-being.

- **Place**

  Many charities run shops which raise significant funds.

- **Promotion**

  Public relations, sponsorship and promotions play a significant part. There is an increasing use of direct marketing to gain support and donations.

- **Price**

  The amount of money generated and the cost of the programme.

- **People**

  The interaction with the public is very important as it provides an extremely important income stream for a charity.

- **Physical evidence**

  Quality literature setting out how the money has been used.

- **Process**

  Making it easy to donate money. Solicitors supporting the charity will offer a free will service to those willing to donate from their will.

Implementation and control

Controls will be based around the services mix to ensure quality of services are maintained. There also must be financial controls monitoring the funds generated and the distribution of these to potential beneficiaries.

Charities are not the only form of not-for-profit organisation. The following are classified similarly, due to their goals being essentially non-profit-making, although they may be seeking commercial outcomes from their operation.

- Colleges and universities
- Hospitals
- Medical practices
- Social organisations.

Another group of important not-for-profit marketing organisations are public bodies such as government departments, agencies and local authorities. In the UK, these have become increasingly more goal-oriented and have used marketing plans to achieve this. Some good examples include campaigns to promote healthy living, through reducing smoking and alcohol consumption, increasing physical exercise and encouraging better diets.

6 The international and global dimension of marketing planning

6.1 Introduction

Although the key principles of domestic marketing and international marketing remain the same, there are some factors that need to be taken into account when undertaking marketing planning in an international context, compared with marketing in a single country situation (Table 13.9).

Table 13.9   Differences between domestic and international marketing

Domestic marketing	International marketing
Single dominant language	Many languages
Dominant culture	Multi-culture
Market research quite straightforward	Market research more complex
Relatively stable environment	Relatively unstable environment
Single currency	Exchange rate risks
Low political risk	Political risk
Business conventions clear	Business conventions very diverse

Given the more complex nature of international marketing, why do organisations take the decision to move into new country markets?

- Intensity of the competition – There may be less competition overseas
- A saturated domestic market – Exploring market growth and development elsewhere
- Excess capacity – Excess capacity may be available to produce goods for other markets
- Product life cycle differences – Opportunities for products overseas at different stages of life cycle
- Financial reasons – Possible investment incentives not available for home market
- Organisational issues – Mergers and acquisitions may bring opportunities overseas
- Geographical diversification – To avoid intense competition, organisations may expand into new areas to diversify risk

The decision to exploit international marketing opportunities will be a strategic one.

There are various levels of international marketing:

- **Domestic/regional marketing** – An example would be trading with the regional market of Europe.
- **Export marketing** – Where an organisation trades in goods and services across national boundaries. There are two types, direct and indirect.
  - Direct exporting – Where goods and services are sold direct to customers in overseas market.
  - Indirect – Where with limited resources the organisation uses various market entry methods such as agents or an export house.

- **International marketing** – Operating in a range of different markets with significant differences between markets. The controllable variables such as distribution networks, advertising and costs will also vary.
- **Global marketing management** – A more complex international operation. An integrated global effort, taking advantage of opportunities, exchange rates, different tax rates and labour rates.

THE REAL WORLD

Diesel S.p.A. is an Italian design company. It is best known for luxury, prêt-à-porter clothing aimed at the young adult market. The company is owned by its founder Renzo Rosso, and is based in the former Laverda building area in Breganze, northern Italy. Rosso said that they learnt marketing from the US, creativity from Italy and systems from Germany.

In 2001 there was a revival to focus on an everyday garment with gender differences towards jeans with fashion and styling considerations for female customers and brand importance for males. It is a very crowded market with Levis as the brand leader and Diesel with 5% of the market. Own/private label accounts for 17% of the market. As an Italian brand it has a youthful appeal with innovative designs and is seen as stylish and edgy. But it has international competitive pressure to constantly connect with global fashion trends.

Porter's 5 forces model can be used to assess the internal factors of the micro-environment that influence the affairs of Diesel.

- Threat of new entrants: As the designer jean market is set to grow, Diesel needs to be aware of potential new international competition entering the marketplace.
- Threat of substitutes: Diesel has attracted a host of copies into the marketplace that could impact on its current dominant marketplace position.
- Power of suppliers: As Diesel is in 5th place (brand share by value) according to Mintel, it is important to maintain and develop mutually beneficial relationships with its suppliers to protect its position.
- Power of customers: It is clear that women are more particular about their style and fashion status of the jeans they purchase, which could mean that they are more fickle when it comes to purchasing jeans. Diesel needs to make sure its strategy for an increase in international market share takes this concern into account and promotes brand loyalty.
- Competitor rivalry: As the market for jeans is becoming increasingly fragmented and segmented, a variety of brands is able to address different consumer groups. Diesel needs to ensure that the global growth strategy focuses on a particular niche area in each of the fashion markets it serves.

When considering the external macro-environment that can influence Diesel, it is useful to refer to the PESTEL model.

- Political factors: These are likely to include trade agreements (crucial as Diesel relies heavily on export), minimum wage rates that impact on costs and EU directives that affect trading climate.
- Economic factors: These include the state of the global economy, income levels–particularly disposable income, as Diesel is a luxury fashion brand.
- Social factors: These are crucial as consumers can modify or change their opinion of a brand as fashions alter over time. Diesel will need to understand the different social factors from different countries and continents.
- Technological factors: This will include developments in manufacturing and distribution technology as well as information communication technologies and the use of the internet. Diesel's web site and 'Club Diesel' are vital parts of the brand's overall strategy and help to differentiate it from the competition.
- Legal factors: It is crucial to monitor the changes in the law within the different countries where Diesel operates. This will include contracts of supply, and sale of goods and services.
- Environmental factors: These have become more important as customers become more environmentally aware and expect global brands to behave in a socially responsible manner. As Diesel is a lifestyle brand its behaviour is particularly important.

6.2 Market entry strategies

Once the decision has been made to enter international markets, various ways of achieving this can be adopted.

- **Agents**

  Agents are effectively overseas sales personnel, who operate on behalf of different client organisations. Agents normally work on a retainer with additional commission or on commission only.

- **Licensing**

  Licensing is based on a contract that permits another party to produce products or services. This method of market entry requires low levels of investment.

  Advantages are reduced market entry costs but contact may commit the organisation to long-term relationship.

- **Franchising**

  This is a very common method of market entry. Franchising requires franchisees to provide capital which makes this mode of entry cost-effective for the franchisor. There are many examples of successful franchising, McDonald's, Pizza Hut and The Body Shop.

- **Acquisitions**

  Gaining market entry through the acquisition of an organisation in the country in which you want to trade. This is a fast mode of entry because an established business is acquired. However, this mode of entry is high risk, requiring very careful research and due diligence.

- **Wholly-owned subsidiary**

  One of the most expensive modes of entry, which requires substantial amounts of capital, is to set-up the organisation overseas.

- **Joint ventures (JV)**

  Instead of setting up a wholly-owned subsidiary, a joint venture can be established. The venture may be based on technological know-how, access to distribution network or for a competitive reason. There are many advantages including shared market research, shared product development, reduced capital and possibly less political risk. However, there may be conflict and trust, shared aims and objectives and strategies are essential.

- **Barriers to entry**

  Sometimes difficulties exist that hinder the ability of a business to expand internationally.

  Barker and Kaynak (1992) identified the following as potential barriers to entering new international markets:

  - Trade barriers
  - Language barriers
  - Lack of competitive products
  - Transportation difficulties
  - Slow payment by buyers
  - Red tape (bureaucracy)

The more informed the organisation, the clearer the country profile, the easier it will be to identify the best method for the organisation.

6.3 The implications for international marketing plans

6.3.1 Product

New products for international markets will need to go through the same review process used in the product development process for domestic markets. Screening should consider the following factors as outlined in Table 13.10.

Organisations will also need to consider the issue of branding. Will the brand be meaningful in the country they wish to operate in?

Table 13.10   Screening factors for international new product

Customer needs and wants	Customer expectations
Standardised or adaptation	International (and local) safety standards
Fit with product portfolio	Capability of potential buyers to purchase
Patent and trade mark agreements	Technology demands
Technical support	After-sales support

6.3.2 Pricing

The pricing of products is a greater challenge than for domestic markets. Consideration must be given to the economic indicators and economic situation of the host country. Major influences will be local legislation, tariffs, tax rates, currency movements as well as the costs of manufacture and distribution. Credit terms, method of payment and speed of payment will be critical issues to consider when setting prices.

Price sensitivity will vary from country to country and pricing policy will be critical to obtaining and sustaining competitive positioning and market share. A significant implication will be that cultural diversity will have a large influence on the perceived value proposition.

6.3.3 Place

There are many logistical challenges with distribution. The selection of an appropriate market entry strategy will influence the way in which distribution can be effectively managed.

Management of channel members will require serious consideration.

The following points should be borne in mind:

- Set-up costs of the channel and members
- Level of investment required
- Level of incentive
- Synergy with local/domestic channels
- Management and control of the overall process.

The growth of the internet is changing the dynamics of distribution and many organisations now deal on a more direct basis with customers overseas via the internet, leading to a reduced role for distributors.

6.3.4 Promotional mix

This area is a challenging and complex area for the marketing planner. The characteristics and cultural differences will differ between countries and the factors influencing international promotion must be considered.

Internationalisation involves selling products across borders and trade increases at an international level. Globalisation is when there is not only an increase in the volume and value of goods exchanged internationally, but where there is:

- Trans-national segments of consumers emerging
- Global brands are promoted worldwide
- Increased interdependence of international business.

Table 13.11   Factors influencing international promotion

Culture	Tolerance of advertising
Language	Advertising methods
Product range	Available advertising media
Product image	Use of agencies
Packaging	Literacy levels
Literature	Relationships
Corporate identity	Marketing ethics

The key success factor in achieving any marketing strategy, including globalisation, is to ensure that the organisation keeps a constant watch on the global marketing environment. Organisations should monitor changes and identify strengths, weaknesses, opportunities and threats.

6.4 Standardisation versus adaptation

Globalisation is often characterised by the standardisation of the marketing mix. Alternatively marketers may plan to adapt the marketing effort to local market conditions. Standardisation is cost-effective and a very efficient approach, but it may not be the most competitive.

An organisation seeking to globalise would need to consider standardising some or all of the following elements of its marketing:

- Market access
- Products
- Promotion
- Distribution
- Communications
- Services
- Technology
- Approach to competition.

The marketing planner needs to remember that moving towards a standardised marketing mix will not guarantee success across all markets.

Adaptation means that part or even the whole of the marketing mix has to be changed to meet the changing needs of different countries.

An adaptation of the *product* involves many companies changing their products to meet local needs and conditions, and organisations will either adapt or change the promotional strategies. The names of products can cause conflict and misunderstanding, so may need to be changed.

The Chartered Institute of Marketing

Price can be used to position the product accordingly in the market to take account of its perceived value that may be delivered through the brand. Pricing must however take account of local factors such as the costs of production, exchange rates, disposable income, taxes amongst other things. Similarly *place* may change depending on the factors that affect distribution such as market accessibility and the structure of retailing.

The ultimate decision whether to standardise or to adapt products can only be based upon knowledge and a wide range of information about each foreign market, its characteristics, cultures and channels.

7 Marketing planning for the virtual marketplace

> ▶ **Key term**
>
> **Virtual marketplace:** web-based marketplace.

The internet has changed the way we do business. It is no longer necessary to have face-to-face contact with a sales person or supplier. The 'pure' internet companies have created strong online brand recognition, provided good customer service and are open 24 hours a day, 7 days a week and 365 days per year. The ability to customise service allows these organisations to develop a relationship with their customers. The internet has made substantial inroads into both the B2C and B2B markets and online business is forecast to be the biggest growth area of the next decade. Traditional companies, often referred to as bricks and mortar company, have been pressurised to respond to the competitive threat from both 'pure' e-businesses and the traditional companies that have added e-business activities.

Key trends in the virtual marketing environment are:

- Convergence of technologies
- Development of digital technologies
- Consumer time poverty
- Consumers looking to take control.

Marketing via the internet has increased dramatically over the last 15 years. Marketing planners need to consider how best to incorporate this medium into their planning.

The internet can be used in many ways to support marketing activities:

- Online sales – Online catalogues and purchases

- Promotion – Advertising banners on web sites

- Customer service – Provision of customer information via the internet

- Public relations – Channel for news

- Marketing research – Collection of detailed information from web sites for customer profiling, which can be added to databases.

Evans and Wurster (2000) identified three bases of competitive advantage:

- **Reach** – Referring to access and connection
- **Richness** – Referring to detail and depth of information to customers
- **Affiliation** – Referring to whose interests the business represents.

These bases need to be considered when planning. Technology is converging and more organisations are using digital marketing to reach and retain customers, ie to attract customers initially and build and manage relationships with them.

Mobile marketing is also growing in its usage with digital information, such as videos, text messages and voice messages sent to mobiles.

Companies can benefit from embracing blogging and utilising it as a marketing tool. A blog on a company web site enables a wide audience to be reached.

According to Wright (2006), company blogging is about three things:

- **Information** – Telling your customers what you are doing and finding out what they think
- **Relationships** – Building a solid base of positive experiences with customers
- **Knowledge management** – Obtaining and communicating knowledge within the organisation to the right people at the right time.

Blogging enables a company to obtain valuable information about the types of customers that are buying products and services. Instant qualitative information about customers and ideas to improve products and services can be obtained without the expense associated with market research.

Marketing planning in virtual environments needs to take account of the way that consumer behaviour is changing with regard to new information and communications technologies and how they are being used to achieve a competitive advantage.

> ▶ **Assessment tip**
>
> When considering the approaches to implementing the process of marketing planning it is vital that the background knowledge is understood, it can be evaluated and that there are plenty of examples to demonstrate application.

Summary

Marketing planning, implementation and control are intrinsically linked. Whether marketing planning is in a FMCG, B2B, services, SME or not-for-profit context, the fundamentals remain the same. Similarly, the principles of marketing planning apply equally in international marketing as they do in domestic markets. However, a range of factors affect marketing planning in different settings and marketing mangers need to be aware of these when developing and implementing plans in different contexts.

The Chartered Institute of Marketing

CHAPTER ROUNDUP

- Marketing planning for FMCG
- Marketing planning in B2B markets
- Marketing planning for services
- Marketing planning in SMEs
- Marketing planning for not-for-profit
- The international and global dimension of marketing planning
- Marketing planning for the virtual marketplace.

FURTHER READING

De Pelsmacker, P. *et al.* (2010) *Marketing Communications: a European perspective*. 4th Edition. Harlow, Prentice Hall.

REFERENCES

Dibb, S. *et al.* (2006) *Marketing: Concepts and Strategies*. 5th edition. Boston, Houghton Mifflin.

Evans, P.B. and Wurster, T.S. (2000) *Blown to Bits: How the New Economics of Information Transforms Strategy*. Boston, Harvard Business School Press.

Mudie, P. and Cottam, A. (1999) *The Management and Marketing of Services*. 2nd edition. Oxford, Butterworth-Heinemann.

Parasuraman, A., *et al.* (1985) A Conceptual Model of Service Quality and Its Implications for Future Research. *Journal of Marketing*, 49(4), pp41–50.

Red Cross (2012) www.redcross.org.uk [Accessed on 20 June 2012]

Schollhammer, H. and Kuriloff, A. (1979) *Entrepreneurship and Small Business Management*. New York, John Wiley.

Wright, J. (2006) *Blog Marketing: The Revolutionary New Way to Increase Sales, Growth and Profits*. New York, McGraw Hill.

QUICK QUIZ

1   Distinguish between the key characteristics of B2B and B2C markets and how this influences differences in marketing planning.

2   What are the unique characteristics of services? How do these translate into differences in marketing activity in practice between services and physical goods?

3   For international markets, list the various market entry strategies.

4   How would an organisation need to consider price when seeking to globalise their activities?

5   How can the internet can be used to support marketing activities?

Activity 13.1

For a FMCG company the most common communications used by companies are advertising and sales promotion. High levels of expenditure are made by FMCG organisations on marketing communications each year and include a variety of elements from the marketing communications mix to communicate to their audience. Major FMCG organisation such as Proctor and Gamble, Unilever and Cadbury have developed thought-provoking and entertaining television advertisements to engage with their audience. In December 2008, Unilever ran an advertisement for PG tips, the monkey's Christmas speech. Cadbury ran a campaign in 2007 with a gorilla playing the drums which became a very successful viral campaign.

Activity 13.2

For your chosen service organisation you should show how the services marketing mix establishes a high-quality service. Typical examples are a clean and fresh physical environment (evidence), well-informed and trained staff (people) and easy navigation in the interaction with the customer (process).

QUICK QUIZ ANSWERS

1   B2C characteristics are driven by primary demand, purchases by individuals who can be grouped together and require immediate satisfaction. B2B have derived demand, based on group decisions and economic need, and where each customer has a different set of needs.

2   The unique characteristics of services are intangibility, inseparability of production and consumption, perishability, heterogeneity and lack of ownership. The further 3Ps of physical evidence, people and processes give the opportunity to establish a high-quality service.

3   They are agents, licensing, franchising, acquisitions, wholly-owned subsidiary and joint ventures

4   Price can be used to position the product accordingly in the market to take account of its perceived value that may be delivered through the brand. Pricing must however take account of local factors such as the costs of production, exchange rates, disposable income and taxes.

5   The internet can be used through:

  ■   Online sales – Online catalogues and purchases

  ■   Promotion – Advertising banners on web sites

  ■   Customer service – Provision of customer information via the internet

  ■   Public relations – Channel for news

  ■   Marketing research – Collection of detailed information from web sites for customer profiling which can be added to databases.

Section 4:

Senior examiner's comments

On completion of Section 4, students should have a detailed knowledge and understanding of:

- The dimensions of marketing planning implementation including, structures, systems, responsibilities, budgets, timescales and monitoring and control procedures

- The barriers to implementing marketing planning and plans

- The ways in which ineffective marketing planning may be addressed

- The range of contextual marketing planning situations that face different organisations in practice

- The parameters of different marketing planning contexts that need to be taken account of when shaping detailed marketing plans to achieve organisational marketing objectives.

Candidates must be able to apply their understanding of implementation of marketing planning to different business and organisational settings. To achieve this, they should recognise that successful marketing planning and implementation of plans leading to desired results require the right structures, internal systems, finance, monitoring and control mechanisms, and cultural determination to provide support to ensure that it happens.

It is important to find examples of good marketing planning leading to effective action and outcomes. However, students should also be aware that poor marketing and the ineffective implementation of plans can easily come about if barriers to planning are encountered, such as limited resources and lack of support from senior management. Examples of these positive organisational characteristics as well shortcomings should be sought from outside the candidate's own organisation in addition to any they have encountered from their own experience.

Means of addressing barriers to planning should also be well understood and examples sought of how this may be undertaken through such initiatives as cultural change brought about by internal marketing. Particular implementation issues may be encountered in specialised marketing contexts which result from organisational characteristics or specific aspects of the markets served or products offered. It is important that students are familiar with such circumstances and seek illustrative examples of how relevant theory in such contexts is applied in practice. They also need to be able to evaluate how well this translates into reality and its effectiveness in achieving intended outcomes.

Index

Advantage, 158

Allocation of resources, 35
Audit, 74

Balanced scorecard, 45

Barriers to the implementation, 186
BCG matrix, 108
Behavioural segmentation, 137
Benchmarking, 187
Benefits, 130
Brand positioning, 160, 164
Brand, 158
Budget allocation, 35
Budgeting, 183, 184
Business ethics, 30
Business-to-Business (B2B), 200

Competition, 166

Competitive, 158
Competitive advantage, 17, 95
Competitive positioning, 159
Competitor analysis, 87
Corporate governance, 30
Corporate objectives, 41
Corporate Social Responsibility, 51
Criteria to create differentiation, 159
Cultural, 70
Cultural context, 30
Culture, 176
Cyclical change, 50

Demographic segmentation, 134

Drivers of organisational change, 50

Economic, 70

Environment, 70
Environmental analysis, 71, 84, 85
Environmental factors, 152
Evaluate, 151
Evolutionary change, 50

Fast moving consumer goods (FMCG), 198

Financial objectives, 43
Financial performance, 188
FMCG, 198
Forecasting and Budgeting, 182
Frequency of an audit, 62, 67
Functional objectives, 41

Gap analysis, 112

GE matrix, 110

Generic strategies, 90
Geographic segmentation, 133

Heterogeneity, 205

Hierarchy of objectives, 40
Human aspects of management, 24

Implementation, 174

Individual marketing, 149
Inseparability of production and consumption, 205
Intangibility, 205
Internal environment, 61, 73
Internal forces, 73
Internal marketing, 192
International Marketing Plans, 217
International segmentation, 139
Internet, 219

Lack of ownership, 205

Leadership, 176
Legalisation, 70

Macro-economic environment, 48

Macro-environment, 83, 85
Market factors, 151
Market orientation, 47
Market segments, 151
Marketing, 4
Marketing audit, 61, 64, 98
Marketing environment, 83
Marketing environment audit, 74
Marketing function audit, 77, 79
Marketing mix, 198
Marketing mix for SMEs, 211
Marketing objectives, 41
Marketing organisation audit, 76
Marketing orientation, 5
Marketing planning, 6, 15
Marketing planning process, 8, 19
Marketing productivity audit, 76
Marketing strategy, 17, 82, 128
Marketing strategy audit, 75
Marketing systems audit, 76
Marketing's interface, 6
Micro environment, 61
Micro-economic environment, 49
Micro-environment, 71, 83
Micromarketing, 148
Mission statement, 30, 31
Monitoring and control, 186

Not-for-profit organisation, 212

Operational framework, 34
Organisational objectives, 43
Organisational structures, 178
Organisational values, 30

Perceptual, 159
Perceptual maps, 162
Performance measures, 35, 188
Performance metrics, 188
Perishability, 205
Pestel, 70, 85
Political, 70
Porter's five forces analysis, 90
Porter's Five Forces model, 88
Positioning, 158
Product life cycle, 106
Psychographic segmentation, 135

Resource-based approach, 47

Scenario planning, 183
Segmentation, 129
Segmentation variables, 132
Segmenting, 130
Service marketing mix, 206
Services, 203

Skills, 177
SMEs, 210
Social, 70
Social responsibility, 150
Stages of the STP process, 130
Stakeholders, 30
Strategic Group Mapping, 93
Strategic marketing plan, 22
Strategic options, 116
Strategy, 176
Success Factors, 175
SWOT analysis, 115
Synergistic planning process, 14
Synergistic planning, 14
Systems, 177

Targeting strategies, 146
Technology, 70
Time series analysis, 182

Undifferentiated, 146

Value chain analysis, 111
Values, 32
Variance analysis, 187
Virtual marketplace, 219
Vision, 30

The Chartered Institute of Marketing

Notes

The Chartered
Institute of Marketing

The Chartered
Institute of Marketing

The Chartered
Institute of Marketing

The Chartered
Institute of Marketing

Review form

Please help us to ensure that the CIM learning materials we produce remain as accurate and user-friendly as possible. We cannot promise to answer every submission we receive, but we do promise that it will be read and taken into account when we update this Study Text.

Name: _____   Address: _____

_____

_____

1. How have you used this Text?
(Tick one box only)

☐ Self study (book only)

☐ On a course: college_____

☐ Other _____

3. Why did you decide to purchase this Text?
(Tick one box only)

☐ Have used companion Assessment workbook

☐ Have used BPP Texts in the past

☐ Recommendation by friend/colleague

☐ Recommendation by a lecturer at college

☐ Saw advertising in journals

☐ Saw information on BPP website

☐ Other _____

2. During the past six months do you recall seeing/receiving any of the following?
(Tick as many boxes as are relevant)

☐ Our advertisement in *The Marketer*

☐ Our brochure with a letter through the post

☐ Our website www.bpp.com

4. Which (if any) aspects of our advertising do you find useful?
(Tick as many boxes as are relevant)

☐ Prices and publication dates of new editions

☐ Information on product content

☐ Facility to order books off-the-page

☐ None of the above

5. Have you used the companion Assessment Workbook?   Yes ☐   No ☐

6. Have you used the companion Passcards?   Yes ☐   No ☐

7. Your ratings, comments and suggestions would be appreciated on the following areas.

	Very useful	Useful	Not useful
Introductory section (How to use this text, study checklist, etc)	☐	☐	☐
Chapter introductions	☐	☐	☐
Syllabus learning outcomes	☐	☐	☐
Activities	☐	☐	☐
The Real World examples	☐	☐	☐
Quick quizzes	☐	☐	☐
Quality of explanations			
Index	☐	☐	☐
Structure and presentation	☐	☐	☐

	Excellent	Good	Adequate	Poor
Overall opinion of this Text	☐	☐	☐	☐

8. Do you intend to continue using BPP CIM products?   ☐ Yes   ☐ No

On the reverse of this page is space for you to write your comments about our Study Text. We welcome your feedback.

Please return to: CIM Publishing Manager, BPP Learning Media, FREEPOST, London, W12 8BR.

TELL US WHAT YOU THINK

Please note any further comments and suggestions/errors below. For example, was the text accurate, readable, concise, user-friendly and comprehensive?